Quality

Peter Dahler-Larsen

Quality

From Plato to Performance

palgrave
macmillan

Peter Dahler-Larsen
University of Copenhagen
Copenhagen, Denmark

ISBN 978-3-030-10391-0 ISBN 978-3-030-10392-7 (eBook)
https://doi.org/10.1007/978-3-030-10392-7

Library of Congress Control Number: 2018967709

This Palgrave Macmillan imprint is published by the registered company Springer Nature Switzerland AG
The registered company address is: Gewerbestrasse 11, 6330 Cham, Switzerland

Preface

I wish to thank numerous colleagues and sources of inspiration, in particular Evert Vedung for his selfless inspiration and encouragement to study evaluation and Thomas Schwandt for his continuous intellectual inspiration and friendship. My many dialogues with these two intellectual beacons have created ideas which cannot be sufficiently recognized through conventional academic references. I have taken their intellectual contributions into directions with which they may not be comfortable and for which they cannot be held accountable.

No secret should be made of the fact that in 2008, I wrote a book in Danish with the title "Kvalitetens Beskaffenhed" published by University of Southern Denmark Press. It was written in the context of a national public reform of quality. This new book is written with another audience in mind, and it incorporates new theory, reflecting a change in my thinking. The organization of the material is new. *Quality: From Plato to Performance* is not a translation of my earlier work. It is a separate book. I reference my earlier work according to academic conventions, but some ideas have slipped through and can be found in both books.

I want to thank University of Southern Denmark Press for their cooperation over the years and for the support that made both the earlier and the new book possible.

I am grateful to the wonderful colleagues at University of Cape Town for their generosity and hospitality that made the writing of this book possible.

Copenhagen, Denmark Peter Dahler-Larsen

Contents

1

Introduction

Among the many words and numbers which circulate in our contemporary world, descriptors of quality are particularly numerous. Ratings, rankings, metrics, indicators, auditing, accreditation, benchmarking, smileys, user reviews, dashboards, international comparisons, and various forms of quality reports are used to capture quality.

Quality is one of the most widely used terms in our time. Three observations testify to its contemporary relevance as a social phenomenon which deserves to be studied (Dahler-Larsen 2008).

The first observation is that discourses of quality have proliferated to a broad range of social domains. Quality is expected to occur not only in art and music but also in consumer goods and service provision. We expect quality in schools, hospitals, universities, and housing. We expect quality in the air we breathe and in our personal relations. More recently, it has even become legitimate to talk about "quality of life" both as something personally and existentially relevant and as something that institutions and polities must take into account. The discourse on quality thus claims to encompass our life, as such. It has become a meta-discourse describing how we live; a mirror in which we should see our existence. This is no small accomplishment.

P. Dahler-Larsen, *Quality*, https://doi.org/10.1007/978-3-030-10392-7_1

The second observation is that organizations play important roles in relation to quality. Organizations are providers of goods and services characterized by more or less quality. Organizations have recipes, standards, and prescriptions for how to measure and document quality. Some organizations make a living from the construction and implementation of such quality regimes. Organizations make sure that particular inscriptions of quality travel through time and space. They do so in the form of pre-arranged quality statements (reviews, rankings, websites, and reports) that are filtered through some organizational machineries and which hold other organizational machineries accountable. Organizations not only provide quality, they also hold each other accountable for the provision of quality, thereby also defining quality in practice in terms of dimensions and standards pertaining to goods and services.

Organizations are linked in chains and networks and organizational fields (DiMaggio and Powell 1983). In some views, the smallest unit of analysis that works as an organizational field independent of other organizations is the world (Meyer 2008). Many of the organizations that help define regimes of quality relevant for others do in fact operate on a global scale. On the micro level, however, organizations are also the sites for practical negotiations about what quality might mean faced with the dissonance possibly occurring in the friction between universal standards and the contingencies of the local situation at hand (Stake 2004; Stark 2009).

It is not up to each individual to invent quality from scratch; the organizational world is already defining quality for us and making it relevant in many ways.

The third observation is that quality today relates to public matters. Quality has invaded the public space. We demand quality from hospitals, schools, foundations, and governments in their capacity as public institutions. Quality has become an important way of dealing with that which ancient Rome discovered as *res publica*: the public thing. The res publica (the etymological source of political units such as the republic) is basically all of the matters connecting us in a society, as they represent our common destiny. The public thing stands between us and connects us, because what *you* do with it influences *my* life. Take the quality of the air we breathe: Once the issue of air quality is raised, we have to talk about pollution from industry and cars. We also have to talk about the regulation of smoking. As much as we may disagree on how we balance the different and opposing interests of drivers, smokers, industry, and so forth—and correspondingly, what constitutes various dimensions of the notion of air quality—the matter is a public one simply because people affect each other's lives through the air, like it or not. Addressing an issue of quality is often a particular way of mobilizing others or regulating the behavior of others around a matter of public relevance. Or rather, it has *become* that way.

There is a particular socio-historical particularity to the contemporary status of the concept of quality. Society has changed how it talks about its res publica. Schools were formerly supposed to bring education, equality, progress, dannelse, or Bildung[1] (Dahler-Larsen et al. 2017). Today, their primary obligation may be quality. We deal with the management of public services in terms of *quality* management. We now see public issues in the light of how they are framed and presented as issues of quality. Perhaps we are even at a turning point where we see them as quality issues *rather than* as public issues.

The constitution of something as a quality issue creates a fundamental hermeneutical contradiction undergirding social life. On the one hand, quality can be understood as collection of subjective viewpoints. You like some things—I like others. *De gustibus not est disputandum*, as the Latin maxim goes. Personal taste simply cannot be discussed. With such a fragmentation of viewpoints, there can be no collective reasoning about res publica.

On the other hand, the definition of quality can be delegated to an institutional arrangement, so that common criteria, goals, and instruments are made possible. The institutionalization of quality, however, is afflicted with uncertainty (Boltanski 2011: 275). Which definition of quality is at play? Who speaks on behalf of which institutional arrangement? With which consequences?

So if we want to understand the contemporary form and shape of public matters, we should attend to quality as a concept as well as its social and institutional embodiment.

---

[1] Yes, there can be goals which are not easily translated into English! Both *dannelse* and *Bildung* refer to how education can contribute to socialization into culture and civilization at the same time as personal character is built.

There exists other concepts in society, which also help structure common social realities, which are also more or less institutionalized, and which are more or less contested. In this perspective, academics have analyzed security (Buzan, Wæver, and de Wilde 1998), sustainability (Gorz 1980; Latour 2004), equality (Rasmussen 1981), and risk (Beck 1992; Power 2016). Some of these discursive constructions have overlapping or competing relations with quality.

However, we are still lacking an academic analysis of the politics of quality itself. Such analysis should be sensitive to institutionalizations of the concept through metrics and other documentation practices, as well as the socio-political consequences hereof. At the same time, an analysis should pay attention to the uniqueness of quality as a concept. How does *quality* in particular help structure reality?

The Many Meanings of Quality and One Thing That Keeps Them Together

Given the broad applicability of the concept of quality, it is hardly surprising that quality is one of the richest terms in our civilization, perhaps superseded only by "culture." The term is used in a variety of meanings, such as: Quality referring to properties of things and human beings. It can refer to a wide range of phenomena, such as physical attributes, artistry of performance, taste, freshness, conformity with norms, durability, user satisfaction, and others; each of which, in turn, embodies multiple dimensions.

Quality can be used in the singular and in the plural ("qualities"). Quality also occurs as a quantified variable, since there can be more or less quality. Quality may refer to both absolute scores on some scale and relative rankings. It may be based on standards or a responsive appreciation of the specificities of the situation that takes into account that quality is relative to human experience (Stake 2004).

Quality can refer to phenomena in a category in itself, parallel to excellence.

Quality can be used in the context of globalization or in the most specific contexts in time and space. It can stand alone or be combined with a number of other terms (quality management, quality indicators, quality assurance).

It may be futile to seek any core meaning inherent in the term. It may be more realistic to think of a number of meanings that may be mobilized with flexibility and in different combinations. The concept would be threatened by fragmentation, however, unless it was used with at least one common denominator. There is one: Quality is positively loaded. Higher quality or more quality is always better.[2] Even without further qualification, if your friend describes a new restaurant simply as "quality," then you know it is good. When negative instances occur, a negative qualifier is mandatory: The other restaurant is "bad quality."

In the absence of further qualification, quality itself tilts toward the positive. As a consequence, even if quality is technically speaking a noun, it can appear as a positive adjective, as in "she is a quality musician." At the same time, a similar combination of terms occurs in, say, "quality management." More often than not, what is meant is presumably "management of quality" (two nouns), although, if you look at the structure of words, it could also be "good management" (with quality as a positively loaded adjective).

Quality may take on many meanings, not *despite* the one principle uniting them all but rather *because* this single, unifying principle—its positive loading—is exactly what allows it flexibility in almost all other respects, each time making people see it as something irrefutably good. An appeal to quality itself allows one to add positive stardust to a variety of projects and initiatives with a simple rhetorical sleight of hand.

It is very difficult to speak against quality. Quality is a concept without opposition. A Google search for "the national association against quality" gives you the National Association for Healthcare Quality and the National Association for Clean Air, and so forth.

Whatever there is to analyze in the term, quality may lie not in any hidden, essential meaning inherent in the concept but instead in its social use. There is a link between the conceptual structure of the term "quality" and its socio-political usefulness. A key part of that use is that quality always appears under a flag of positivity. This is useful for those who want to create alliances, gain support, and act with legitimacy.

---

[2] Evidently, the term "quality" also occurs without valuation attached, as in "physical qualities." My argument is merely that when there is a valuation, it tilts toward the positive.

Very different projects that aim at the improvement of quality may understand and operationalize quality in very different, perhaps contradictory ways. Yet it is not enough merely to say, "I want to create an alliance and act with legitimacy." A specific appeal to quality hooks a particular quality initiative up with a particular quality object understood in a particular way and, most importantly, provides a positive flag under which operations can take place. These operations are interesting because they have a bearing on how we deal with the res publica.

From Common Misunderstandings to Analytical Principles

Before proceeding with analytical steps, it is important to remove obstacles and misunderstandings. Since quality is already entangled in our world in so many ways, and since it is positively loaded, we are standing too close to be able to see it clearly—the proverbial forest for the trees. Berger et al. (1973) talk about different types of relevance structures. Relevance structures are ways we see and talk about the world depending on the type of engagement we have in it. Some relevance structures are very practical in our daily lives. Distinct from these are theoretical relevance structures, which are guided more by our intentions to analyze things. In a practical relevance structure, for example, money is a good thing. In a theoretical relevance structure, however, we can analyze various economic systems in a cool way apart from our personal fascination with money. In a similar vein, we need to overcome some common misunderstandings and dead ends in our everyday understanding of quality if we want to proceed with analytical thinking. The following analytical principles are recommended.

1. Do not let the goodness of quality trap you

We have seen that positivity might be the only principle holding the various notions of quality together. Yet, positive (or negative) connotations of objects of study are not good guides. Positivity is an impediment to cool analysis. Cool evaluations may point out that prematurely labeling things "good" can end badly, and positive as well as negative effects may wander in interesting ways across individuals, social units, and levels of analysis. Quality finds itself in the midst of a variety of social and political values. A particular notion of quality is always a choice between particular values, albeit usually guised in a general veil of goodness.

2. Study quality as a social, not a transcendent phenomenon

An encounter with genuine quality fills anyone with awe. We find quality in food, music, literature, and many other domains of life. Quality does not occur as frequently as we would like, and it is hard to define; like happiness, we simply know it when we see it. Quality fascinates. Quality comes to us as a gift. It appears to us as sent from above, something transcendent. Quality lets us forget ourselves.

As fascinating as it is, quality is therefore a dangerous object of study. The most recent good book about quality (not about a particular quality regime, not about quality assurance, not about quality in this or that sector, but about quality as such), and an often-cited one, is Robert Pirsig's (1974) *Zen and the Art of Motorcycle Maintenance*. While the author maintains that quality itself remains undefinable, the narrator alter ego becomes insane as a result of his inquiry into metaphysical quality.

Let us not forget ourselves. Let us stay on this side of the moon. Quality should be studied as social phenomenon through the lens of social science, including the history of socio-political concepts, and not mixed with a preoccupation with motorcycles, drugs, nor Buddhism. In this book, quality is understood in entirely earthly terms. We have a res publica to deal with.

3. Beware of synecdoche

A synecdoche is a figure of speech where a part is taken for a whole or a whole is taken for a part. Its literal meaning in Greek is "simultaneous understanding." While the notion of quality in its entirety is very rich, in the practical world quality usually comes to us in a particular, enunciated form as some aspect of something in a particular situation.

In many instances of quality assurance, there is a preoccupation with minute details that need to be documented. Yet, the umbrella term given to all of these matters is "quality" even if not all aspects of quality are taken into account. That would be impossible given the richness of quality in its totality. The specific version of synecdoche used here is *totum pro parte*. A grand and positive term is mobilized to describe a range of more specific phenomena. Totum pro parte provides a creative lack of clarity about exactly which parts of the larger unspecified set of meanings are actually referred to in the specific case at hand. Through this figure of speech, all of the positive connotations of quality may be taken onboard a particular project, even if this particular project is fairly pedestrian. The totum pro parte may help create support for a project, because if you are not supportive of the project, the rhetorical figure will position you as an adversary of quality, as such. Therefore, beware of synecdoche. Without this awareness, you will fall victim to anyone who uses the term for any purpose and thereby claims all of the positive connotations of quality in toto, regardless of what is specifically done practically and rhetorically.

4. Do not conflate a situated experience and a quality standard

Let us consider a solution to a problem in a particular situation in the form of a quality initiative. For example, nursing homes for the elderly have been subjected to cutbacks, and there is now concern for the level of personal care and hygienic standards. A political party suggests a legally mandated quality standard at two showers per week for all elderly citizens under care. Once this criterion is applied to a number of different situations, new problems occur. Some of the elderly have skin diseases that make showers uncomfortable. Some prefer bathtubs instead of showers due to the risk of falling. Some have simply never taken two showers a week. Evidently, the elderly individual must have the right to *refuse* the showers. But does that mean that those who cannot speak, the mentally ill, and the senile should have two showers, whether they speak up or not? Perhaps wisely, the proposal was dropped. The elderly and the local staff simply had to figure out how they would handle the problem from day to day, from situation to situation, as they usually did.

There is a long, rich, and respectable tradition in the literature on practice to conceive of quality as sensitive to the specifics of the situation (Schwandt 2002). The tricky part, as the example shows, is that once a criterion of quality becomes incorporated into a quality standard, the concept of quality travels when the standard travels. Standards do not always specify their own limitations. They constantly lend themselves to new situations. If you buy into a quality standard that is relevant in one situation (S1), you often also accept it being applied to other situations even if there is no way in the world in which you can think all of the contingencies through that characterize the next situations (S2, S3, etc.). In a political or organizational perspective, however, it is not enough to think of either S1, S2, or S3. Policies, standards, management instruments, and recipes by definition operate across situations.

An important thing to watch then becomes how and when specific experiences from specific contexts translate into quality criteria that travel across time and space as parts of a concept of quality that are then talked about as quality, as such. It is difficult to dissect a particular notion of quality in order to determine the boundaries of the settings to which it applies, because all of these possible variations in settings are not known. However, opponents of any given general notion can be positioned as an "enemy of quality" even in Situation 1, where the application of that notion may be very reasonable. In order to reduce opposition, it is therefore rhetorically tempting to operate with general notions of quality without situation specificity.

In phenomenology, an interesting concept is the *indexicality* of typifications (Schutz 1978; Schwandt 1994). It means that a given situation lends itself to various ways of seeing the "typical" features of that situation. Interpretation mediates so to speak between the typification and its situation-specific application. Because of the indexicality of typifications, we cannot be sure that a particular typification will actually be put to use in that situation—until it actually happens. Once you buy into a given quality standard as relevant for a set of situations, however, you have also typified those situations as "fitting" the type of quality you are about to deliver (consistent with the standard), even if you have yet to encounter these new situations.

People sometimes buy into a notion of quality that has very little contact with even one practical, situated experience. Broad discourses about quality without contact to practical situations are problematic. For example, students occasionally interview childcare workers about how they see quality as part of the practices of childcare. The childcare workers then talk broadly about respect for children as human beings and the wonderful experience of seeing them growing up. Students believe that these concerns permeate pedagogical practices, but the interview perhaps never makes a connection between the wider quality discourse and practical situations.

Thus far, we can conclude that quality within a specific situation and quality as a concept (potentially relevant outside that situation) have a precarious relationship. While they can mutually inform each other, it is also (too) tempting to think that once one of them is known, the other is also. Sometimes they have little to do with each other. What is interesting is what brings a particular notion of quality and a particular understanding of a situation together. Defining a situation is problematic, defining quality is problematic, and connecting the two is problematic.

An analytical key is to decompose notions of quality depending on the relevance structures that enunciate them. In plain language, this means: Who is asking? In what situation(s)? What is his/her/their project? If we understand the relevance structure in which a notion of quality is anchored, then we may understand better (analytically) which exact version of quality we are talking about and what it might afford. Each quality notion should be taken seriously as representative of a particular relevance structure, but not literally as evidence of quality in any universal sense. To understand how the "same" concept can operate so differently, what is necessary for an analysis is a controlled shift in our grasp of quality in a theoretical relevance structure. It does not help to just insist what quality *is*.

5. Do not believe that descriptors are only descriptors

It is common to talk about quality indicators as if they "indicate" an underlying objective reality. We gauge our descriptors based on whether they provide us with valid and reliable accounts of the aspect of reality we wish to describe. This notion is particularly problematic in the case of quality. Quality descriptors do not relate to quality in the same way as thermometers relate to temperature. Even if we accept what has to be found in the sociology of science—that our understanding of physical phenomena depend to a large extent on paradigms and conventions—it is obvious that there is a high degree of consensus about temperature, whereas the notion of quality remains fragmented, contested, value-laden, and situation-dependent.

A claim to measure quality cannot be understood as referring to an already-existing reality, but as an attempt to define reality in a particular way. It is performative (Butler 2010). It seeks to enact what it claims to describe. When people react to the measurement, it may happen that they take the definition of quality inherent in the quality measurement for granted and base their actions on that understanding in which case the measurement has constitutive effects (Dahler-Larsen 2014). The measurement interferes with reality, sometimes colonizing minds and practices (Erkkilä and Piironen 2014; Shore and Wright 2015), sometimes leading to new uncertainty, risk, paradox, or controversy (Barry 2012; Dambrin and Robson 2011; Jensen 2011; Pollock et al. 2018; Roberts 2018).

There is a close link between the conceptual structure of quality and the capacity of quality measurements to interfere with reality. It is *because of* the openness and flexibility inherent in the concept of quality that metrics and other forms of documentation have such a wide space for not only measuring quality, but in fact also *defining* what it means. The conceptual structure of quality helps pave the way for the socio-political influence of people who operationalize it. In addition, the positivity bias inherent in quality provides this endeavor with a sugarcoating, at least on the rhetorical level.

Purpose of the Book

It is an interesting challenge to write against something which appears to have transcendent origins, which usually involves confusing relations between the concept and the situations to which it is applied, and which turns around the relation between an object and its measuring. Furthermore, what makes the concept of quality particularly "unhintergehbar" as the Germans would say, meaning "something you cannot go behind," is the ever-present positivity of quality. It is tempting to criticize one enunciation of quality for not being "real quality" (as if the author knows what that is). But the ambition here is to go behind even the idea that there is an underlying real quality apart from the socio-historical practices in which it is dealt with.

I apologize if my writing might appear speculative in some passages and my terminology unconventional. The intention is to achieve a kind of *Verfremdungseffekt* (an "alienation effect"). This effect helps create distance from everyday thinking, which is necessary for analysis.

The first and primary purpose of this book is to take the obviousness out of any statement that claims to be based on evident knowledge about quality. My intention not to prescribe any particular specification of quality does not mean I am uninterested in quality. I just have different kinds of interests in it. These are analytical interests.

The first of these interests relates to my engagement in the field of evaluation. I am a researcher, teacher, and sometimes consultant. Since quality takes up much discursive space, I want to understand what kind of evaluative statements and practices are produced with the help of the notion of quality. Without going too deep into evaluation theory (which has been done elsewhere; see Dahler-Larsen 2012; Schwandt 2002, 2015; Vedung 1997), let me briefly say that some of the key concerns are how objects of evaluation are conceived, how values matter in evaluation, and what difference evaluations make for policy and practice. I am particularly interested in how evaluative statements work as arguments to help shape practices, minds, priorities, and the broader social order (Dahler-Larsen 2012). Obviously, quality relates to all of this.

As mentioned earlier in this introduction, quality is so prominent in contemporary discourse that we have reason to believe it plays an important socio-political role. Other books have studied evaluations and audits as socio-political phenomena (Dahler-Larsen 2012; Power 1997; Taylor and Balloch 2005). This is the first book to explore the socio-political implications of evaluative statements with a specific focus on the contribution of the concept of quality to these processes.

More specifically, I want to know which understandings of quality are in play and what might be accomplished by appealing to quality. I explore the *dynamics of the relation between the conceptual and social aspects of quality*. What are the conditions of possibility for producing statements about quality that reach across time and space, sometimes even in a global perspective?

What is the role of quality, and more specifically quality inscriptions, such as measurement? And finally, if the concept of quality reigns under present socio-historical conditions, what happens to the collective reasoning about public issues?

The concept of quality is so rich that the only place where all of its meanings meet is in a dictionary. In practice, quality enunciates itself as something more specific. Quality perspectives are ways of talking about quality that conceptually only highlight a particular conceptual aspect. A quality perspective is logically linked to an understanding of a quality problem in a given quality situation. I will map and discuss some prominent quality perspectives and show their relativity and, sometimes, instability. On that basis, I will argue that quality measurement plays a critical role in keeping a notion of quality fixed. In other words, I turn a common argument on its head. Conceptual unclarity does not make measurement difficult. Instead, measurement controls quality in a way that the concept itself is too confused to do. In fact, the social function of measurement expands exactly because measurement plays a key role in regulating the meanings and social implications of an otherwise elusive phenomenon.

The centrality of measurement and quality inscriptions (forms of quality documentation) raise important questions for public issues related to democracy, particularly when they occur without deliberation about quality. To shed light on quality as a socio-political problem, it is necessary to draw on a variety of theoretical sources.

Theoretical Approaches and Intellectual Debts

Neo-institutional theory in the so-called sociological version has delivered much-needed criticism of functionalistic, rationalistic, and individualistic models of organizational life. Instead, neo-institutionalists argue that most of what takes place in organizations are not rational solutions to well-defined problems but rather reflections of norms, values, scripts, and recipes that circulate in the social environments of organizations; hence the "sociological" label. For the key contributors to this school of thought, such as DiMaggio and Powell (1983) and John Meyer (2008), conformity with modern organizational environments first and foremost implies the institutionalization of bureaucratic rationality (Stark 2009: 168). The critical edge here is that, in this understanding, rationality has less to do with technical problem-solving than with achieving a particular kind of legitimacy. In this theoretical light, regimes of quality are regimes for creating legitimacy. Organizations in the modern world are surprisingly similar in terms of how they conform to the same rationalized myths about quality. Quality may appear as a positive word that can be used to improve the world in a "warm" way in contradistinction to "cold" bureaucracies. Bureaucracies may engage with quality in order to renew the moral framework they are otherwise lacking (Boltanski 2011: 204). Tragically, however, bureaucracies do not stop being bureaucracies just because they engage in quality management.

In one of the key texts that inaugurated the neo-institutional era, Meyer and Rowan (1977) offer hypotheses about how organizations handle evaluations. They predict that organizations will protect their operative core from evaluations of quality. Evaluations of quality will primarily be used as "window dressing."

Meyer and Rowan possibly underestimated how invasive evaluations of quality ultimately proved to be. Today, external inspectors have ways to enforce quality assurance. Digital networks help diffuse massive amounts of data in and between organizations. Quality measurement is now connected with legal and financial sanctions in a manner that Meyer and Rowan did not predict. Quality has become more invasive, and there are specific mechanisms which ensure that managers must respond to ratings and rankings (Espeland and Sauder 2007).

There is a camp of scholars studying quality indicators, whose critical view is almost antithetical to the neo-institutional paradigm of window dressing and decoupling. Instead, quality indicators, metrics, and other forms of documentation are neoliberal instruments which colonize practices and undermine professional values (Shore and Wright 2015; Bruno et al. 2014). Sometimes these critics assume, however, that this form of governing-at-a-distance works in a linear way. It is as if when the instruments used to govern people have been identified, we also know that the steering is successful.

Instead, paradox, tension, and the active, but ambiguous involvement of people under measurement could be attended to and understood as a part of how quality inscriptions operate (Dambrin and Robson 2011; Kauko et al. 2018; Kaltenbrunner and de Rijcke 2017).

Vocabularies are needed that connects the concept of quality with practical situations and practical consequences. Theoretically, we find inspiration in measurement theory, which describes the social and practical tensions regarding metrics (Desrosières 2009, 2014; Porter 1994); and in aspects of Actor–Network Theory (Latour 2004), which explains how actors and mechanisms that produce inscriptions are connected in complex ways. My purpose is not to contribute specifically to each of these fields of theory but to distill only what is helpful for the understanding of quality and its journey through the world.

Stark uses practice theory to describe how actors find their ways through conflicting orders of worth (Stark 2009). He focuses not on isomorphism as an outcome of rationalization (as neo-institutionalists do) but on dissonance in organizational life that results from the meeting of rationalizing forces with concrete situated practices. Dissonance—the simultaneous presence of multiple values and concerns—increases the need for a theoretical focus on distributed intelligence, diversity, recombination, adaptability, multivocality, and heterarchical organization (Stark 2009: 172, 187). Stark brings action in organizations back into alignment with notions of situated action (Hay 2012) and the long-standing tradition of theories of practice (Schwandt 2002). In the light of this tradition, practice is complex and often embedded in situations that call for attention to multiple (if not conflicting) evaluative principles.

While Stark's work resonates with classical tenets in practice theory, he adds special attention to the dynamics and complexities of technologies and quickly changing markets. Consequently, actors cannot merely take recipes for action "for granted" (Stark 2009: 189). Clever practitioners engage in "trading zones" where multiple orders of worth are negotiated. Stark argues that heterarchical organizations help us curb the total dominance of one order of worth and one single metric: market value. He also argues that heterarchical organizations have a high capacity for learning, adaptation, and discovery. They actively develop tools that allow them to construct their world anew (Stark 2009: 186).

While one might have sympathy for a world that gives space for multiple orders of worth, perhaps Stark's model of the heterarchical organization is more normative than descriptive. If descriptive, does Stark's model not tend to underestimate the strength of the social forces that make organizations isomorphic and subordinate to general systems of auditability (Power 1997)? If normative, how about the weaknesses of the heterarchical, networked world, such as the exhaustion of the committed individual and the evaporation of accountability? Which, to be fair, Stark (2009: 205) acknowledges but does not analyze in depth.

Another question begs itself that is not sufficiently attended to by Stark. Let us generously acknowledge some of the positive aspects of a heterarchical organizational model, including its contribution to learning, adaptation, and discovery. But how should one evaluate an organization that reflects multiple orders of worth? Is there an order or worth appropriate for the evaluation of orders of worth?

My favorite philosopher, Gianni Vattimo (2005), would respond that, in the present era, which he describes as postmodern in the sense of "post-metaphysical," there can be no ultimate principle guaranteeing the prioritization of the rest of the principles in this world.

While I hope to have made my intellectual debt to several of the above-mentioned literatures clear, my intention is not to contribute to these fields. I am merely interested in understanding how the present construction and use of quality as a concept helps structure social order in particular ways. *My analytical entry point is the concept of quality*. This project is embedded in a problem-oriented research frontier, of which there are many in social science but which do not necessarily converge into "high" theoretical knowledge (Mjøset 2009: 64).

In tying my research strategy to the social life of a concept, I have found the kind of conceptual analysis suggested by Reinhard Koselleck particularly helpful. In Koselleck's terminology, a word becomes a concept when loaded with a set of socio-political meanings, experiences, and expectations (Koselleck 2007: 71).

While any concept is a result of particular history and social order, it is also a socially productive factor in itself. It enunciates expectations. In modernity, social expectations are "emancipated" by means of concepts (think civil rights, think sustainability, think learning, think development, think identity, think quality!), which helps accelerate social change. However, the concept–social order relationship goes both ways; it is sometimes relaxed, sometimes tense, and only sometimes productive (Koselleck 2007: 73).

A conceptual history allows us to uncover layers of meaning that no longer resonate with an existing social order, but we can also uncover implicit, taken-for-granted meanings that are integral to the contemporary use of the concept (Koselleck 2007: 77). A generally positive concept should not be used without concern for its unanticipated consequences (Palonen 2002: 99). Koselleck's thinking can be used to uncover the values and norms at play when generalizing concepts are used in specific situations, which they in fact always are (Palonen 2002: 103).

A particular methodological challenge is that meanings wander in and out of words over time. Based on this observation, two methodological strategies can be chosen (Koselleck 2007: 73): An onomasiological strategy studies how the same idea is expressed in different terms, whereas a semasiological strategy begins with a term and proceeds to uncover its various meanings under different circumstances. Still, it is no easy thing to identify quality. When quality is transformed into an adjective, "quality" and "good" can be used almost interchangeably (see, e.g. "good regulation" [Radaelli and De Francesco 2007]), but the nominalization of good may be both quality or goodness or even positivity.

It is important to keep an eye on neighboring concepts, such as well-being, happiness, satisfaction, and excellence. Lines of demarcation cannot be drawn in any general way. Quality borrows meanings from other phenomena. One example is test results in schools that are later used as indicators of school quality even if they were not originally intended as such. I will discover what my semasiological strategy allows me to see, neither more nor less, as my point of entry will be the concept of quality itself, but the semasiological approach is a guiding principle, not a mechanical rule.

Structure of the Book

Chapter 2 tells a history of the concept of quality, showing its variety of meanings and the critical junctures over time when displacements of meanings took place.

Chapter 3 describes nine quality perspectives, each referring to a slice of quality, given particular pre-understandings. In my discussion of the inter-perspectival relations, I will show that quality as a concept encompasses perspectives that are, at least partly, in mutual conflict. I shall also discuss the (lack of) intra-perspective stability.

Chapter 4 analyzes quality inscriptions and in particular the role of measurement. I begin with those who make quality inscriptions, their organizations, and the hinterlands in which they are embedded that influence the form and shape of how quality is understood and measured. I argue that measurement plays an important role in keeping a notion of quality fixed. Measurement does not reflect an already-existing essence in the concept of quality itself. Instead, measurement holds an otherwise elusive concept in place. In that light, I shall discuss the socially constitutive consequences of quality measurement.

Chapter 5 examines qualitization as a speech act that sets quality inscriptions in motion. I describe three styles or models of qualitization: the metrological, the deliberative, and the configurative model.

Chapter 6 draws perspectives concerning qualitization and democracy. I argue that there are constitutive effects of qualitization that are neither subject to government control nor to democratic deliberation. The implications of quality without democracy are discussed.

I discuss what can be done with quality in the epilogue in Chap. 7.

A Quality Vocabulary

When referring to "the concept of quality" in the remainder of the book, what I mean is, following Koselleck, the term "quality" as it presently manifests itself with a baggage of socio-political meanings, experiences, and expectations or quality as it appears for us in its present incarnations. This is also what I mean, unless otherwise stated, by quality without brackets.

More specifically, my frame of reference will include the following terms combined with quality:

Quality situation:	A specific practical setting in time and space where a dissonance of values is at stake and where the term "quality" is invoked as relevant.
Quality script:	An intuitive approach to what quality might mean in the situation at hand.
Quality perspective:	A way of talking about quality that conceptually highlights only a particular conceptual aspect. A quality perspective is logically linked to an understanding of a quality problem.
Quality problem:	A lack of quality (as defined from a quality perspective) perceived to require attention and action.
Quality recipe:	An institutionalized approach to producing and circulating quality inscriptions across time and space.
Quality inscription:	A documentation of quality, usually in the form of quantification.
Quality object:	The "thing" that a quality inscription talks about or claims to measure. Equivalent to "evaluand" in evaluation theory.
Quality zone:	The bounded time and space in which quality objects are comparable through the use of a quality inscription.
Quality infrastructure (or machinery):	The network of documents, computers, reporting mechanisms, experts, and so on that make quality inscriptions possible.
Quality agents:	Actors related to quality such as "consumers," "producers," "inscriptors" of quality, their helpers, and their adversaries.
Quality configuration:	A particular network of quality agents held together by expectations, inscriptions, infrastructure, and so on.

Quality work: Any kind of effort, choice, action, improvement, learning, and so on that relates to a quality object and its position in a quality configuration.

Qualitization: A speech act that makes quality relevant in a given instance by mobilizing, connecting, and setting in motion several of the above.

References

Barry, Andrew. 2012. Political Situations: Knowledge Controversies in Transnational Governance. *Critical Policy Studies* 6 (3): 324–336.

Beck, Ulrich. 1992. *Risk Society. Towards a New Modernity*. Thousand Oaks: Sage.

Berger, Peter L., Brigitte Berger, and Hansfried Kellner. 1973. *The Homeless Mind: Modernization and Consciousness*. New York: Vintage Books.

Boltanski, Luc. 2011. *Pragmatisk Sociologi* [Pragmatic Sociology. A Reader]. Copenhagen: Hans Reitzel.

Bruno, Isabelle, Emmanuel Didier, and Tommaso Vitale. 2014. Statactivism. Forms of Action between Disclosure and Affirmation. *Partecipazione e Conflitto* 7 (2): 198–220.

Butler, Judith. 2010. Performative Agency. *Journal of Cultural Economy* 3 (2): 147–161.

Buzan, Barry, Ole Wæver, and Jaap de Wilde. 1998. *Security: A New Framework for Analysis*. Boulder: Lynne Rienner.

Dahler-Larsen, Peter. 2008. *Kvalitetens Beskaffenhed* [The Nature of Quality]. Odense: University Press of Southern Denmark.

———. 2012. *The Evaluation Society*. Stanford: Stanford University Press.

———. 2014. Global Inscription Devices and the Politics of Education. *Knowledge Cultures* 2 (4): 90–109.

Dahler-Larsen, Peter, Tineke A. Abma, Maria Bustelo, Roxana Irimia, Sonja Kosunen, Iryna Kravchuk, Elena Minina, Christina Segerholm, Eneida Shiroma, Nicoletta Stame, and Charlie Kabanga Tshali. 2017. Evaluation, Language, and Untranslatables. *American Journal of Evaluation* 38 (1): 114–125.

Dambrin, Claire, and Keith Robson. 2011. Tracing Performance in the Pharmaceutical Industry: Ambivalence, Opacity and the Performativity of Flawed Measures. *Accounting, Organizations and Society* 36 (7): 428–455.

Desrosières, Alain. 2009. How to be Real and Conventional: A Discussion of the Quality Criteria of Official Statistics. *Minerva* 47: 307–322.

———. 2014. Statistics and Social Critique. *Partecipazione e conflitto* 7 (2): 348–359.

DiMaggio, Paul, and Walter Powell. 1983. The Iron Cage Revisited: Institutional Isomorphism and Collective Rationality in Organizational Fields. *American Sociological Review* 48 (6): 147–160.

Erkkilä, Tero, and Ossi Piironen. 2014. (De)politicizing Good Governance: The World Bank Institute, the OECD and the Politics of Governance Indicators. *Innovation: The European Journal of Social Science Research* 27 (4): 344–360.

Espeland, Wendy N., and Michael Sauder. 2007. Rankings and Reactivity: How Public Measures Recreate Social Worlds. *American Journal of Sociology* 113 (1): 1–40.

Gorz, André. 1980. *Ecology as Politics*. Boston: South End Press.

Hay, Colin. 2012. Interpreting Interpretivism Interpreting Interpretations: The New Hermeneutics of Public Administration. *Public Administration* 89 (1): 167–182.

Jensen, Casper Bruun. 2011. Making Lists, Enlisting Scientists: The Bibliometric Indicator, Uncertainty and Emergent Agency. *Science Studies* 24 (2): 64–84.

Kaltenbrunner, Wolfgang, and Sarah de Ricjke. 2017. Quantifying 'Output' for Evaluation: Administrative Knowledge Politics and Changing Epistemic Cultures in Dutch Law Faculties. *Science and Public Policy* 44 (2): 284–293.

Kauko, Jaakko, Risto Rinne, and Tuomas Takala. 2018. *Politics of Quality in Education. A Comparative Study of Brazil, China, and Russia*. New York: Routledge.

Koselleck, Reinhart. 2007. *Begreber, Tid og Erfaring. En tekstsamling* [Concepts, Time and Experience: An Anthology]. Copenhagen: Hans Reitzel. Collection of chapters originally published in Koselleck, R. 2000. *Zeitschichten: Studien zur Historik*. Frankfurt am Main: Suhrkamp Verlag.

Latour, Bruno. 2004. Why Has Critique Run Out of Steam? From Matters of Fact to Matters of Concern. *Critical Inquiry* 30 (2): 225–248.

Meyer, John W. 2008. Building Education for a World Society. In *Changing Knowledge and Education*, ed. M.A. Pereyra, 31–49. Frankfurt am Main: Peter Lang.

Meyer, John W., and Brian Rowan. 1977. Institutionalized Organizations: Formal Structure as Myth and Ceremony. *American Journal of Sociology* 83: 340–363.

Mjøset, Lars. 2009. The Contextualist Approach to Social Science Methodology. In *The SAGE Handbook of Case-Based Methods*, ed. D. Byrne and C.C. Ragin, 39–68. Thousand Oaks: Sage.

Palonen, Kari. 2002. The History of Concepts as a Style of Political Theorizing: Quentin Skinner's and Reinhart Koselleck's Subversion of Normative Political Theory. *European Journal of Political Theory* 1 (1): 91–106.

Pirsig, Robert M. 1974. *Zen and the Art of Motorcycle Maintenance: An Inquiry Into Values*. New York: William Morrow.

Pollock, Neil, Luciana D'Adderio, Robin Williams, and Ludovic Leforestier. 2018. Conforming or Transforming? How Organizations Respond to Multiple Rankings. *Accounting, Organizations and Society* 64: 55–68.

Porter, Theodore M. 1994. Making Things Quantitative. *Science in Context* 7 (3): 389–407.

Power, Michael. 1997. *The Audit Society*. Oxford: Oxford University Press.

———. 2016. Postscript. On Riskwork and Auditwork. In *Essays on the Organizational Life of Risk Management*, ed. Michael Power. Oxford: Oxford University Press.

Radaelli, Claudio M., and Fabrizio De Francesco. 2007. *Regulatory Quality in Europe: Concepts, Measures and Policy Processes*. Manchester: Manchester University Press.

Rasmussen, Erik. 1981. *Lighedsbegreber* [Equality Concepts]. Copenhagen: Berlingske.

Roberts, John. 2018. Managing only with Transparency: The Strategic Functions of Ignorance. *Critical Perspectives on Accounting* 55: 53–60.

Schutz, Alfred. 1978. Phenomenology and the Social Sciences. In *Phenomenology and Sociology*, ed. T. Luckmann, 119–141. Harmondsworth: Penguin.

Schwandt, Thomas A. 1994. Constructivist, Interpretivist Approaches to Human Inquiry. In *Handbook of Qualitative Research*, ed. N. Denzin and Y. Lincoln, 118–137. Thousand Oaks: Sage.

———. 2002. *Evaluation Practice Reconsidered*. New York: Peter Lang.

———. 2015. *Evaluation Foundations Revisited: Cultivating a Life of the Mind for Practice*. Palo Alto: Stanford University Press.

Shore, Cris, and Susan Wright. 2015. Governing by Numbers: Audit Culture, Rankings and the New World Order. *Social Anthropology* 23 (1): 22–28.

Stake, Robert E. 2004. *Standard-Based and Responsive Evaluation*. Thousand Oaks: Sage.

Stark, David. 2009. *The Sense of Dissonance, Accounts of Worth in Economic Life*. Princeton: Princeton University Press.

Taylor, David, and Susan Balloch. 2005. *The Politics of Evaluation: Participation and Policy Implementation*. Bristol: Policy Press.

Vattimo, Gianni. 2005. *Nihilisme og Emancipation. Etik, Politik, Ret* [Nihilsm and Emancipation. Ethics, Politics, and Law]. Aarhus: Aarhus University Press.

Vedung, Evert. 1997. *Public Policy and Program Evaluation*. New Brunswick: Transaction.

2

A History of the Concept of Quality

Given the centrality of the concept of quality and the complexities related to it, which I described in the introduction, it is surprising how little the history of the concept of quality is discussed—how often it is completely neglected, in fact.

Neither Blond's *Encyclopedia of Education* (Blishen 1969), *Webster's Dictionary of Word Origins* (Merriam-Webster 1995) written "for the occasional browser," the *Encyclopedia of Governance* (Bevir 2007), nor the *Encyclopedia of Quality of Life and Well-being Research* (!) (Michalos 2014) provide any entries for the term quality.

In many other situations, a definition is given as in the following example: "Quality: A parameter of action describing those properties of the product which will be critical for the potential consumer's perception of the product and preference for the product" (Management Leksikon 2001: 219). Notice how much is already taken for granted (e.g. products and consumers and preferences and the whole economic regime in which these terms make sense).

Whether no definition is given or whether a definition is provided without further reflection, taken-for-grantedness reigns. Even among researchers who deserve respect for the fine intellectual analyses of quality, there is sometimes a tendency to distill the meaning of quality from

P. Dahler-Larsen, *Quality*, https://doi.org/10.1007/978-3-030-10392-7_2

one relevance structure with only one socio-historical origin. For example, Power (1996) finds a very important source in industrial concepts of quality control, while Callon et al. (2002) define qualities in terms of aspects of a product wanted by consumers in a market.

Instead, this chapter provides a history of the concept, which shows its multiple meanings and their contingencies over time.

A concept is a product of particular history and social order; it refers back to social structures, cultures, and roles. At particular times, particular people are guided by social positions, projects, interests, ideas, and experiences altogether comprising relevance structures, which necessitate particular concepts. A concept is also a socially productive factor in itself (Koselleck 2007). It embodies expectations. People refer to a concept to mobilize expectations as socially relevant arguments for change. Concepts such as rights, equality, and democratic deficit are words with built-in expectations of a better world. Particularly in modern times, social expectations are "emancipated" by means of concepts which in themselves make an argument for social change.

A history of a concept is therefore two things at the same time: a map of relevance structures that represent an existing "demand" for the concept and a manifestation of new demands. A concept is both construct*ed* and construct*ive*. In Koselleck's terminology, it embodies experiences and expectations, both of which change over time.

According to Foucault (1984), too many histories of concepts claim to reveal a golden, definitive origin of a concept. Too many histories tell a story of how a concept is perfected over time as if guided by metaphysical forces. Instead, he proposes a genealogy that shows the ancestor's "logical inadequacies" and "the hazardous play of dominations," including "invasions, struggles, plundering, disguises, ploys," and unfulfilled potentials, which characterize the shifting interpretations of a concept over time.

There is no empirical access to what quality "really meant" in past historical times. We must rely on etymological accounts, dictionaries, and histories of philosophical concepts. Yet, their typicality is somewhat the result of how events are presented in a particular narrative. In my history of the concept of quality, I sacrifice empirical depth and detail in order to capture what I believe to be broad, long, and significant trends in the history of quality. I have searched for answers to questions related to my understanding of the present role and function of the multi-headed monster called "quality." The result is *a* history of quality, not *the* history. The story can be told in many ways and will be retold in the future. With these caveats in mind, my version is as follows.

The Ancient World: Qualia and the World of Ideas

Quality was first coined in Ancient Rome by Cicero (106–43 BC) in the form of the term *qualis*. The term can best be translated into "how-ness," "of what sort," or "of what kind." A *quale* (in plural, *qualia*) is a singular sense of a property of things, usually materials. It is also a property of a mental state that determines what it is like (Cambridge Dictionary of Philosophy 1995: 762).

Cicero coined the term *qualis* after the Greek *poiotes*, another artificially constructed word. This was used by Plato (app. 428–348 BC) in his report on the dialogue between Socrates (470/469–399 BC) and Theaetetus (Klein 1977: 114). The two discuss deep questions in what we would later call epistemology, particularly the role of the sense perception for the construction of knowledge. If knowledge is built on sense perception, a key question then becomes what can be done with the fact that when the same wind blows, one person perceives it to be cold and another does not? Things do not speak directly to us. Human perception must play a role.

The dialogue introduced an important distinction between a thing and the sensations of its properties (the qualia). A precondition for sensing qualia is the human capacity to recognize or recollect the corresponding properties. So, for example, the notion of whiteness is logically different from, but a precondition for, the sensation of something actually being white (Klein 1977: 114). Whiteness exists as an idea distinct from its being embodied in particular phenomena. The sensation of white related to the thing is therefore not totally a property of the thing itself. The quality of a thing depends, at least partly, on an idea that is not inside the thing.

One question that follows is also whether a thing has a separate existence apart from the sum of the qualia describing it, or, in other words, whether the essence of the thing is fully exhausted through a number of qualia used as descriptors. Plato would say no. He would argue that it is possible to recognize all of the letters in Theaetetus' name and still not grasp the idea of the name, as such.[1]

Plato continues to insist on the role of ideas. There are ideas about objects that are not grasped simply by adding up a number of qualia that characterize the object. Furthermore, qualia themselves only make sense because they are supported by ideas, such as the idea of color, weight, or extension. A "world of ideas" explains how it is possible for human beings to "know" something about "things" through "sensations." The world of ideas is a bit of a deus ex machina. In the interpretation of later philosophers, this is an immensely metaphysical solution (Vattimo 2005).

According to Plato, human insight remains linked to a basis of human virtue; or in modern terminology: Epistemological success depends on the virtue of human beings (plato.stanford.edu/entries/plato-Theaetetus). The ultimate harmony of these domains is secured by the metaphysical canopy overarching Plato's thinking.

The dialogue ends inconclusively, which has stimulated curiosity among philosophers. Is Plato consistent in his account of the dialogue and in his position (Klein 1977: 4)? Is Plato's account of the dialogue a smokescreen hiding the fact that he himself has no firm understanding of knowledge (Bostock 1988: 270)? Or is his mission merely to get away with a few common misunderstandings, really just playing with a number of philosophical training exercises (Klein 1977: 4)?

In practice, Socrates' dialogue with Theaetetus ends as Socrates leaves the scene to go to the courthouse to attend the trial against him, which ended in his death sentence. So much for epistemology.

[1] You might recognize this question in its present version: Does a set of indicators fully describe a public service exhaustively?

Primary and Secondary Qualia

The meaning of quality as a set of properties which characterize objects has been long-lived. In 1425, medicine was known to produce the qualities of hot/cold and moisture/dryness (Barnhart and Steinmetz 1988). Mention of the qualities of water occurs in 1533. In 1725, the qualities of ideas were described as "clear" or "obscure" (Oxford English Dictionary 1989). Qualia also referred to the qualities of sound and color.

Philosophers continue to struggle with the question of how much of qualia are due to objects and how much to human beings. With the advent of empiricism, this question was answered by a simple move, namely splitting qualia into two categories: primary and secondary qualities. No issue in the history of the concept of quality is more extensively dealt with among philosophers than this distinction.

According to Locke (1632–1704), the primary qualities reside in things themselves. The secondary ones are human perceptions somehow triggered by our perceptions of the things. This distinction is important because it paves the way for a split between objective and subjective dimensions of quality. The primary (or objective) qualities can only be measured and objectively gauged if technical difficulties in measurement are resolved and proper instruments developed. All of the paraphernalia of modern science can help us here, guided by Galilei's dictum: Measure everything, and make measurable everything that is not yet measurable.

This dictum obviously also challenges the daring scientist to conquer the world of all qualia hitherto categorized as "secondary." As the terminology itself suggests, they are second-order derivatives of something measurable. Paradoxically, then, human sensations and emotions might one day be given mechanistic explanations not in spite of the distinction between primary and secondary qualities but because of it (Hegge 1978: 127). The distinction is philosophically important not only for the construction of knowledge but also because it influences the perception of the human being. All aspects of the human that can be studied as primary qualities are relegated to a mechanistic worldview known from the natural sciences, while the rest becomes an epiphenomenon. The distinction in itself is potentially reductionist from the view of a phenomenologist

(Luckmann 1978) or any other philosophical viewpoint, which sees phenomena such as soul, spirit, and meaning as central to human life.

Moreover, a critical question becomes how and where the distinction is to be drawn. A way to learn about the distinction between primary and secondary qualities is to observe how it is drawn at different points in time. For example, weight, extension, and movement were categorized as primary qualities from the earliest days of the distinction. Locke held that heat was a secondary quality because, as Plato already had shown, the same wind could be felt to be either hot or cold (Cambridge Dictionary of Philosophy 1995). Evidently, heat has moved to the other side of the distinction after the notion of temperature was discovered and thermometers invented. The paraphernalia of measurement obviously had the capacity to displace this quality from one category to the other.

Phenomenological philosophers have argued that the human world is constituted through human sensation, experience, and sense-making (Luckmann 1978). It is unacceptable and reductionist to perceive of a Chinese wall inside the human being which separates the domain of the natural sciences from humanities (the measurable from the unmeasurable). In practice, however, history shows that wall to in fact be non-existent for all the reasons that the same philosophers have feared. The worldview of the empirical natural sciences first establishes a domain for themselves in contradistinction to the "subjective" remainder of the world. The former then expands continuously, in fact colonizing the latter, according to Luckmann (1978).

Measurement does not stop in the face of some metaphysical and pre-social properties inside things or inside human beings, for that matter. In fact, measurement helps move around our fundamental categorizations of things.

For Latour (1987, 2004, 2005), there is no "guarantee" for the thingness of things in things. Instead, knowledge about things is a result of networks and associations that make measurement and inscriptions of qualia possible.

Interestingly enough, the distinction between primary and secondary qualities is made and upheld by those interested in an empirical (i.e. anti-metaphysical) approach to the world only to establish a peculiar metaphysical basis for the categorization of what can be studied. Latour also insists that the primary/secondary qualities distinction is politically problematic; if primary qualities define the world we already share (objectively determined) and the secondary divide us (because they are subjective), then the bulk of the political work has already been carried out by the distinction itself (Latour 2004: 47)!

From the standpoint of more recent sociology of science, this observation reveals a lot about both the constructive character of measurement as well as the problematic nature of ontological distinctions such as the one between primary and secondary qualities. The fact that the drawing of the distinction can be so easily moved by means of practical measurement makes clear that the basis for the epistemological distinction should not be sought in the domains of ontology and metaphysics, but in the practical life of methodology.

The implication is that measurement of quality plays an important role. It helps constitute both the ontology, epistemology, and politics of quality even in present times.

Quality, Morality, Esthetics… and Commerce

While the term quality continues to play a role in the realm of epistemology and the discussion about qualia and their status has remained of great concern to philosophers, the term quality entered entirely different domains in the centuries following 1300. We now turn to the use of the term quality in morality, esthetics, and trade. Unfortunately, philosophers and other specialists who describe the history of concepts have paid much less attention to the meaning and use of the term quality in these areas of life than to the epistemological properties of qualia. This is paradoxical, because the goodness of quality that continues to be quintessential for the use of the term today was constituted through this transposition of quality into these new domains.

One of the conditions of possibility for the entry of the term quality into the moral domain was secularization and the loosening of a religious and theocratic grip on human life. The Reformation was one of the conducing factors to this long, historical transformation.

Quality also becomes generally known as something good and positive. Already before 1396, it is used to refer to a grade of excellence

(Barnhart and Steinmetz 1988). This opens two very common meanings of quality, which have remained in use since then: Quality as a category (of something excellent) (similar to nobility but now used in a general sense) and quality as a variable (degree of excellence). These remain the most prominent and frequent connotations of quality. The positivity of quality infuses or overrides almost any other aspect of the concept of quality and its application to a variety of phenomena. Whenever you encounter it, quality is something good, absolutely or relatively, but good nevertheless.

These connotations of quality remain (Encyclopedia Britannica 1972; Webster's Ninth 1990; Oxford Advanced Learner's Dictionary 2000). Quality is absolute (a category of good in itself) or relational, where it depends on its position in relation to something else. Either way, it is not common. It is not ordinary. It is extraordinary, fine, rare, or at least comparatively good.

This meaning of quality (as extraordinary and/or comparatively good) builds on the epistemological configurations of qualia known since Antiquity, but it adds entirely new evaluative dimensions. It is presumably no coincidence that these meanings break through in the centuries after 1400, perhaps most clearly from 1600 to 1700. As mentioned, one can imagine that a slow, gradual loosening of the control of religious dogma over society would allow greater space for the moral and esthetic dimensions being woven into the concept of quality.

One might also imagine that merchants would like to talk about the sublime quality of the silk and spices they brought home from the new world. Quality is an incredibly useful term in trade and commerce for explaining why similar quantities of goods should not cost the same. Once there is more than one type of something, once there is a diversity of goods available, it becomes pertinent to describe their variations. To the extent that variation in prices must be explained, grades of quality become relevant.

We know from the history of metrology that attempts were already made in ancient Rome to standardize cubic measures (for standardized amounts of, e.g. olive oil and grain). We also know that the invention and implementation of the metric system in Europe was instrumental in replacing a plethora of various local measures. How much is a foot? That depends on your foot. The same with inches, pounds, ounces, yards, and so on. Examples were given of how, when the price of flour went up, bakers started baking smaller loaves of bread to make ends meet. They were restricted by conventional or feudal price-setting, and they were expected to bake traditional bread in traditional ways. The only logical response therefore became to be "flexible" concerning the size of "a normal loaf of bread."

The standardized metric system rendered it easier to trust that a particular amount of something was in fact objectively defined. With the opening of markets, prices became variable. Quality became a necessary factor for explaining variations of price given the same standardized amount of a particular type of good.

To understand how quality can become as widespread as it is today, we must revisit one more domain where quality peaks and then disappears. It has to do with the quality of human beings.

Already around 1300, quality takes on the meaning of character, disposition, and temperament. After 1400, the term quality is also referred to in terms of rank or position in society or nobility. Quality becomes something fine, something above the extraordinary. The positivity of quality has remained with us to this day, but quality as a label on social rank has become rare and archaic (Oxford English Dictionary 1989). J.L. Heiberg (1791–1860) could meaningfully state that "A man of quality is the term for one whose rank forbids him to pay his tailor," but a dictionary suggests that this use of the term expired by the beginning of the twentieth century (Ordbog Over Det Danske Sprog 1976).

In the modern world, quality can only be used to imply class or rank in a subtle, indirect sense, such as when intellectuals talk about the lack of "quality" in mass culture products, while not explicating their view as elitist. Other political forces can seek to remove the term from official policies (cultural policy in particular) as an appeal to populist or anti-elitist sentiments (Husz 2012). This move has been primarily observed in policies related to "the fine arts" and to reiterate, only by implication.

Another meaning of quality (known to be used in 1596) which is now lost is that of party or side (in contradistinction to enemy). If quality creates distinctions between people, this function is not visible anymore, except by indirect implication. In the contemporary world, distinctions between people are implemented much more smoothly when not managed through a system making these distinctions explicit and thereby deprives human beings of their dignity (which is one of the reasons why Apartheid was such a horrendous system). So quality presumably increased its chances of remaining in circulation in modern times when it disconnected itself from all explicit connotations of social rank.

The only common way in which the term quality continues to be used as a label on people is when a person's intellectual, moral, or other qualities are praised. To reiterate, these are moral qualities and individual qualia, not categories of people.

Exactly as Foucault warned, it is tempting to overstate the later usefulness of particular displacements of meanings as if there were an inherent teleological drive in the history of the concept. Nevertheless, I do emphasize that a very productive rhetorical opening was made possible by movements in the concept of quality described above: the identification of quality with excellence and with a grade of good plus the elimination of the ability of quality to explicitly refer to categories of people. These displacements of meaning make it possible to refer to quality in a way where it can be used everywhere where there is a market, and it can gain support and establish alliances, not fronts, because it operates under an unconditionally positive flag. Quality becomes ever-positive. The road becomes paved for a broadly applicable concept without opposition. In addition, the positivity of quality infuses other aspects of quality with ever-positive meaning.

Quality, Norms, and Statistics

While the meaning of something unquestionably good is maintained, another radical turn in the history of quality takes place with the advent of industrialism. An early precursor occurred in the US, where systematic production of small arms already took place in 1850 without the kind of craftsmanship known from Europe. The key was conformance to specifications to enable interchangeable machine parts to fit together (Reeves and Bednar 1994).

While the excellent, the sublime, and the rare have constituted important dimensions of quality since around 1400, quality under industrialism ushers in an understanding of quality with almost opposite connotations. In industry, a quality product is one that conforms to standards. Variation is deviance. Deviance is bad. Quality and norm become equivalents. Minimum standards of quality must be met in all aspects of production. As technological advances and division of labor render mass production possible, workers are separated from the responsibility for their final products (Berger 1964). While the quantity of produced goods increases rapidly, questions about their quality become relevant, especially in the absence of the pride and self-consciousness of the craftsman. In the industrial era, the dominant relevance structure sees quality as a matter of control over all aspects of industrial production at the expense of the perspective of the individual worker.

As a consequence, in the first half of the twentieth century industrial organization invents a special organizational function with responsibility for the quality of products.

Published in 1931, Shewhart's *Economic Control of Quality of Manufactured Product* lays down the principles for the quantification of quality so that the quality function has a measurable "object" and can document its progress from one period to the next. It is epistemologically supported by statistics that make it possible to draw conclusions about large numbers of phenomena based on a representative sample (Reeves and Bednar 1994). All variation not induced by sheer chance should be controlled and eliminated. Statistics gauge how much chance can account for. The rest is the responsibility of quality management.

World War II intensified the need to ensure that products were actually functioning in the moment of use and, thus, the need for systematic quality control.

The second half of the twentieth century is characterized by attempts at obtaining systematic and holistic grip on quality in the production sphere. Dictionaries introduce entries such as quality control, quality assurance, quality management, quality control officer, and so on. These numerous composite terms pave the way for grammatical use of quality as an adjective, which occurs from the 1960s onwards.

Several recurring problems and trends seek to define that holistic grip more specifically. Despite several attempts at improving the quality of the final product, however, some forms of production continue to fail.

This problem becomes particularly intense when the production process is long and labor-intensive, and when customers are ready to turn to other products (International Encyclopedia of Business and Management 2002). It then simply becomes too expensive to postpone quality control until the manufacture of final product.

Consequently, quality becomes more process-oriented. Attention to quality is necessary in each step of the production process. Checklists, algorithms, and other tools are developed to enforce the idea. Over time, it becomes clear that quality requires the active participation of all employees, guided by some form of organization-wide coordination and management. The full price must now be paid for the degradation of the craftsman so characteristic of industrialism.

An additional influence on the concept of quality comes from consumerism. While engineers hold a production-oriented view on quality, marketing personnel focus more on how products fit into people's lives and how consumers perceive brands. In addition to changing quality recipes in fundamental ways, the consumerist perspective also adds another layer of relativity to quality. Maybe a cheap, unhealthy product, a product without durability, or an otherwise inferior product can be a quality product as long as consumers are willing to pay for it. The right of consumers to purchase and throw away products was seen as new and progressive (compared to the scarcity they had experienced earlier) (Husz 2012).

Ads now claim how many times a product has been bought, not sold. New paradigms for understanding consumers emerged. Qualitative methods proved useful in this endeavor, as focus groups became popular and ethnographic studies helped marketers understand consumer perspectives. Qualitative methods were sold partly as socially progressive, partly as pragmatically useful (Patton 2002). Gone are the days when philosophers in ivory towers relegate consumer perceptions to the almost derogatory category of "secondary qualities." Phenomenology, culture theory, and semiotics are mobilized in order to understand—and commercially exploit—consumer perspectives.

Marketers, market analysts, and strategists seek influence on how an industrial corporation defines quality with reference to consumer views. Marketing discourse installs a logic of its own (Bauman 2001). Service packages and other initiatives that moved products and (eventually also design) closer to consumers become relevant for the understanding of quality. In this light, Callon et al. (2002) talk about qualification and re-qualification, that is, processes where qualities of products are attributed, stabilized, objectified, and arranged in the light of passes as a sellable good on a market. In their view, the old distinction between primary and secondary qualities becomes increasingly obsolete, as everything that helps position a product in a favorably in relation to other products can be "a quality" (Callon et al. 2002: 200).

Processes of qualification and re-qualification are demanding for the producer. Companies struggle to incorporate the concern for quality—however defined—into their planning, production, and even their organizations, as such. An impetus into the conceptualization of quality in production is articulated along with an interest in organizational culture. Especially in the 1980s, American automobile manufacturers found themselves outcompeted by their Japanese counterparts. Japanese cars were smaller and more fuel-efficient, giving them a competitive advantage after the energy crises in the 1970s. They were also reasonably priced and not lacking in design or durability compared to American cars. American business consultants began asking questions about the secrets behind the Japanese success. They found the answer in organizational culture: Japanese workers were devoted to their company. They also practiced particular forms of working together, now known as "quality circles." Quality circles are immediate, on-the-spot forms of cooperation where employees across functions and levels contribute to the identification and solution of quality problems as they appear on a daily basis in the company. Although many of the stories about Japan may in fact have been fabricated and the importance of organizational culture overrated, the notion of organizational culture as a key to excellence was a vehicle that could be used to massage a notion of quality into the hearts and minds of all employees (Peters and Waterman 1982).

While the ideals of Taylorism, which dominated the early phases of industrialism, focused on the structure and division of labor but ignored the meaning of work, organizational culture was a new paradigm that filled the gap. Organizational culture as a paradigm built on the earlier notion that quality required the attention and involvement of all employees; more than that, however, it added the importance of commitment and conviction.

It did so in a very optimistic spirit. The somewhat unspecific definition of culture might have been conducive to this project. Enthusiasm is needed to win hearts and minds, and enthusiasm sometimes thrives on what is not specified very clearly.

The notion of culture thus became a vehicle for a broad spectrum of factors, partly intangible, which nevertheless had to be mobilized in order to enhance quality and excellence (Harvey and Stensaker 2008). Organizations cannot leave important factors to chance.

The underlying tension between structure, surveillance, and measurement control, on the one hand, and culture, conviction, and enthusiasm on the other—in other words between the "hard" and "soft" forms of control in organizations—went unresolved. It continues to be an issue in organizations, whether or not the tension is articulated clearly (Dahler-Larsen 2015; Läubli Loud and Mayne 2013). While it is easy to agree that the post-hoc quality measurement typical of the early days of industrialism is no longer viable, a "culture-oriented" approach can be seen as an attractive alternative (Harvey and Stensaker 2008), but process-oriented inspection regimes also claim to address the problem of how to secure quality in a preemptive manner before quality problems occur. In this view, quality assurance, inspection, and audit resemble risk management, which is famous for its own set of problems regarding the social definition of risk (Beck 1992; Power 1997, 2016).

So, not long after industrialism made it clear that quality was an aspect of human-made products, and thus became something for which someone could be held accountable, a new era was inaugurated in which the control of quality became a problematic industry itself.

Quality, Service, and Audits

As the overall economic structure in modern society gradually puts extra emphasis on the service industry, quality also becomes important in that sector. Around 1970, debate addressed whether service is so different from production that it deserves its own notions of quality; for example, service is produced and consumed simultaneously. It cannot be stocked. Services are processes, not products. They are perishable and somewhat intangible. They also involve customers in a way that makes it difficult to measure quality after the conventional model known from the quantification of (primary) qualities of physical objects (Reeves and Bednar 1994: 426) as well as after the conventional industrial model. However, Levitt (1972) argued that the most important problem in services was lack of consistency; in his view, the technocratic mentality of the manufacturer should be adopted rather than the so-called erratic elegance of the artisan (Reeves and Bednar 1994: 427).

In Power's (1996) view, one of the most important keys to understanding the contemporary form and shape of the concept of quality is the imprint it received from quality control as conceived in industrial production (Pflueger 2016; Power 1996). This imprint remains integrated in the concept as quality wanders into service organizations. With this imprint, there is a relentless focus on the prevention of quality problems through detailed norms, inspection, audit, and documentation.

A wide range of notions for how to steer quality in organizations (e.g. Total Quality Management) is already available. Quality is articulated as a special function in organizations that also becomes visible as identifiable parts of organizational structures. Special quality functions are mentioned in job postings related to quality development, quality measurement, and quality control. Quality managers and quality consultants develop their own particular way of thinking, supported by the establishment of their own organizational field with paraphernalia such as conferences, journals, associations, and organizational recipes (DiMaggio and Powell 1983; Meyer et al. 1994). All that is further required is a transfer of existing infrastructure for dealing with quality into the service sector.

The corollary imaginary of a perfect social world is one where people follow handbooks, prescriptions, checklists, and standards. It is also a world in which inspection is needed and warranted. It is a world that celebrates consistency with minimal standards (or what might be called defensive quality). This is not the kind of imaginary you would expect from someone aspiring to the excellent and sublime (or what we might call offensive quality).

Power (1996, 1997) explains how quality as a general recipe for an organization results from an interplay between internal and external forces. Organizations are subject to external audits, reviews, and control mechanisms. To manage these external demands, organizations set up their own departments, offices, and functions. In turn, quality managers seek to make the organization "auditable" in the light of the external demands. Quality thus becomes a product of a chain of organizational procedures as well as an entire set of tools and infrastructures that render quality inscriptions possible, including surveys, report cards, metrics, handbooks, and so on. In health care, for example, this instrumentation of quality has taken place since 1970 (Pflueger 2016: 19). Computerization helps make the collection and management of large amounts of data possible.

Documentation enhances the possibilities for external audit. Inspecting organizations are also inspected. Lindeberg (2007) further explains the importance of quality documentation by showing how organizations not only combine internal and external factors but are in fact linked in chains of control which are surprisingly long and complex. Inspired by Power and Luhmann, Lindeberg stipulates the existence of a whole differentiated social system that governs quality in a self-referential manner. Kristoffersen and Lindeberg (2004) show how, at the end of the chain, quality-bestowing organizations use peer-review and mutual recognition to seek to bestow legitimacy upon each other and thereby themselves.

This configuration of control mechanisms seems to signify an increasingly high level of abstraction as quality is defined in terms of what organizations see when looking at other organizations, at a great distance from actual products and services. It also produces an interesting closure to the open question as to why quality is not in need of a broader (and, some would hope: critical) discussion of which values constitute the "goodness" that is so inherent in quality. This discussion becomes functionally superfluous when quality organizations legitimize quality organizations.

A precondition for organizations inspecting organizations is that quality has become abstracted from the specificities of goods and services and, as the social equivalent of this, when organizations dealing with quality have organized themselves into a self-referential system. Social and political legitimacy, one can argue in critical opposition to Luhmanian theory, cannot be bestowed by a system upon itself.

Quality in the Public Sector

Finally, let us consider the introduction of the discourse of quality into the public sector. In many countries, this took place from around the late 1980s (Bergh 2011). The introduction of the quality discourse is particularly problematic in the public sector, which deals with "wicked problems" (Harmon and Mayer 1986). These are problems where people disagree about the boundary and definition of problems, where multiple values are involved, and where criteria for the solution of the problem are contested.

One of the factors making the introduction of the quality discourse possible is that schools, universities, hospitals, and childcare institutions have become conceived of as *organizations* (Ahrne and Brunsson 2008). In that capacity, they participate in fields of organization in which general recipes for good and legitimate management are defined and circulated (Røvik 2005). Furthermore, New Public Management as a movement helped neutralize the public/private distinction, thereby allowing the transport of quality regimes inspired by private industry and service into the management of public service organizations. This move is often interpreted as the "pushing" of a new (neoliberal) ideology into the public sector. Perhaps a collapse of meanings undergirding the belief in the public sector as a trustworthy provider of grand narratives about progress, equality, *Dannelse/Bildung*, and democracy (Lyotard 1982) had already happened. Perhaps a vacuum had occurred that helped pull in the quality discourse. The general positivity of the notion of quality helped take the focus away from what might be lost when other discourses lost attraction. Quality also helped nullify potential social contradictions and conflicts. Quality is for all, and apparently without opposition. Perhaps quality helps portray wicked problems as if they are more tame and more manageable.

Yet, the quality movement has its own problems in the public sector. A particular problem related to the notion of quality is its overtones of excellence (something rare and special, not the ordinary). How can this aspect of quality be maintained together with a political imagery that demands the equal rights and worth of all citizens?

Here, the quantification of quality probably plays an important role. If quality is conceived of as a variable (where the scores in one end of a continuum are defined as "excellent"), any absolute, categorical contradiction is dissolved. There is also intense ideological work going on, especially in welfare states such as those in Scandinavia to redefine the quality–quantity relationship so as to enhance an imagery where high quality can be accessible to everyone. In practice, the working class should also have access to quality education, "high culture," and so on (Husz 2012). Others argue, however, that in practice what is formerly seen as elite higher education cannot simply be extended into mass education without the addition of resources and without consequences for "quality." However, this argument can only be stated carefully—and perhaps implicitly—inasmuch as quality cannot refer to categories of people. Quality is, apparently, for all. At the same time, the continued attraction of the notion of quality rests with its continued reference to something particularly good.

* * *

Modern public organizations are characterized by complexity, specialization, and fragmentation. In the public sector, the need for the overall coordination of organizational quality is as pressing as it was in industry. Quality offers itself as an overarching concept, as do other concepts.

Each has a worldview that vies to become the most prominent principle for the organization of the organization. We have seen "communication," "sustainability," and "innovation" become headlines for such conglomerates of management principles, recipes for legitimate organization, and job titles. All specialists in all of these areas claim expertise. They want good salaries, an office close to top management, recognition, and influence.

A particularly prominent set of recipes relates to risk management. Quality control and risk management share a number of practices, including audit, inspection, checklists, and control mechanisms. There is also an overlap in worldviews: Steps should be taken before problems occur. A defensive view of quality resonates well with a preemptive risk management perspective. Do not do anything surprising. Stick to the norms. As risk management develops its own perspective embodied in conferences, bodies of literature, education programs, and management positions, there can be competition between a quality management view and a risk management view. They also tell different stories about the world. Quality suggests improvement. The risk perspective talks about how to secure survival in a world that is becoming insecure, unpredictable, and violent. The integration of these narratives presumably requires an interweaving of elements into local stories.

In organizations in the real world, there may be overlaps, displacements, ploys, and reorganizations under different—sometimes equivocal—headlines. Quality is only one of these headlines, albeit an important one.

The abstraction following from meta-regulation that we identified earlier also surfaces in relation to public governance. At least from around 2005, prominent international organizations such as OECD, the World Bank, and EU develop publications and guidelines about the quality not of services but of public regulation (Radaelli and de Francesco 2007). At the same time, the ideals regarding regulation are pushed in a particular direction and regulation is depoliticized (Erkkilä and Piironen 2014). Quality does its best to hold on to the role of meta-regulator.

What the History of Quality Has Brought

Quality has a long, rich history. It has gained in prominence. Its journey from a classical philosophical dialogue into a discourse relevant for millions of teachers, managers, consumers, journalists, consultants, evaluators, and others—if not for the structuration of our society as such—is nothing less than amazing.

Its flexibility and its ever-positive loading (since 1300 onwards) have contributed to its successful history over the centuries. The incredible success of the concept is not due to its precision, because it is not very precise. Its meanings are rich, varied, and change over time. Some important significations remain, while others are lost. The dimensions in the concept of quality are partly in tension with each other, such as the offensive/maximalist and defensive/minimalist versions of quality. The implications of reaching for the stars versus not falling below minimum standards are very different. They represent quite different aspirations and fears, quite different mentalities, and set in motion different practical initiatives, but both can be appealed to using the notion of quality.

Some issues remain unsettled, such as the ontological versus the practical-methodological position regarding the distinction between primary (measurable) and secondary (non-measurable) qualities.

Some of the domains in which quality occurs, such as the moral/esthetic and the epistemological, are also in underlying tension or have not resolved their differences.

The underlying warrants for when and how quality implies statements of the good have not been in focus among philosophers. This lacuna regarding valuation stands in stark contrast to the many pages one finds about the epistemology of qualia, particularly the categories of primary and secondary sense qualities. While the link between quality and knowledge has been an object of intense philosophical scrutiny, the incorporation of value into quality is under-cultivated and under-reflected. Sometimes, the value-laden aspect of quality surfaces when the utility for customers is compared to price (Reeves and Bednar 1994). Here, value is evidently reduced to its economic sense.

Apparently, quality has been able to live a life over the course of centuries without interference in the type of philosophical and practical discussions we otherwise have about values. In recent years, the abstraction, reification, and self-referentiality of quality systems have contributed to parking this issue. From the perspective of social and political science, the tacit neglect of important value issues is exactly what demands our attention. The lack of explicit attention to controversies about values is surprising to an evaluator who is trained to see such deliberations as an integral element in any proper evaluation process. One might also wonder how it has been possible to maintain a separation between two key domains in the concept of quality: the domain that deals with values versus the domain that deals with epistemology (except in one very important sense, which is that quality is infused with ever-present positivity). Remember that these domains were linked together in the days of Plato. Has quality become a way of *not* thinking about values and not linking values and cognition? Is the use of the term quality in fact a functional replacement of debates we could otherwise have?

The history of the concept of quality has produced a rich variety of meanings, which one can draw from, often without further specification, and often with positive stardust attached. In a rhetorical perspective, the notion of quality is attractive because even a carelessly selected set of meanings of quality is never negatively loaded. At the same time, given its many layers and avenues of meaning, the concept of quality itself can be used haphazardly, without specification and clarification. Ambiguity and positivity go hand in hand.

When the discourse of quality also enters everyday realities, we can imagine these realities becoming "trading zones" (Stark 2009) for different notions of quality. So, in practical situations, people will have to deal with the specificities of quality or qualities.

Rather than merely subscribing to a myth of general positivity, I shall propose that quality can be good in particularly selective ways, in specific situations, and relative to varying perspectives. I shall delineate nine such perspectives. I do not suggest that in a situation in daily life, only one perspective counts. I propose that a responsible evaluative statement about quality would be based on some kind of explicitly and reflexive reference to these nine perspectives or a frame of reference of a similar sort rather than merely a vague, unspecified notion of something good. In that sense, a vocabulary of quality perspectives can be used to analyze what an otherwise broad, vague, or multifaceted concept might mean and which potential tensions might be at play among its many meanings.

References

Ahrne, Göran, and Nils Brunsson. 2008. Organizing the World. In *Transnational Governance*, ed. M.-L. Djelic and K. Sahlin-Andersson. Cambridge: Cambridge University Press.

Barnhart, Robert K., and Sol Steinmetz. 1988. *The Barnhart Dictionary of Etymology*. New York: H. W. Wilson.

Bauman, Zygmunt. 2001. Consuming Life. *Journal of Consumer Culture* 1 (1): 9–29.

Beck, Ulrich. 1992. *Risk Society. Towards a New Modernity*. Thousand Oaks: Sage.

Berger, Peter L. 1964. Some General Observations on the Problem of Work. In *The Human Shape of Work: Studies in the Sociology of Occupations*, ed. P.L. Berger. New York: Macmillan.

Bergh, Andreas. 2011. Why Quality in Education – and What Quality? – A Linguistic Analysis of the Concept of Quality in Swedish Government Texts. *Education Inquiry* 2 (4): 709–723.

Bevir, Mark. 2007. *Encyclopedia of Governance*. Thousand Oaks: Sage.

Blishen, Edward. 1969. *Blond's Encyclopedia of Education*. London: Blond Education.

Bostock, David. 1988. *Plato's Thæetetus*. Oxford: Clarendon Press.

Callon, Michel, Cécile Méadel, and Vololona Rabeharisoa. 2002. The Economy of Qualities. *Economy and Society* 31 (2): 194–217.

Dahler-Larsen, Peter. 2015. Book Review: Enhancing Evaluation Use: Insights From Internal Evaluation Units. *American Journal of Evaluation* 36 (2): 283–286.

DiMaggio, Paul, and Walter Powell. 1983. The Iron Cage Revisited: Institutional Isomorphism and Collective Rationality in Organizational Fields. *American Sociological Review* 48 (6): 147–160.

Encyclopedia Britannica. 1972. London: Encyclopedia Britannica Inc.

Encyclopedia of Quality of Life and Well-being Research. 2014. Ed. A.C. Michalos. Dordrecht: Springer.

Erkkilä, Tero, and Ossi Piironen. 2014. (De)politicizing Good Governance: The World Bank Institute, the OECD and the Politics of Governance Indicators. *Innovation: The European Journal of Social Science Research* 27 (4): 344–360.

Foucault, Michel. 1984. Nietzsche, Genealogy, History. In *The Foucault Reader: An Introduction to Foucault's Thought*, ed. P. Rabinow, 76–100. London: Penguin.

Harmon, Michael M., and Richard T. Mayer. 1986. *Organization Theory for Public Administration*. Glenview: Scott, Foresman and Company.

Harvey, Lee, and Bjørn Stensaker. 2008. Quality Culture: Understandings, Boundaries and Linkages. *European Journal of Education* 43 (4): 427–442.
Hegge, Hjalmar. 1978. *Mennesket og Naturen* [The Human and the Nature]. Oslo: Universitetsforlaget.
Husz, Orsi. 2012. The Morality of Quality: Assimilating Material Mass Culture in Twentieth-Century Sweden. *Journal of Modern European History* 10 (2): 152–181.
International Encyclopedia of Business and Management. 2002. Ed. W. Malcolm. London: Routledge.
Klein, Jacob. 1977. *Plato's Trilogy: Theaetetus, the Sophist, and the Statesman.* Chicago: University of Chicago Press.
Koselleck, Reinhart. 2007. *Begreber, Tid og Erfaring. En tekstsamling* [Concepts, Time and Experience: An Anthology]. Copenhagen: Hans Reitzel. Collection of chapters originally published in Koselleck, R. 2000. *Zeitschichten: Studien zur Historik.* Frankfurt am Main: Suhrkamp Verlag.
Kristoffersen, Dorte, and Tobias Lindeberg. 2004. Creating Quality Assurance and International Transparency for Quality Assurance Agencies: The Case of Mutual Recognition. *Quality in Higher Education* 10 (1): 31–36.
Latour, Bruno. 1987. *Science in Action: How to Follow Scientists and Engineers through Society.* Stony Stratford: Open University Press.
———. 2004. Why Has Critique Run Out of Steam? From Matters of Fact to Matters of Concern. *Critical Inquiry* 30 (2): 225–248.
———. 2005. *Reassembling the Social: An Introduction to Actor–Network-Theory.* New York: Oxford University Press.
Läubli Loud, Marlène, and John Mayne. 2013. *Enhancing Evaluation Use: Insights from Internal Evaluation Units.* Thousand Oaks: Sage.
Levitt, Theodore. 1972. Production-Line Approach to Service. *Harvard Business Review* 50 (5): 20–31.
Lindeberg, Tobias. 2007. *Evaluative Technologies: Quality and the Multiplicity of Performance.* Copenhagen: Copenhagen Business School.
Luckmann, Thomas. 1978. Philosophy, Social Sciences and Everyday Life. In *Phenomenology and Sociology*, ed. T. Luckmann, 217–253. Harmondsworth: Penguin.
Lyotard, Jean-Francois. 1982. *Viden og det Postmoderne Samfund* [The Postmodern Condition: A Report on Knowledge]. Aarhus: Sjakalen.
Management Leksikon. 2001. Ed. S. Hildebrandt and C. Waldstrøm, vol. 3. Copenhagen: Børsens Forlag.
Meyer, John W., John Boli, and George M. Thomas. 1994. Ontology and Rationalization in the Western Cultural Account. In *Institutional Environments*

and Organizations, ed. W.R. Scott and J.W. Meyer, 9–27. Thousand Oaks: Sage.

Ordbog Over Det Danske Sprog [Dictionary of the Danish Language]. 1976. Det Danske Sprog- og Litteraturselskab. Copenhagen: Gyldendal.

Oxford Advanced Learner's Dictionary. 2000. A.S. Hornby. Oxford: Oxford University Press.

Patton, Michael Q. 2002. *Qualitative Research and Evaluation Methods*. Thousand Oaks: Sage.

Peters, Thomas J., and Robert H. Waterman Jr. 1982. *In Search of Excellence: Lessons from America's Best-Run Companies*. New York: Harper and Row.

Pflueger, Dane. 2016. Knowing Patients: The Customer Survey and the Changing Margins of Accounting in Healthcare. *Accounting, Organizations and Society* 53: 17–33.

Power, Michael. 1996. Making Things Auditable. *Accounting, Organizations and Society* 21 (2/3): 289–315.

———. 1997. *The Audit Society*. Oxford: Oxford University Press.

———. 2016. Postscript. On Riskwork and Auditwork. In *Essays on the Organizational Life of Risk Management*, ed. Michael Power. Oxford: Oxford University Press.

Radaelli, Claudio M., and Fabrizio De Francesco. 2007. *Regulatory Quality in Europe: Concepts, Measures and Policy Processes*. Manchester: Manchester University Press.

Reeves, Carol A., and David A. Bednar. 1994. Defining Quality: Alternatives and Implications. *Academy of Management Review* 19 (3): 419–445.

Røvik, Kjell A. 2005. *Moderne Organisasjoner: Trender i Organisasjonstenkningen ved Tusenårsskiftet* [Modern Organizations: Trends in Organizational Thinking at the Millennium]. Bergen: Fagbokforlaget.

Simpson, John A., and Edmund S. C. Weiner. 1989. *The Oxford English Dictionary*. New York/Oxford: Clarendon Press/Oxford University Press.

Stark, David. 2009. *The Sense of Dissonance, Accounts of Worth in Economic Life*. Princeton: Princeton University Press.

The Cambridge Dictionary of Philosophy. 1995. Ed. R. Audi. Cambridge: Cambridge University Press.

Vattimo, Gianni. 2005. *Nihilisme og Emancipation. Etik, Politik, Ret* [Nihilsm and Emancipation. Ethics, Politics, and Law]. Aarhus: Aarhus University Press.

Webster's Dictionary of Word Origins. 1995. Ed. Merriam-Webster. New York: Smithmark.

Webster's Ninth New Collegiate Dictionary. 1990. Springfield: Merriam-Webster.

3

Quality Perspectives

Why Distill Quality Perspectives?

The previous chapter showed that, in its totality, the concept of quality is enormously rich. It carries a number of meanings, some of which are in tension with each other. Although its ever-present connotation of something good is always attractive in social use, the concept of quality in toto is, if explicated, too big and unhandy to move around with. The only place where all meanings of quality meet is in the dictionary. In practice, people do not look up all these meanings; they usually talk about something less.

The manner in which quality is rhetorically condensed into something more specific is particularly interesting because of the ever-present goodness in quality. In all evaluative contexts, it is appropriate to ask: What do we mean by "good"? Good in what sense? Good with respect to what? While the previous chapter took a historical-thematic approach, the following analysis is conceptual-analytical. The previous analysis was diachronic. The following is synchronic: Which perspectives do we have today?

A quality perspective is a way of seeing and talking about quality that conceptually highlights a particular aspect. It is what Weick (in Dean and Bowen 2000) would call a rudimentary structuring of further selections. A perspective makes one look in one direction rather than another in

P. Dahler-Larsen, *Quality*, https://doi.org/10.1007/978-3-030-10392-7_3

order to find what is relevant and meaningful. It resembles what is called frames in policy analysis (Fischer 2003).

The nine quality perspectives presented in this chapter all resonate with literature. They also resonate with viewpoints you can meet in practical life, although not always in a pure form. The practical world is ambiguous. People do not always talk about quality in a systematic manner; in fact, they may talk more in terms of quality "scripts," which are tentative and implicit grips on what quality might mean in the situation at hand.

Expressed in the terminology of quality scripts and quality perspectives, I can imagine several sources of ambiguity. One is that a quality script is held intuitively. It remains implicit. It does not "clinch" in terms of a particular quality perspective.

People might talk about quality as if they subscribe to one particular quality perspective without taking responsibility for both plusses and minuses related to that perspective. They may even shift between views from one sentence to another. I could imagine a rhetorical strategy that evokes quality but which benefits from "floating" around and seeking to subscribe to the benefits of several perspectives without binding commitments to the blind spots or disadvantages of any of them. It would be similar to cherry picking all of the advantages of several perspectives and not taking responsibility for any disadvantages.

If people want a little bit from one perspective and a little bit from another but they prefer not to think of the downsides of any of the involved perspectives, we can bring clarity to a discussion about quality by offering a purified, ideal-typical list of pros and cons of each perspective.

When quality scripts are made articulate, reflected, explicit, and justified, they often come close to one of the quality perspectives covered in this chapter. I shall deal with each of these perspectives as systematically as possible—let us take clarity as far as we can. Only then can quality perspectives allow us to lay bare choices that are made explicitly or implicitly when talking about quality in practice.

In practical life, we may not afford the luxury of just choosing between such ideal types, but after an analysis of ideal types, we at least think more clearly about choices, pros, and cons. We also learn something about the concept of quality as such if it really hosts all of these nine perspectives.

To get to that insight, however, it is necessary to analyze each perspective in a cool, systematic manner. This chapter offers a definition of each perspective. I will describe what that perspective identifies as a typical quality problem. I will describe in which value framework the quality perspective makes sense and which kind of actors would be likely to find that quality perspective meaningful. I do this having in mind that the identities of actors are not given but can be co-constructed, that modern human beings play multiple, shifting roles, and that actors must create alliances through arguments that convince others. Nevertheless, the rough sketch of the (socially rooted) perspective from which a quality perspective makes sense is a heuristic key; it helps us understand what sense a perspective may make in the social world. Among the factors which keeps a quality perspective rooted in social life is how well it fits with the normative landscape in the social context at hand and how easily the perspective can be made operational so that it can produce data, facts, comparisons, assessments, and recommendations which paves the way for practical action.

So even if the main emphasis in this chapter is conceptual rather than historical, the conceptual analysis is not disconnected from social realities. In fact, the emphasis upon each of the quality perspectives may shift over time (Harvey and Stensaker 2008). Near the end of this chapter, I will return to the question of whether particular trends in our time tend to favor particular quality perspectives over others.

A caveat: Perspectives are not categories of things; rather, they are ways of looking at things. The fact that a given phenomenon plays a role in one quality perspective does not mean that it is totally excluded from another. Perspectives do not categorize phenomena; they merely typify different ways of looking them. As such, perspectives "enroll" phenomena and provide them with a definite meaning. Two or more perspectives may overlap in making judgments about an object. However, coincidental overlap is not the same as conceptual convergence.

Rhetorical devices such as *totum pro pars* may even be applied to accomplish alliances between otherwise diverse perspectives. It is analytically imperative, however, to take the *totum* out of the *totum pro pars* rhetorical figure. Parts should be understood as parts—no more, no less. Once the relativity of perspectives is revealed, we can then discuss whether each and every part deserves the same slice of the overall positivity connected to quality.

Without a notion of quality perspectives, it would be impossible to recognize differing principles as fundamentally different. The precondition necessary for this endeavor is clarity. However, one could philosophically imagine a commitment to a particular quality perspective that still did not lead to a fixed, stable, and secure notion of quality. The metaphor for this project is peeling an onion without ever getting to the core. Is there a stable, essential center of meaning inside a particular quality perspective, meaning that continued work within a perspective will only confirm and verify one operational definition of quality? Or is continued, loyal work within the perspective in fact unable to hold a fixed version of quality in place? The ambition is to get as much clarity as possible, but also to recognize that clarity cannot be imposed on what is messy and ambiguous.

Bearing in mind that quality perspectives can surely be carved out in different ways (Harvey and Green 1993; Reeves and Bednar 1994), here is my list.

Quality as an Accomplishment of Official Political Goals

Definition and Meaning

In this perspective, quality is defined as the accomplishment of set goals and objectives, which are qualified in a particular democratic way. Only goals and objectives that have been officially sanctioned in a legitimate system of government based on representative democracy are considered valid (Vedung 1997). This principle works as a bulwark against actors in a polity pursuing their own private goals. In education, for example, quality is not just what teachers and pupils think it is, but rather the achievement of goals in a curriculum that have been approved by legitimate authorities in a parliamentary chain of control.

Quality as an accomplishment of official political goals is not only relevant from the perspective of politicians, but also relevant for citizens who have legitimate expectations that organizations in the public sector will deliver what politicians have promised (Vedung 1997).

Many problems contribute to the lack of fulfillment of goals. If humans are lazy or forgetful, they will not focus the right amount of energy on the accomplishment of goals. Next, research in policy implementation has demonstrated that organizations hesitate to implement what has been officially decided. A number of problems result from a lack of communication, lack of enforcement of policy, and lacking knowledge or capacity among key people in all of the stages of the chain of implementation. There may also be deeper political reasons, including ideological tensions or conflicting interests that explain why some stakeholders hesitate to work for the accomplishment of officially binding policy goals. All of these difficulties should be overcome. The very meaning of a quality perspective that ties into official goals is to serve as a reminder of the continued relevance of these goals.

The goals are politically and legally binding even without the notion of quality. The term quality is therefore not mandatory in this context. There can be policy research, implementation research, and evaluation without the term quality. The term quality is nevertheless frequently occurring in policy contexts. Presumably, it adds an extra layer of positivity to policy and its implementation, thereby contributing to the reduction of opposition.

Limitations and Ambiguities

There are a number of problems with using policy goals as quality criteria.

Goals can be multiple or unclear, in which case they do not constitute a precise framework for operationalization of evaluation criteria, which implies finding appropriate and valid indicators of quality. Unclarity can even be a good thing in policy. The fact that many recent public sector reforms are enunciated as "quality reforms" suggests that there is presumably good reason to appeal to the concept of quality in a policy context. When a policy issue is conceived of not in classical policy terms but as a question of "lack of quality" in schools, universities, hospitals, and so on, the rhetorical function may be exactly to seek to mobilize the masses while presenting the reform as a generally good thing, not highlighting specific goals and value choices except for the enhancement of "quality." That is why governments of varying political colors seek to implement one quality reform after another. Quality is a concept without opposition, but it is also something that always requires improvement.

Whenever there is demand to measure and operationalize quality, anything that appears to be quantifiable, such as "results-based" quality, easily takes precedence over a careful delineation of quality as accomplishment of goals, which may be less easy to measure (Bergh 2011), although the slippage between the two may pass unnoticed.

Bereiter (2002) reminds us, however, that an operationalization of a hitherto un-operationalized concept changes the concept at hand. Paradoxically, this mechanism is sometimes an inherent part of policymaking. The responsibility for figuring out what overarching goals might mean in a particular context is occasionally delegated to lower levels of the implementation chain. Predictably, ambiguous transformations of meanings follow.

Political systems can be polycentric and exert multilevel governance. Given a fragmented, multilevel, and sometimes global configuration of systems of governance, the political chain of representation in which this perspective finds legitimacy is sometimes difficult to identify. It is therefore not always entirely clear when policy speaks in the name of quality or whether quality speaks in the name of policy.

Although OECD consists of nations with independent governments, it does not speak *for* governments; nevertheless, OECD statements are often influential in political discourse. While political chains of command may be unclear in complex governance structures, one often has the sense that producers of quality statements speak as if authority is clear. Harvey and Stensaker (2008) find considerable ambiguity when quality is referred to in an international context, across national governments with their own politically defined notions of quality. So, lack of clarity is one problem with defining quality in terms of official goals. Another is lack of attention to side effects.

With official goals and objectives as the only valid criteria, side effects are not considered. Official goals are frozen ideas. Learning about side effects is not included. Goals are sanctioned at official meetings, imprinted in strategies and policy documents, and difficult to change. Large-scale organizations with official goals as their guiding legitimate principles talk more than they listen; they struggle with feedback and responding to it quickly.

Three is a parallel issue relating to the distinction between explicit and implicit goals (Dörner 1996). In a rigorous understanding of this perspective, where quality is defined as the accomplishment of goals, only initially articulated (i.e. explicit) goals can count. Otherwise, subsequent assessments would be based on guesswork. As life unfolds, however, people gain experience, and some of this experience does count in an evaluative perspective, also politically, but it sometimes counts in relation to criteria that were not initially stated as important. Why not? Because life is unpredictable and human beings only know particular criteria are relevant when there is a clash between these criteria and specific experiences. Without these experiences, the corresponding criteria do not matter at all.

Here is a practical example. A person accepts a demanding job in another city because it helps her achieve (explicit) professional goals. She commutes too much and does not get enough sleep. Her new lifestyle gives her stress symptoms. Only because of this experience does she begin to include her health in her career decisions. It was hitherto taken for granted. She held it as an implicit goal.

An analysis of implicit goals has much in common with an analysis of side effects. However, the analysis of implicit goals is one step more advanced. In principle, side effects can be positive or negative, foreseen or unforeseen with reference to a given set of goals and preferences. The notion of implicit goals, however, reminds us that goals and preferences themselves may be dynamic depending on the flow of experiences. Their degree of articulation changes because their relevance changes over time. It is not only the effects which matter but also our changing constitution of them as relevant.

Official goals are sometimes met with resistance by local people who work with the implementation of policy. The counterargument from advocates of the "quality as official goals" perspective is that political legitimacy (remember, this is representative democracy) trumps what is defined locally as relevant. In that case, "quality" may in fact become more contested than the ideal-typical perspective suggests. However, if local contestation is strong enough or politicians wish to take local experiences into account, policies are sometimes adapted or revised.

If politics includes the making of collective experiences in the face of a dynamic reality, a perspective that only considers initial and explicit goals is unsophisticated. However, the clear legitimacy of the perspective of quality defined as the accomplishment of official goals rests with the initial, explicit goals. When official goals are ripe for change but have not officially been explicitly changed, an evaluative gaze that seeks legitimacy in official goals is caught in an interesting situation where it seeks firm ground but finds potential instability.

In sum, we have found a number of reasons why a perspective that defines quality as the accomplishment of political goals may be much less clear and stable than would initially appear. Goals may be unclear, their origins and interpretations be distributed in unclear ways, implicit goals or side effects may complicate the picture, and the dynamic relationship between experiences and the articulation of experience may make the perspective practically and philosophically unstable.

Social Conditions Favorable to Quality as an Accomplishment of Official Political Goals

The context most favorable to this perspective is one where a political authority and the goals it sets are seen as legitimate. Furthermore, there should be stable social environment so that goals do not change too often and too much. Finally, goals should be articulated clearly in a way that makes it possible to measure the degree of their attainment.

Quality as Utility

Definition and Meaning

Especially in the sphere of industrial production, it has been common to define quality in terms of utility. The idea is that although products can be characterized in terms of a number of properties, which can be more or less controlled in the production process, a production-oriented view does not pay attention to how the product can be used. Simple little products have proven incredibly useful. Similarly, just because particular products can be mass-produced, it does not follow that they are useful for anyone.

This observation has paved the way for a utility-oriented approach to the definition of quality. As notions of quality expanded beyond the sphere of industrial production, the utility-oriented approached made the same journey. In education, for example, the utility-oriented view would say that it is of less importance whether a particular educational program lives up to symbolic traditions of the past and whether a group of professionals feel that the education program is consistent with their values. Instead, what counts is that students learn competencies that are useful in solving real-world problems. If they do, they are also likely to find gainful employment. The employability of its students is therefore used as a proxy for the quality of an education program.

The underlying assumption is that the concept of utility enables one to "cut through" some superfluous layers of symbolism and subjectivity. There is a functional reality in utility.

This notion of utility is reminiscent of earlier distinctions made in economic theory between exchange value and use value. Whereas exchange relates to the value of a good in exchange for other goods on the market, the use value of a good relates to how it makes life livable or pleasant for human beings. Use value stands in a relation to human needs. Utility-oriented economic theory provides the ideological superstructure for such thought. Ideologically, the notion of quality as utility has gained considerable traction as the ideology of economic thinking permeates modern society.

Limitations and Ambiguities

It is tempting to see exchange value as a social construction defined by the market in contradistinction to use value understood as a real function, but the distinction does not hold. Once again using the example of education: The "exchange value" of an education program may be that it gives entry into another program that is known to lead to income, status, success, or other aspects of life to which human beings strive. Although one may criticize some education programs or policies for being excessively oriented toward careers and incomes, the problem is not that careers and incomes are artificial constructions. In the search for "exchange value," people invest in bonds, diamonds, housing, and education, and they do not do so because these phenomena are artificial in any sense. These phenomena have a "use" or "use value" because they have an exchange value. In turn, as the sociology of economic life has shown, exchange values hinge on property rights, on the organization of markets, and so on. Ultimately, there is no way of talking about the "value" of something, be it exchange value or use value, without running into a wall of social organization. For example, the "use value" of a car rests with the existence of infrastructure, roads, gas, and police.

It is therefore an illusion to assume that quality as utility rests on a rock-solid reality; it is as fluid and evanescent as the social reality within which it is embedded.

The definition of "use value" therefore ran into problems when confronted with the views of customers on specific goods and products. Unless expanding the term "use value" almost ad infinitum, it is difficult to explain why consumers are fascinated with diamonds and why they pay extraordinary prices for brand products. In turn, we may understand these phenomena if we inquire into the "secondary qualities" of products as subjectively perceived in the light of the needs, expectations, and wishes of users, but that journey can only be made if we are not restricted by a rigid, reified notion of what constitutes utility.

Social Conditions Favorable to Quality as Utility

This perspective is likely to thrive in combination with a rational view of the human being. The world should be one in which symbols and the imaginary play a limited role, so utility can be objectively defined in terms of a few measurable dimensions. Tacitly, a form of authority is assumed so that utility can be defined for others. If people speak for themselves, they often have all kinds of wishes and desires.

Quality as the Fulfillment of the Needs, Expectations, or Wishes of Users

Definition and Meaning

In this perspective, quality is defined as the fulfillment of the needs, expectations, and/or wishes of users. Although a large part of the historical roots of this perspective emerged from consumers in a market, I use "user" more generically. It refers to all of the addressees of a service or product, including patients, students, clients, and other recipients of public services.

One of the main justifications for this perspective is that manufacturers and service providers are often large organizations that talk more than they listen. Their managers and professionals maintain the status quo, they hold a production-oriented view, they are technically or professionally privileged, and they speak management language or Latin either metaphorically or in fact (as do some medical doctors).

The common consequence of these maladies is a lack of attention to the needs, expectations, and wishes of users. The remedy is more feedback regarding the same factors.

More attention will not only lead to greater user satisfaction with the provided services and goods. Differences in power can be reduced. More legitimacy can be bestowed on the organization that provides the product or service. And the organization will be able to deliver better services as a result of a better understanding of the situation of users (Dahlberg and Vedung 2001).

Here is an example. A pharmaceutical company had invented a new product that effectively reduced symptoms of psoriasis. It was marketed as a cream in a tube.

At one point, the company hired anthropologists to study how patients used this product in everyday life. The anthropologists found patients putting an old newspaper on the floor. They would then open the tube, leave it on the newspaper, step on it to make the cream come out, and then use the newspaper to apply the cream to their skin. When asked why they did so, patients would explain that because of the arthritis and weak joints that many of them suffered from in addition to their psoriasis, their hands were not strong enough to squeeze the thick cream out of the tube. The marketing people then went back to production and told them that patients had a problem with getting the cream out of the tube. Funny enough, said the production people, because we have a problem with getting it in. The next immediate step was to transform the product into a gel that could be applied much more easily. The company then also developed a new version of the product where the active ingredients were put into a spray so that patients could apply the product to parts of their body they were unable to reach, such as the back. However, the company had to work on a new kind of mechanism that would release the product at a lighter touch compared to conventional spray cans.

Limitations and Ambiguities

The perspectives of various users are not always compatible. As Julnes (2012) has convincingly shown, the need for an algorithm synthesizing various views is situation-specific. In public services where users share the same service, this need is indeed pressing. One example is a public library in which some users are expecting church-like tranquility. Others might use the library for group work (students) or play (children). These groups cannot all agree on appropriate noise levels. Yet they share the same public space, so some solution must be found. Care facilities for the elderly are often marked by an inherent tension regarding the use of common spaces, such as dining rooms. Some elderly persons find it uncomfortable to eat together with persons with severe problems with behavior and eating. At the risk of loneliness, some prefer eating in their private rooms. A "user perspective" without attention to balances and dilemmas between different users is sometimes an abstraction.

Instead, it makes more sense to understand quality statements issued from this perspective as a specific *interpretation* of a composite configuration of needs, preferences, and wishes informed by a particular understanding of value priorities in the situation at hand.

The plasticity of the user perspective renders it particularly prone to someone stepping in, interpreting what users need, and speaking on their behalf.

When data about the preferences and assessments expressed by users are quantified, they sometimes take on a particularly "objective" quality that possibly stems from their standardization and their similarity to measurable primary qualities of objects. Consequently, there can be a stark difference between objectified and typified viewpoints from average users, on the one hand, and the views and lives of specific users on the other (Schwandt and Burgon 2006).

Users have experience but no sure way of knowing what to expect. Expectations are highly amenable to social construction, if not manipulation. Users may put too much emphasis on kindness and comfort in service delivery at the expense of the professional knowledge and skill which characterizes good teaching, health care, social services, and so on.

Users may not always be aware of what will satisfy them in the future. While needs, expectations, and wishes all help define what counts as quality from a user perspective, they are not the same. What users immediately wish may not be good for them or may not be a good predictor for that with which they later turn out to be happy. Henry Ford is quoted for saying that if he had asked people what they wanted, they would have said faster horses. Similarly, many customers reportedly rejected a pilot version of the Xerox machine because they believed carbon paper provided the same result (Sower and Fair 2005: 15).

For example, a qualitative inquiry into travelers' perspectives on train travel revealed that what they desired most was seating with as much privacy as possible. Nevertheless, when asked to recall their most enjoyable train rides, they typically mention coincidental meetings with new, interesting people.

Users may need something they cannot explicate, which becomes painstakingly clear when they cannot talk reasonably about their own situation (e.g. small children, Alzheimer's patients). These instances exemplify to an extreme extent that deriving a definition of quality then requires an interpretation of what the world might look like from the user's perspective. This interpretation involves a moral responsibility as it interferes with another person's life; indeed, it involves a person in a situation where they depend on others. The tricky part is how one should speak on behalf of others.

Paradoxically, users themselves also take others into account when expressing their "own" wishes. Atul Gawande's (2014) book "Being Mortal" describes the terrifying dilemmas concerning how the terminally ill spend their last days. Ineffective and painful treatments are all too often chosen at the expense of how the persons in question would most enjoy the last days of their life. Doctors typically overrate the potential success of treatments and overestimate how much time is left. On top of which comes an unpleasant observation: Patients themselves sometimes accept further treatment because their relatives cannot accept having to say farewell, which moves one step closer psychologically if further treatment is refused. Out of love and fear of loss, family cannot tolerate what might be best for the patient, foregoing futile attempts at combating the illness, focusing instead on their wishes for their last days. The example reveals that statements from users are not essentially and purely "their own" solutions. Users' preferences and wishes resonate with social expectations.

Indeed, the very definition of a legitimate "user" of something is constituted through social conventions, some of which are institutionally sanctioned and change over time. The normative validity of a given user perspective is contingent upon these changing social frameworks. A quality statement based on this perspective can therefore be caught between the norms of the past and the norms of the future.

A user perspective can be evoked to induce change in business strategies or policies. Market mechanisms make service providers sensitive to customer preferences. Even without proper market mechanisms, however, public policy can use instruments emulating market mechanisms and stimulate similar effects, such as free choice between service providers, ongoing user feedback to which service providers must respond (e.g. student evaluations, customer satisfaction surveys), with the option of publishing this data to inform the choices of potential future users. The voices of users, such as patients, can thus be used to hold service providers accountable (Pflueger 2016: 23).

However, Pflueger (2016) convincingly shows how survey instruments tapping into the patient perspectives in health care have changed over time, in fact thereby constituting the socially valid voice of the user in different and more restricted ways. For example, methods that tap into the troubles, worries, and stress of individuals gradually become "purified," the survey instead focusing on what is seen as more objective and actionable from an organizational perspective. A methodological "improvement" (cleansing the survey for subjectivity) goes hand in hand with making the measure more "reasonable" and more "actionable" from a managerial perspective.

In return for becoming more "accountable" for quality as seen from a user perspective, service-providing organizations in turn redefine the user perspective, stripping it of particular, subjective experiences and instead counting only dimensions compatible with the kind of quality management deemed possible from a particular organizational perspective.

In a similar vein, Young (2006) describes how accounting information has been streamlined to fit into user needs. Little is known about specific individuals, however. Instead, a particular, socially defined category of users is carved out that allegedly requires a peculiar, streamlined, and standardized form of accounting information.

Hermann (2007) explains how changing visions of children have fitted changing visions of pedagogy in the school and corresponding visions of society. The most recent version of the "user" of the school is one in which the child is reconfigured into someone who can contribute to the economic competition among countries in a global world.

Some regimes that aim to deliver transparent quality information about public services also imply or construct an abstracted consumer. Thus, the user not only uses information; the "user," as such, is also "used" to promote a particular configuration of roles and a particular government regime.

Not surprisingly, the control of the social definition of what constitutes a proper user perspective is sometimes contested. Quality, as defined from the user perspective, is on the one hand a "liberating" and "emancipating" perspective that makes a variety of user needs and wishes more socially visible, which might trigger service renewal, but there is also a risk of unleashing high or unreasonable expectations. Quality has played a complex role in debates about consumer rights and the moral overtones in consumerist outlooks on life (Husz 2012).

Since the introduction of the customer perspective in the public sector, a long-standing debate has taken place over the tension between the roles and views of customers and users and broader social obligations (Fountain 2001). These broader obligations connect, in part, with specific roles, such as the role of the student, which is broader, more active, and has more responsibility than that of the consumer (Cheney et al. 1997). Broader obligations are also connected to the roles of citizens (e.g. paying taxes to finance services). The user perspective must therefore be subsumed under a citizen perspective (Dahlberg and Vedung 2001).

One interpretation of recent policies is that while neoliberal currents in governments employed a consumer perspective to induce public service innovation, the same political forces are now realizing that they may have unleashed an insatiable monster that has demanded too much from the public sector (Olsen 2016).

Not long ago in Denmark, the emphasis was on strengthening the voice of students in the evaluation of teaching as part of quality assurance in higher education. The political emphasis has since shifted to making the students move quickly through the education system so that they can contribute to the national economy as soon as possible. Not many years ago, if students complained about an exam grade, an independent committee would reevaluate the assessment. The committee could award the same or a higher grade, but the grade already given could not be lowered, since the achievement of that grade was perceived as the user's inalienable right. Teachers were told that this arrangement was carved in legal stone. In recent years, however, the system was changed so that an independent committee can award any grade it wishes. So user rights are in fact flexible social constructions. The current version of the student is one who completes a study as quickly as possible. It is a production factor that contributes to the economic vitality of the nation-state. Present policies are consistent with Brown's (2015: 83) analysis of neoliberal policies where the individual (hitherto conceived as is a self-interested homo economics) is now expected to sacrifice its own well-being to larger economic purposes.

Appeals to the user perspective are sometimes ambiguously caught between concrete users and the space for user perspectives designated by wider legal, political, and ideological frameworks. This ambiguity can also be found in some contemporary discourses, which cherish co-production and other forms of cooperation between service users and producers. Even if co-production is cast in a very positive official light (as the road to innovation, common understanding between citizens and professionals, democracy, and cost savings at the same time), concrete users do not always wish to "co-produce." For example, some elderly citizens just want to passively receive the services they think they deserve after many years of paying taxes (Andresen and Fjordside 2015). The discursive mobilization of the user and the concrete user do not always overlap.

In concrete cases it is contestable who has the right to speak in the capacity of being a user of services. An example: Some elderly people suffer a stroke. Attempts at saving their lives sometimes have meager results, for example, when a patient ends up being paralyzed. In some hospitals in Denmark, a code was inserted in the patient's file to indicate that doctors should not treat a patient if a stroke occurred. Hearing about this practice through the media, some patients' relatives were shocked. They felt that they should have been consulted and that their rights as health services "users" had been violated. Technically speaking, however, they had no rights that were violated. As a patient's relative, you do not have any influence on the decision to treat the patient. Hospital staff are mandated by law to treat the patient. There are only two conditions that may exempt staff from this obligation: One is that sound medical judgment says that the treatment is ineffective or harmful, the other is the existence of a signed declaration from the patient which precludes treatment in case of a stroke. Evidently, the practice with the code in the file is highly problematic, but not because of the violation of any user rights of the relatives; that would be an inappropriate extension of user rights that does not in fact exist, at least in legal terms.

In other situations, however, changes in laws and norms in fact bestow users of services with rights which constitute or strengthen their social position. Kreutzmann (1994) carried out the first evaluation of care for children in Greenland placed outside of their respective homes. For ethical reasons, she abstained from interviewing the children themselves. At the same time, she recommended that the right of children to be heard should be enhanced in future cases. She was writing her report in times when children were becoming recognized as legal subjects to an increasing extent in various spheres of life (e.g. when parents divorce). The tension between her methodological choices and her recommendations are indicative of the changing social norms concerning the pros and cons of children's right to be heard.

This interpretation is occasionally consistent with the values of the past and sometimes ushers in values of the future. The tension between experiences and expectations, between the past and the future, are sources of ambiguity. The same is, evidently, the tension between the perspective of the users as "their own" and seeing it as a construction depending on social context.

Social Conditions Favorable to Quality as the Fulfillment of the Needs, Expectations, or Wishes of Users

The user perspective is relevant when the users are seen as having a relevant role in a market (as consumers) or in a regime of social policy, where they are recipients of services. They are relevant as users to the extent that their preferences, needs, expectations, and so on play a role for the design, marketing, or delivery of products or services. The perspective is often portrayed as a progressive one which strengthens the position of the user and thereby reduces social inequality.

Ambiguities follow when "autonomous" users are fitted into larger social, political, and ideological agendas, such as economic growth and neoliberal competition.

At the same time, in a management context, if a quality perspective attends to all aspects of reality seen from the perspectives of all users it becomes impossible to handle. Large organizations often reduce this quality perspective to a limited number of dimensions, while maintaining that the perspective still speaks on behalf of users.

Quality as Expert Judgment

Definition and Meaning

Some objects of quality assessment are complex. A holistic view of quality is sometimes called for. Users do not always have the insights and the experience to fully appreciate all aspects of a phenomenon. Especially in the arts, music, and literature, quality assessments require connoisseurship (Eisner 1976). Quality inscriptions come in the form of reviews. Reviews have genre characteristics and are performances in themselves.

A good expert performs in the same way as a connoisseur. Through training and expertise, experts cultivate their sensibilities toward subtle aspects of quality in a quality performance. Expertise rests with perceptual differentiation and insight, which is trained through experience (Eisner 2003). In contrast to a user or consumer of music, who may like or dislike a particular piece, the expert appreciates and articulates valuations of genre, composition, style, tonality, performance, improvisation, and other complex aspects of musical artistry. While arts, music, and literature are particularly illustrative of the role of connoisseurship, the notion of expertise evidently also extends into such domains as technology, science, and policy.

Expertise is shaped not only by knowledge, insight, professionalism, and experience but also by values and theories (Eisner 2003) and by taste. The definition of "holistic" assessment is up to the expert. Consequently, the expert may talk about any or all of the aspects of a performance found relevant—holistic or not.

The uniqueness of this perspective is that it is the expert who decides. Explicit criteria may or may not be used. Parts or whole objects can be evaluated. The strength of quality as expert judgment is that the trained expert is trusted to have a particularly qualified view and remains free to focus on whatever aspect is found relevant.

Expert judgments have an educational function. Experts can sometimes see what others cannot, and they can train the perceptual differentiation of non-experts and experts-to-be by appreciating qualities in an object that otherwise would have been neglected. Scientific peer review is one example of a practice based on expert judgments and a good illustration of how much one can learn from experts in a field.

Expert judgments require attention and care. The self-understanding of experts is therefore important and more than a sign of self-ascribed importance and status. The self-conscious experts will continue to cultivate their skills and be humble about the limits of their expertise (Lamont 2009).

Limitations and Ambiguities

While experts may produce insightful quality statements, their reliability may be very low. Any two experts, even within the same field, often produce divergent evaluative statements. Expert views rely on training and theory, and these theories can be very diverse in some fields. Experts' views sometimes reflect what is a fashionable trend in a field.

Expertise is limited and relative to fields, disciplines, and subjects. Economists may talk about ethical issues without hesitation, but that does not mean that their expert status will be respected. Here, the problem is that "field" is not a category of persons, but rather a perspective on life defined by a discipline or theory. Many phenomena can thus be viewed from multiple perspectives, each with their own experts.

Some experts become defensive about their status. They are sometimes insensitive toward those who do not share their insights. Some experts restrict their view to a particular paradigm that was dominant in their field in the formative years of their career. Some architects design houses that are meant more to impress other architects than to fulfill the needs of commissioners or future users.

Returning to scientific peer review: Even though it might well be the "least bad" way to assess the quality of an academic product, it has serious flaws. Peer experts tend to conform conservatively with existing, already-established paradigms. Peers are connected in networks that cite and review each other's work. Two peer reviews of the same text may be at odds with each other and give different recommendations for improvement. Peer reviews are sometimes terrible performances in terms of structure, care, and courtesy.

In its worst version, quality as expert judgment represents an uncomfortable combination of power and subjectivity. Several tendencies in recent years exemplify attempts at reducing the power of expert judgment, to make it more attentive to broader social voices in society (Sismondo 2008; Stilgoe et al. 2013), or to partially replace it with more mechanistic or standard-based perspectives on quality.

Social Conditions Favorable to Quality as Expert Judgment

Under social conditions favorable to this perspective, expertise is recognized despite the social inequality which comes with it. There is also a rich supply of experts in various areas. There may be rules for how and when experts are used, including rules regarding limits of expertise and conflicting interests. If experts disagree among themselves, there should be social space for a respectable deliberation among them so that their collective judgment can be respected by themselves and others (Lamont 2009).

If organizations hire experts to produce quality assessments, these organizations may run into problems if the judgments of these experts are unreliable or in disagreement. Even if experts are guided by common guidelines and manuals, they may go their own way. It has proven difficult to make experts comply with such requirements. The expert judgment is difficult to codify.

The expert perspective also runs into problems when experts are scarce or their time is precious or too expensive. A pressing example is peer review of scientific work, where it has become difficult to find the necessary number of peer reviewers for the increasing amount of research evaluation which is carried out at many levels. The increasing popularity of bibliometric measures in research can to some extent be explained by the alleged subjectivity and the costs associated with peer review.

Classical factors such as money and power also influences the role of experts. In music, for example, the role of expert reviews has been reduced compared to the "common opinion regime" (sales and popularity measures) which is more simple, unidimensional, and more in line with dominant economic interests (Beuscart and Mellet 2013).

Quality as Compliance with Standards

Definition and Meaning

A standard is a formula that prescribes uniformity among a class of products or services or in the processes of their production. Moreover, some definitions mention that standards are "for common and repeated use" and that they are "aimed at achievement of the optimum degree of order in a given context" (Brunsson and Jacobsson 2000: 15).

A key moment in the history of standards is industrial production, where a need emerged for substitutable machine parts. Standards help create uniformity.

While an official definition of standards emphasizes that they are "established by consensus and approved by a recognized body" (Brunsson and Jacobsson 2000: 15), there are in fact many bodies issuing standards. They can emerge out of authority, custom, or consent (Stake 2004: 13). Sometimes standards emerge as social constructs out of a particular, calculative practice. An average is sometimes used as a standard for comparison even if there is no "consensus" or "recognized body" that has reflected normatively regarding the appropriateness of that standard.

Standards assume many forms, such as forms of planning, ways of organizing, product specifications, ways of measuring things, milestones against which things can be evaluated, and ways of legitimizing things such as certification and accreditation. Standards can be more or less mandatory. Standards can be binding in practice, even if there is no legal sanction for non-compliance. Most people in the West type on QWERTY keyboards, even if there is no sanction for not doing so. It is just extremely difficult to purchase any other kind of keyboard. This observation highlights an important aspect of standards: They are not always adopted because they are technically superior, but they are useful when some degree of compatibility and coordination is needed within a larger socio-technical system.

In the light of quality understood as compliance with standards, a quality problem is defined in terms of unexplained variation around a standard.

Even if a particular standard is not necessarily a good indicator of all of the aspects of quality, stark deviation from a standard is often indicative of a problem requiring attention, say advocates of standards. One example is the monitoring of accounting data for institutions providing child care. If one of these homes has extraordinary costs on items such as vehicles, travel, or representation, it may indicate unsound management practices or improper use of public funds.

Monitoring of the prescription practices of general practitioners against a simple average may help identify a few who overprescribe due to inappropriate relations with drug addicts. At the very least, a strong deviation from the standard requires an explanation, and usually also action. The advocates of standards therefore often emphasize the operational advantages of standards.

Notice how closely a quality perspective and definition of a problem are linked. Once you see the world through the perspective of standards, quality objects displaying variation immediately pose a problem if this variation is "unexplained." The perspective puts an explanatory burden on those who are responsible for the quality object. This is true for all quality perspectives, but the rhetorical move is even more smoothly made with the standards perspective, as it depends less on an external normative justification, such as "legitimate political goals" or "real user needs."

In the standards perspective, "not normal" is enough. A quality problem defined in this way does not rely on a lengthy justification. Once you measure some dimensions of quality objects, some will almost by definition score above or below average or above or below a statistically determined regression line. *Voila*! Unexplained variation! Standards are extremely functional for the lazy evaluator; or, more specifically, the evaluator who is not keen on lengthy arguments about the deeper origins of values. Instead, standards can be in functional operation quickly without much deliberation and/or afterthought.

As Reeves and Bednar (1994: 431) explain: "Conformance to specifications is the most parsimonious, appropriate, and easily measured definition of quality. The more subjective definitions of excellence, value, and meeting and/or exceeding expectations become unnecessary."

Standards do not always materialize just because we need them. In most evaluation work, there are no fixed standards and no good way of fixing them (Stake 2004: 8). Here, Stake presumably means normatively good, broadly socially acceptable, and/or good with respect to a thorough understanding of the local situation at hand. In that respect, he is right. However, standards may function as standards (prescribing uniformity) even without such normative justification. Functionally speaking, there may even be "too many" good ways of fixing standards. As Stake (2004: 227) says: "Often standardization is increased not because the quality of activity is enhanced, but because standardized activity is more easily monitored and controlled."

My point—that standards sometimes emerge almost involuntarily out of social processes—can be illustrated with examples. A municipality kept digital records of the visits that caretakers made to elderly people who remained in their own homes. The records documented whether standards were met both in terms of frequency and duration of visits. These factors were measured against standards of units of care that were allocated to the elderly person based on an analysis of need (defined by an "allocation specialist," not the caretakers themselves). An administrator explained that a main function of this meticulously standardized documentation was that it provided a strong defense against filed complaints from the relatives of the elderly who questioned whether sufficient care was provided. It was always possible to explain that care was allocated according to standardized principles and, furthermore, that a given number of visits of a given duration actually took place. This provided a strong argument against stories about "lack of care" that sometimes circulated among the relatives of the elderly and who relied, in turn, on the faulty memory of their elderly kin. The somewhat tragic paradox here is that standards and standardized documentation were not primarily needed to manage care but to defend the care provider from complaints from (someone who claimed to represent) recipients of care.

Another example: Universities are interested in documenting the impact of social research. Researchers are interested in keeping this concept open and multifaceted. Researchers also want recognition of their contribution to turning research into something with an impact (e.g. being in public committees, appearing in media, doing policy-related work, working collaboratively with stakeholders). If some of this work is compensated in terms of work hours or pay, however, they want the compensation system to be transparent and fair. This requires some standard ways of measuring and documenting impact and a way to transform uneven forms of impact into a few variables (e.g. hours or money). Management may also be interested in a standardized way of setting expectations for impact and for the comparison of researchers or comparisons across departments.

In other words, while a professional understanding of impact supports a differentiated view, a sense of justice and fairness pulls in the direction of standards. If standards are some day established, there may be complaints about the lack of perfection in capturing all forms of impact and about the burden of documentation. Which of the tendencies in the example are more compatible with the views of university management? The point is, however, that standards may emerge out of social processes involving people who are otherwise not keen on standards as such. Even if nobody loves standards, they serve important functions and are therefore in demand. They make measurement, comparison, and transparency possible. Standards and their ongoing development are sometimes a result of different principles, such as expertise, user orientation, representation, and participation (Hallström 2000: 93). The function of standards is to help bring different principles together in a single organizational form.

Standards may be socially attractive because they appeal particularly to bureaucracies, which manage them while simultaneously facilitating coordination and a sense of fairness. If there is a lack of tolerance of variation (e.g. variations between service providers, between institutions, or between municipalities), then standards present themselves as the answer. Certain trends in society, such as the publication of indicator scores, focus on individual rights, and media representing variations in service as a great scandal, help make variations intolerable. Standards are fundamentally helpful in promoting a sense of social order (Furusten 2000: 84) in a manner that may be particularly in tune with contemporary socio-historic tendencies.

Limitations and Ambiguities

The view that quality is the same as compliance with standards is often criticized. Standards and standardized ways of measuring and testing things often become goals in themselves. While uniformity becomes an aspiration (Eisner 1976), its main focus on defensive quality (securing compliance, not reaching for the stars) stifles creativity and prevents paradigm-shifting discoveries (Sower and Fair 2005).

If a standards-based definition of quality governs the establishment of organization structure, reward systems, and human resource practices (e.g. selection and training in an organization), an escalation of commitment toward these practices may occur (Galbraith 1983). The standardization necessary for a conformance-to-specifications definition of quality sometimes works against an adaptive organization that has the flexibility to respond to a changing market (Reeves and Bednar 1994: 432).

Understanding quality as compliance with standards, the concept is deprived of all overtones of the sublime, the extraordinary, the sensitive, and the carefully calibrated. Consequently, this perspective is antithetical to productive idiosyncrasy (Eisner 1976). Standards are insensitive to the particularities of situation and locality, because their very meaning is to enhance uniformity.

Standards describing services for a category of recipients or users may not be good descriptors of what the individual members of the category need or want. Standards established in the name of concerns for a group of people may not be helpful for specific individuals, but they can still be justified as "serving the users." At the same time, standards may in fact define and limit what individuals can expect.

For example, if a certain number of hours is set aside for a nurse visiting families with newborn babies, a given family may need more or less time than that. An efficient way of allocating hours would be according to need, whereas a strict adherence to uniform standards might comply with management requirements and/or a general sense of justice.

Notice here how standards operate across different types of justifications or without justification. Standards are often followed by a lack of clarity about their value basis and legitimacy. Their construction is also often so lengthy in time and space or their delineation so anonymously and mysteriously contrived that it is difficult to find out who is responsible for them.

Social Conditions Favorable to Quality as Standards

Quality standards have the most favorable social conditions when the makers of standards are recognized as legitimate, when standards are technically and substantially appropriate regarding the objects they describe, when infrastructures are in place to support standards, when opposition to standards is limited, and when the risk of overflows into other domains does not create controversy (Beuscart and Mellet 2013: 406). Sometimes, there are competing quality conventions. The survival of a given quality standard depends on many uneven factors, including bureaucratic or economic interests (Beuscart and Mellet 2013).

Quality as Organizational Recipe

Definition and Meaning

In order to understand the meaning of quality as an organizational recipe, one must first understand the organizationalization of quality.

Quality sometimes rests not with a particular service but with how the services are coordinated and delivered, which is best understood as an organizational phenomenon. Let me give an example: Consider a patient with Alzheimer's disease. Her brain makes her believe she is talking care of small children (as she had many years ago). She now fears that these children have disappeared for her, since she kept looking for them and could not find them. An experienced team of psychiatrists is called in who are specialists in the medication of Alzheimer's patients. Their task is complicated, as people respond differently to different types and doses of medicine: too little medicine would not help her, but too much would leave her comatose. The specialist team prescribes the calculated optimal dosage based on the existing evidence, but wants to fine-tune it to the patient's case after three weeks. In the meantime, her daily caretakers would make schematic, hour-to-hour observations about her fears, behavior, attention, and sleep patterns. Based on this feedback, the medical specialists are able to optimize the medical regime. What worked in the case at hand was neither the medicine nor the specialists in themselves; rather, it was the organizational coordination between the specialists who controlled the medicine and the caretakers who made the necessary observations and provided feedback to the specialists.

In addition to what is required from medical specialists, it is also organizationally difficult to make sure that busy caretakers produce systematic observations on an hourly basis (including weekends) unless they all clearly understand the importance of that endeavor. Everybody should know where to find the necessary documentation when the specialists return for their second visit. All this requires organizational coordination.

In most forms of modern service delivery (e.g. health care), service quality is at least two-dimensional. One dimension relates to the level of knowledge, expertise, technologies, and so on under the aegis of the professions. The other is regarding the organizational coordination between the professions. The need for paying attention to the second dimension increases as professional services become specialized. Medical specializations are not logically constructed; some deal with particular parts of the body, while others deal with particular patient groups defined by gender or age. Others yet deal with particular disease types. No wonder there are overlaps. And patients who fall between categories. Organizational coordination is needed. As a part of this process, professional work is relocated and reconfigured. The changing, and sometimes less autonomous, role of professionals cannot be explained only by neoliberalism and New Public Management. It is a result of a broad and complex set of social factors (Noordegraf 2016).

Professionals often have problems with organizational coordination unless it is under their own control, but multi-professional organizations engaged in cross-disciplinary work need someone to take charge of an organizational perspective; thus, the organizationalization of quality.

Organizational "meta-craftsmanship" is a concept that suggests how to handle organizationalization. It ties together quality improvement, reengineering, customer service, and management.[1] Upon recognizing that organizations have a responsibility for organizational "meta-craftsmanship" in the coordination and delivery of services (one aspect of organizationalization), how the organization handles this responsibility becomes an object of quality itself. How much quality is there in the way organizations carry out "meta-craftsmanship"? Organizations are providers of quality, but they are also quality objects. The quality of how they carry themselves as organizations can be assessed. In a sense, this is a second-order assessment of quality. The dual nature of the organizationalization of quality is a result of the fact that the steering of the provision of quality in coordinated services is itself a quality object.

While meta-craftsmanship may not be a commonly used term, there is an enormous amount of tools that help describe what it might entail: project management, coordination, budgeting, organizational development, organizational learning, management by objectives, performance management.

Many terms even emphasize the term quality: quality management, quality assurance, and total quality management (branded and sold as Total Quality Management or TQM). These are candidates as guiding principles for a perspective that defines quality as organizational recipe. An organizational recipe is a legitimized notion about what constitutes good management. It is legitimized in organizational fields where norms of good practice circulate among prestigious organizations, experts, consultants, and the like (DiMaggio and Powell 1983). Recipes often come in the form of particular management fashions, and their names change quickly.

The defining characteristic of organizationalized quality is that in order to find quality in a given situation, one would look for (the documentation of) organizational procedures, rules, practices, technologies, and structures—all in all: recipes—that are more or less implemented and in place as organizational responses to the challenges of the situation at hand.

To support this documentation, organizations need a special kind of knowledge that deals with quality systems, information, and

[1] http://www.businessdictionary.com/definition/meta-craftsmanship.html (Sept. 1, 2017).

communication technologies. It is also necessary to regulate how registration and documentation take place using these technologies (Wallenburg et al. 2016: 13) in order to secure trustworthy, comparable information.

In the light of quality as an organizational recipe, a quality problem is one where an organization does not take responsibility for its own procedures. The way to solve the problem is to adopt an organizational recipe, to manage it, and document it sufficiently.

An illustrative example is an audit of the quality of teaching at an institution for higher education. Auditors have no expertise in theology, accounting, medicine, or economics. Instead, they look for the documentation of organizational recipes that describe how the institution controls and develops what is called quality in teaching. If auditors do not find enough of this, they recommend procedures and rules for certification and the promotion of teachers, student-based evaluations on the Internet, and annual reports from all study program managers documenting their quality initiatives upwards and outwards. This is called systematic quality work—seen from the perspective of quality as organizational recipe.

Limitations and Ambiguities

A fundamental criticism of this perspective relates to its abstraction. It privileges rules and procedures at the expense of concrete services and concrete persons. It also privileges documented rules and procedures above informal ones. This is because the practical function of quality as an organizational recipe lies in its ability to be externally documented in the face of auditors, evaluators, inspectors, and others of the same caliber (Power 1997). Much of management consists of installing procedures that "make things auditable" toward an external view (Power 1996).

For this reason, quality as organizational recipe is often despised among professionals in organizations. They often view all of this documentation as primarily serving managers and auditors and regard the time spent on documentation as time wasted. They feel that the documentation is less relevant for "real work." Yet at least some forms of documentation are crucial for coordination across time and space (see the initial example of an Alzheimer patient in this section). In addition, what professionals sometimes ignore is that given the demands of taxpayers, customers, clients, competitors, technology, and increasing complexity, classical professional autonomy simply does not suffice.

An underlying conflict here is one of epistemic perspective. Organizational managers and their auditors have knowledge interests and make knowledge claims that are different from those of professionals in disciplines. The tension between them surfaces when auditors check the function and operation of organizational recipes that professionals see as not relevant for the subject matter at hand (e.g. health care, education). In contradistinction, the power of the auditor's epistemic regime hinges on abstractions from particular practices and substantive disciplinary areas. Otherwise, the knowledge produced by auditors cannot travel and cannot be made known to external partners.

The expertise of the auditor or organizational consultant is constituted on the basis of a perspective that traverses time and space. In practice, it is also much easier for the controller to ask for rules, procedures, guidelines, handbooks, and other documents than to observe the professionals in practice. The relevance of this abstraction remains a contested issue in many situations. According to this criticism, auditors check the consistency of documents with other documents but not with other practices.

The "abstraction" that is claimed to be inherent in this perspective is in fact abstraction compared with the "concrete" practical reality that is experienced by professionals such as teachers, nurses, and social workers. Following Latour (1987: 241), for example, there is no reason to assume that the coordination between different organizational documents is not a real, very concrete activity. In Latour's view, there is no "higher order" or more advanced—or more abstract—cognitive activity involved in making organizational documentation, calculations, and so on; it is merely a different set of epistemic and practical endeavors supported by inscription practices in a particular scale.

The criticism that organizationalized quality is defined by its "abstraction" is therefore not actually an analysis, it is merely a viewpoint (held by some, not by others). Latour's intervention is useful in order to maintain a focus not on "concrete" "reality" but on the inscription devices seeking to define reality in particular ways. These inscription devices are likely to be perceived in very different ways from the "inside" and from the "outside" of the networks and alliances of specialists, evaluators, and from different positions in the accountability relations involved.

Organizational recipes that are used by one organization to inform another organization that things are under control are particularly in demand here. The internal evaluators and quality specialists in Organization A may have more in common with their counterparts in Organization B, to whom they report, than with the professionals in their own Organization A about whom they are reporting (Mathison 1991).

It is often an issue how well a particular organizational recipe is adopted and implemented in the organization. Some theories of organization (neo-institutional theory in particular) claim that organizations separate organizational recipes designed for external exposition from the actual internal working practices in the core of their operations (Meyer and Rowan 1977). This is called decoupling or even hypocrisy (Brunsson 1989). But decoupling or hypocrisy cannot always be maintained. External audits of organizational recipes are sometimes exercised with power. Inspection, certification, and accreditation can have substantial consequences for the organization. The same is true if a performance audit is linked to money streams and to the reactions among key stakeholders which influence the reputation or even survival of an organization (Espeland and Sauder 2007). The impact of external audits looking at quality as an organizational recipe is therefore often substantial.

While the internal evaluators spend much of their time securing the documentation needed for external purposes (Mathison 2011), they also have interests themselves and a desire to demonstrate that their work has real consequences. They are often the arbiters who turn the effects of organizational recipes into reality. They do so by translating organizational recipes into locally relevant solutions and by involving organizational stakeholders in quality work, such as organizational learning or teamwork (Dean and Bowen 2000; Øvretveit 2005). There is much effort in organizations to massage the notion of quality as organizational recipe into the sinews of daily life in the organization. The tools to do so oscillate between holistic devices (e.g. integrated learning, systems perspectives, evaluation capacity building) and a strict focus on the control of, say, performance indicators.

These numerous practical tools draw on a variety of schools of thought in organizational theory.

For example, Karl Weick's theory of sensemaking offers a perspective in contrast to the most dominant theories of management. Sensemaking is experience-based and distributed across the organizational landscape. It is a paradox in organizations that, under crisis and up to potential disasters, the organizational capacity to make sense of things is diminished because people's attention becomes blocked and information-processing is concentrated at the top of the organizational hierarchy. What is in fact more needed, in Weick's view, is an involvement of a variety of experience-based, interactive forms of sensemaking that allow the organization to better deal with equivocal phenomena (Weick et al. 2005).

In a similar vein, there is no such thing as "Total Quality Management." "Total" is relevant for external legitimacy but inconsistent with how sensemaking unfolds in practice (Weick in Dean and Bowen 2000). An organizational recipe in the spirit of Total Quality Management does not provide the vocabulary and labels necessary to energize people to explain to themselves and others what they are doing when they are doing quality work (Weick 2000). An organizational recipe is faulty when it assumes that the world is more predictable than it actually is and when it overspecifies directions and precludes adaptive action (Weick 2000: 164).

The theoretical key uniting Weick's work on quality with his perhaps more well-known work on disasters in organizations is the importance of attending to weak or ambiguous signals, cultivating sensemaking, and not burying troubles in normalizing standards and procedures.

Weick's perspective helps explain why the "implementation" of a dominant, comprehensive, or "total" organizational recipe for quality is an impossible mission and (too) hard work. If an organizational recipe works, it is because of all of the local sensemaking it sets in motion; not because of the recipe, as such.

It is therefore difficult to determine the "effectiveness" of an organizational recipe for quality. Confusion about whether any given organizational recipe is effective continues as long as the recipe itself is open and interpretable and most of its use hinges on local interpretations (Øvretveit 2005). The recipe is only a loose idea that has rational appeal, but it has not been qualified through rough encounters with materiality (Røvik 2005). Those who developed and transported it are not responsible for its use and consequences. Sometimes, the pushing away of responsibility is a managerial strategy in itself. Once a particular organizational recipe for "quality assurance" makes particular aspects of organizations transparent, managers manage *only* with transparency, while the responsibility to make sense out of the recipe and make it work in daily life is delegated to subordinates (Roberts 2018).

Many, especially professionals, maintain ambivalence when criticizing quality as an organizational recipe. While it is described as a waste of time, paper, and money, it actually restructures the organizational reality in a way that is full of friction when "the rubber hits the road."

Strides will continue to be made over who has the right to define which of several organizational perspectives should be dominant. Quality is sometimes a subordinate part of an organizational recipe with another name and sometimes a recipe in itself, which may even drive the development of other recipes (Dean and Bowen 2000). In practice, the relative status of a recipe for quality may be up for grabs, for example, in times of austerity, and its anchoring in the organizational landscape may change so that responsibility for quality is moved (Roberts 2018; Sørensen and Foged 2015).

The critique that organizational recipes are merely abstract management jargon underestimates the many steps that specialists take to weave their ideas into organizational operations. It also misses reflection about the philosophical naiveté in saying that some things are "really real" only if we call them "concrete."

The strides about quality as an organizational recipe are likely to continue. While it is true that many factors contribute to a need for organizational coordination of quality, it is also true that many organizational recipes are simplistic victims of fads in management circles and continue to cause frustration among those professionals who must deal with conflicting demands of organizational recipes, users, professional values, and limited time and resources.

Social Conditions Favorable to Quality as Organizational Recipe

Social conditions which make this perspective viable include an increasing skepticism against professionals (from media, politicians, or users), which delegitimizes professional autonomy, a consistency between an organizational recipe and broader social norms such as rationality and individualism (Strang and Meyer 1994) as well as a consistency with fads or fashions, a simplicity in the organizational recipe, which allows it to travel, and last, but not least a strong layer of managers and specialists who have the power to promote organizational recipes and the documentation requirements which follow.

Quality as Impact

Definition and Meaning

The underlying inspiration for understanding quality as impact often comes from (a version of) systems theory vocabulary that is easily adopted in everyday language. In a systems view, there is talk of inputs, processes, outputs, outcomes, and impacts. Another source of influence comes from experimental methodology which offers a way in which interventions and impacts can be causally linked.

From the perspective of this framework, too many people spend too much time focusing on inputs and processes, and sometimes outputs. What counts in the long run are outcomes. In the international evaluation literature, the evaluation of outcomes and impacts is seen as a mature, well-developed form of evaluation (Furubo et al. 2002). The whole point of distinguishing between inputs, processes, outputs, and outcomes is often to motivate people to direct more attention to outcomes and impacts.

Outputs occur in the interface between the delivery system and the recipient, while outcomes are understood as the changes in the lives of people after they have been in contact with some program, intervention, or service. Outcomes are the long-term changes after the contact is over.

Outcomes can be short-term or long-term. Although terminologies may differ, impact often refers to relatively long-term outcomes. Furthermore, while "outcomes" may be desired end-states, where the causal link with the intervention or program is not always implied or clarified (Funnell and Rogers 2011), the term "impact" usually incorporates such a causal link. Impacts are causal phenomena. They are effects of interventions. Impacts and effects are relevant because of their familiarity with broader notions of effectiveness.

Quality as impact is particularly pertinent in medicine and social work (where the vocabulary is often one of "interventions"; see below). It is also becoming pertinent in research, where a typical contemporary question is how research contributes to society.

Quality as impact may overlap other quality perspectives, such as those defined by goals, utility, or user needs. A particularly distinctive feature, however, which the inscription of quality as impact must one way or another take seriously, is how to account for the causality implied in this version of quality. This perspective is born with an inherent methodological challenge, but it also offers a solution.

A randomized controlled trial (RCT) is often seen as the best way to determine a causal link between an intervention and its impact. Once evidence for this causal link is available, a number of initiatives are set in motion to spread best practices. These include education, courses, supervision and manuals (here quality as impact overlaps with quality as standards or as organizational recipes). Together, the experimental design and the strict control of subsequent practices should lead to a maximum impact. This combination of causal thinking and controlled interventions is unique for the perspective here called "quality as impact."

Limitations and Ambiguities

The notions of input, process, output, and outcome are less obvious than they appear. They assume a definition of the system to which these phenomena are related. System is, however, an analytical construct that depends to some degree on the perspective of an observer and their purposes (Bateson 1972). The world comprises multiple, interacting systems, and the "outcome" or "impact" does not always give itself. We are interested in a particular "system" when we want "it" to "do" "something" for us. The definition of system is relative to a relevance structure. Whether we are interested in pest control or in the diversity of ecosystems rests with different relevance structures.

Some interventions influence people who make other interventions, and it is not always meaningful to assume that all of outcomes rest with citizens, and that there is a list of correct outcomes that can be used as the ultimate checklist.

While the notion of impact is often inspired by systems theory, this theory is not a value theory, so it does not help discriminate between good/bad impacts. Nor is that distinction made by the methodological thinking related to the determination of causal links. With quality as impact, a particular "form," "paradigm," or "mentality" is enhanced, but this is often void of exact criteria unless some criteria are taken for granted because of social conventions (e.g. in medicine, where cure and survival rates might do the job). In other areas of life, such as education, there may be less agreement about conventions. For example, is a more boring form of education something desirable if it produces better international rankings of students' performances?

More often than not, criteria are "brought in" to supplement the systems view with ideologies or values that are not strictly part of the definition of quality as impact. While this permeability makes the perspective open and useful for the transportation of many criteria, the perspective itself is unable to sort out conflicts between them. In social work, for example, a particular program might prove to help drug addicts get rid of hard drugs and escape a life of crime, only to become dependent on methadone. Whether or not this means "clean"—for not to mention whether life on methadone is a good life—remains a question for discussion, unless value questions and policy questions are buried under the techno-methodological veil of whether or not the intervention is "evidence-based," in which case quality-as-impact has succeeded as a self-evident perspective on quality. Strictly logically speaking, however, an outcome is an outcome in a system the definition of which cannot be evidence-based.

The indeterminability of value criteria in this perspective remains clearly visible in many instances. An additional example is the impact of research. Although difficult to encircle and even more difficult to measure, there is a need to produce inscriptions of "quality as impact" to justify university funding in times of austerity. While some believe that the impact of science can be measured in terms of patents, technological innovation, and the like, the same criteria are not relevant in social research.

Inspired by the terminology of input, process, output, and outcomes, some argue that the ultimate goal of social research is the use of research results in political decision-making. However, this view runs into a multitude of problems. Some research is basic, whereas other research is applied. The impact of social research unfolds over different periods. Social research plays a cultural role as well as an instrumental role (Biesta 2007). It helps interpret social life in a much broader sense than a focus on political decisions would suggest. Research finds that use of social research is collaborative, interactive, and contextual (Prewitt et al. 2012; Wimbush et al. 2012), so it would be difficult or unfair to attribute it to a particular research result itself and to only one result. It would be fairer to include interactive sessions and dialogue into the notion of the research process itself, but then you cannot subsequently separate the "research" from its "impact."

Sometimes it is a stream of research or school of thought that is influential. Last but absolutely not least, there are some political decisions that researchers would not want their research to support even if they could. Again, the perspective on quality defined as impact cannot identify—but sometimes assumes—the goodness of impacts.

Interestingly enough, the current attempts at capturing the impact of social research are caught between the almost indefinite and unlimited nature of impacts, on the one hand, and the desire to capture them in a methodologically rigorous way on the other. The best compromise currently seems to be asking researchers to provide some form of systematic narratives that illustrate particularly striking examples of the impact of their research. These kinds of inscriptions do not live up to the high ideals advocated by strict causal methodology. Paradoxically, research managers at different levels in the university system who are otherwise proponents of strict, objective, and rigorous methodology are now pulling out their hair as they suddenly have to seek help from otherwise despicable qualitative narrative methods just because of a political need to document impacts. At the same time, there is an intense demand for all kinds of digital devices that capture traces of research, each of them claiming to capture "impact." Perhaps technology here determines what counts rather than the other way around.

Another point of contention is how interventions need to be structured to fit into the imagery connected with impacts. The causal methodologies used to document causal impacts in a trustworthy manner have a structuring force on the interventions, programs, projects, and services, the impact of which is to be measured. More often than not, sound causal judgment depends on rigorous control of a methodological inquiry, at best in the form of a randomized, controlled experiment. It is necessary to implement the intervention with fidelity, which requires training, handbooks, and surveillance. It is also necessary to deny the control group access to the services provided in the intervention to avoid polluting the experiment (Droitcour and Kovar 2008). The point is that the methodology required to identify the causal impacts of an intervention with some degree of trustworthiness has a very structuring force on interventions themselves. The attractiveness of the quality-as-impact perspective therefore hinges upon the willingness to structure interventions as defined preemptively by the inscription device needed to document their impacts. Not all politicians or managers, for example, are willing to explain to beneficiaries that their access to services will depend on randomization; they often leave such tasks to other agents in the implementation chain.

An additional problem with the impact perspective is that although a particularly structured intervention may be shown to have a desired impact, at least statistically, someone who is considering a practical situation may find that the intervention structured in this particular way is impossible, unfeasible, or inappropriate in the practical situation at hand. The given practical situation may be complicated, fuzzy, or difficult to interpret. A wide range of norms and values to be taken into account does not afford a strict separation of means and ends where only ends count as "impacts" (Biesta 2007). In practice, there is often intense pressure to act here and now (Schwandt 2002). So even if the perspective aims at codified information about which interventions work best, the practical applicability of that codified information may be limited. (This problem is parallel to the ones encountered in quality as standards and in organizational recipes).

In practical circumstances, it is also debatable how much rigor is demanded from a methodology that produces causal propositions. In some situations, a preliminary understanding, a tentative causal link, or even a warning about potential side effects may be enough to reduce the uncertainty regarding the choice of a particular practical action. In other situations, methodological standards are set so high that even fairly obvious knowledge is deprived of its right to be called evident. In this light, the problem is not so much the methodology required by the perspective on impact, as such, but rather the normative, political forces that send methodological requirements up and down, depending on expediency. So the key question is not about paradigmatic disagreements in the philosophy of science regarding the ontology and epistemology of causality. The key question is the size of the gap between the methodological textbook and real life. The issue is also who manages that gap and who has the right to issue a waiver exempting us from the strict version of methodological rules (or not) so that we accept or reject findings in a particular case.

Intra-scientific and practical debates have made clear that the concept of causality is not as unequivocal as some of its advocates believe. In fact, there are multiple schools of thought and their many advocates are in disagreement. For example, the search for universal laws that allegedly characterize experimentalism and statistics are criticized by critical rationalists who find causality only in the configurations of contexts, mechanisms, and outcomes (Pawson and Tilley 1997). Diverse practical interests in causality manifest themselves in different practical questions, which require different methodologies and lead to different answers (Stern et al. 2012). In other words, quality as impact does not speak for itself. It is not univocal. Once you start working within the perspective, your statements and conclusions will depend on your own positioning and your specific questions, even if you choose the one perspective that makes highest claims on scientific and methodological rigor. Furthermore, while the best methodological designs to produce causal inference help defend against some of the specific threats to validity, no design offers general protection against all of the threats in all situations (Cook and Campbell 1986).

At the same time, criticism of quality as impact is sometimes overstated. For example, a utilitarian ethic is contrasted with an ethic of duty and/or care. The distinction is sometimes used to make the claim that advocates of impacts and effects only evaluate human activity in terms of its consequences (a utilitarian ethic), while they are blind to other ethical perspectives. While that may be true, it cannot be concluded, as is sometimes implied, that a utilitarian orientation is by definition unethical. Attention to effects and impacts would be ethically warranted when we will be confronted with the consequences of our actions even if these actions are primarily motivated by other ethical principles.

Attention to effects and impacts is important in many practical-political situations. If criticism of methodologies delivering causal claims becomes too sweeping, it is no longer impossible to say that smoking causes cancer or that education influences life chances. On that basis, Latour (2004) recommends that the critical analyst "moves closer" to how causal claims are produced in the detail rather than "moves away" from them at all.

When we move closer to causal claims, we see tensions in the interface between the specificity of methodological rules and the broadness of the impacts we wish to capture, and we will see ambiguity in how rules for causal claims are applied to specific situations.

Social Conditions Favorable to Quality as Impact

This quality perspective enjoys the most optimal social conditions, when there is uniform belief in one way of establishing causal links (such as experimental methodology), when situations are uniform and easy to understand, when interventions are clearly defined, when evidence of their impact has already been found, when there is a machinery which keeps experiments and best practices in place, and when people delivering interventions and services do not question the notion of "best practice."

Quality as Excellence

Quality as excellence is a perspective that builds on one of the classic semantic components in the concept of quality: the sublime, the special, the exquisite, and the rare.

At the same time, it paradoxically shares with a number of other perspectives (standards, organizational recipes and impacts) a particular "emptiness" or "lack of specificity" as regards specific values or substantial criteria according to which quality is defined. Something is excellent if it is in a special category of itself above others, but it can be excellence in any respect. Quality as excellence has to do with relative positioning. Quality as excellence and social competition are therefore often connected.

The general meaning of this perspective often rests with its elective affinity with a social ideology favoring competition, often at the global level. Quality as excellence has gained particular traction in an era of competitive capitalism. A ranking system (e.g. league tables) is the epitome of this perspective on quality. Yet, the term excellence as such does not carry specific meanings that allow it to pinpoint what an excellence perspective *must* mean.

In the light of this vague perspective, a quality problem is often defined as a lack of a good ranking or, more widely applicable, the lack of a strategy or ambition directed toward maintaining or improving one's ranking.

Limitations and Ambiguities

With quality as excellence as a dominant perspective, the whole world is defined as one quality zone, meaning that the same goals, criteria, and ways of thinking are assumed to apply everywhere (Meyer 2008). One problem therefore relates to the relevance of "excellence" in general versus quality in a particular situation. To serve the needs of a specific situation, an "excellent" solution may be less relevant or even inappropriate.

Schools and other educational institutions may be caught between their concern for serving local communities versus an interest in "excellent" results on a ranking scale. In a similar vein, research oriented toward close interaction with local stakeholders and collaborative problem-solving may have problems documenting their "excellent" quality in wider, perhaps international, contexts; but that does not mean that the research did not serve a noble purpose. Locally relevant research may help educate the people, create public debate, and promote social innovation (Chavarro et al. 2017).

Another problem occurs when "excellence" is translated into operational criteria. In particular, the transformation of various quality criteria into a hierarchical ordering is problematic. In the assessment of research quality, for example, geographical arenas are often conflated with hierarchical levels of excellence. If something is nationally recognized, it is therefore by definition not as excellent as that which is internationally recognized. In practice, "international" often means published in the USA or in an Anglo-Saxon language area. Consequently, the researchers living in these areas and by nature publishing in their county's journals are by implication "born excellent." A post-colonial lesson from anthropology seems relevant here: International systems of comparison often have a surprisingly local (and Western) epistemic anchoring. Basic categorizations are not culture-free (Sahlins 1976).

Yet, notions of international and other forms of ranking seem to have a strong impact on minds and mentalities. For this reason, there is demand for "theories" that help explain why the successful have become successful and, by implication, what someone should do to imitate their success. Subscribing to such theory and being a rational actor in relation to a broader social field constitutes what is seen as legitimate behavior (DiMaggio and Powell 1983; Meyer et al. 1994).

Some of the theories explaining what is required to achieve excellence are very soft theories. For example, most sports clubs have a strategy explaining what to do in order to win the league championship one of the following three years. Logically, some of the strategic theories are bound to fail. There is not enough space at the top of the league for so many winners. Quality as excellence is by definition a positional good.

When this perspective is in play, discussion often arises about whether comparison is fair and the playing field level. Universities in many countries are expected to be as excellent as Oxford, Cambridge, Harvard, and

Stanford, without taking into account the differences in financial resources, teacher/student ratios, languages, and other factors.

Competition sometimes leads to peculiar behaviors. In research, the prestige of a journal depends on its journal impact factor (JIF), which is calculated on the basis of the number of subsequent citations of journal articles. Some editors are said to encourage their contributors to adopt citation practices that help enhance the journal's JIF. If successful, the integrity of the JIF is compromised. As an increasing number of scholars wish to publish in the most prestigious journals, the burden on reviewers has increased. If nothing other than publications count for the "excellent" researcher, however, there is no incentive for researchers to carry out reviews. It becomes difficult to recruit reviewers (Bauer 2016). One way to do so is to ask scholars who are cited in the article under review. They are presumably experts in the field and wish to carry out their review with integrity, but they also have their own interest in the publication of articles in which they are cited. These mechanisms are difficult to uncover, because the peer review is anonymous. Yet, if there is a structural bias in favor of positive and mutually beneficial—but hidden—exchanges between editors, reviewers, and authors, then the fairness of the competition is not what it is assumed to be.

The fairness and validity of rankings is often under debate. Shrewd university managers refer to university rankings only when their own position is good or improving. Otherwise they remain silent. Quality as excellence is a perspective that often puts the competitors in ambiguous or awkward positions with regard to which kind of behaviors are legitimate to enhance one's position and when and how much the ranking system should be accepted as legitimate.

Social Conditions Favorable to Quality as Excellence

This perspective thrives in situations where global competition is seen as the relevant context for quality assessment. It requires a center of calculation which is able to capture data and produce quality inscriptions which circulate widely in time and place. The perspective is particularly powerful at the local level when influential stakeholders around an organization add pressure on the organization to comply with criteria of excellence (Espeland and Sauder 2007).

Quality as Practice

Definition and Meaning

Quality as practice is a perspective on quality that is deeply rooted in theories of practice. It resonates with Aristotle's notion of phronesis (practical wisdom or judgment) (Schwandt 2002) and Dewey's notion of situated qualitative thinking (Dewey 1931).

As moral-ethical beings, humankind is already "thrown" into concrete sociopolitical and practical situations. As hermeneutics would suggest, all of our interpretations of life are bound to this thrownness as an inescapable starting point (Schwandt 2002). In Dewey's words, the starting point (also for scientific thinking) is the "experience of the common man" (1931: 101).

Our situations are already "multi-dimensional," meaning they are institutional, historical, political, relational, corporeal, and personal at the same time. Phronesis, or practical wisdom, does not come from compliance with a given set of criteria (be they legal, scientific, utility-oriented, etc.), beginning instead with a careful appreciation of understanding the situation. Over time, good practitioners learn to recognize patterns in situations they consider typical. They incorporate a sense of good practice as part of their habitus or "tacit knowledge" (Polanyi 1966). Habitus is often as much corporeal as it is cognitive. For example, travel to a country where traffic drives on the left side of the road, and your typical, intuitive way of moving around in the cityscape becomes awkward. Even if you intellectually understand where the traffic is, your sense of orientation and your bodily movements are difficult to change.

The corporeal aspect of practice is clearly illustrated in the case of sports stars and musicians. Playing the guitar requires coordinated fingers together with a sense of harmony and rhythm. Learning to play includes overcoming resistance of a genuinely bodily nature.

Becoming a competent practitioner requires training and skill. Malcolm Gladwell has written that mastering practically anything typically requires at least 10,000 hours of training. There is a reason why this training is called "practice." Good practitioners continue to learn as they adapt to changing situations, appreciate ever more nuanced aspects of these situations, and refine their skills. Good practitioners share with experts and connoisseurs (whom we encountered earlier) the cultivation of perceptual differentiation, which is trained through experience. Yet, an expert perspective and a practice perspective are not the same. Expertise travels and can be called in, whereas a practice is collective, interactive, habitual, and situated.

Practice is neither "planned" nor "implemented" but often intuitive and improvisational. Against the backdrop of tradition, competence, and institutional setting, good practice is often defined by small innovations and the understated display of extraordinary skill. Good practice is therefore only partly habitual. It is also sometimes emergent and dependent on play, innovation, and the mood of the day, even if it hinges on skill, experience, and craftsmanship (Sennett 2008).

This becomes clear in the case of a soccer player who sometimes passes a ball into what appears to be a surprisingly empty space, while one of his teammates has already intuitively grasped the idea before everybody else and is moving into that space at exactly the right moment, thereby making the pass a stroke of genius. Exactly how fine an item of practice it is could not be known before the move was made. The good practice almost relied on its own inexplicable execution. But it is possible to examine the situation in toto in awe and simply exclaim, "Oooh, that was good!" In Dewey's (1931: 102) terminology, "translation into specific terms gives a partial and inadequate result."

Schwandt explains this phenomenon in terms of a position that contrasts with a conventional criteriology. Criteriology suggests that there must be some external or transcendent desiderata with reference to which differences in knowledge positions, ethical stances, or practical choices can be reconciled. Criteriology is a quest for permanent criteria of rationality founded in a desire for objectivism and in the belief that we can and must transcend the limitations of socio-temporal frameworks of knowing (a.k.a. "situations") (Schwandt 2002: 95). In contradistinction, practice theory is "anti-criteriological." True enough, good practice may lean on criteria (be they legal, ethical, theoretical, etc.), it may refer to a particular interpretation of criteria, but the point is that there is no algorithm that transforms a given set of criteria into good practice. No criteria exhaust the meaning of good practice. It is "good" in an irreducible sense. In the terminology of the introduction of this book, quality as practice embodies itself as intuitive quality scripts rather than as formalized quality criteria. In the practice perspective, quality rests with the total configuration of the situation into which it is situated.

Lamont (2009) reports on a fascinating study of the practice of professors in a cross-disciplinary panel reviewing applications. They must reach a decision about the allocation of research funds. Their practice is complicated in part due to conflicting understandings of what constitutes good research in the different fields and subfields. Lamont unpacks the different meanings that professors attach to evaluative criteria, such as originality, significance, methods, feasibility, and more "evanescent" aspects of research. She also attends to "cognitive contextualization," meaning that the weight attached to a given set of criteria takes into account what is considered appropriate for the field or discipline of the proposal under review (Lamont 2009: 106).

The interaction between experts takes place with reference to highly advanced norms, but also tact, dialogue, and courtesy. Panelists lose credibility if they push their own field (Lamont 2009: 137). On the other hand, panelists who establish credibility over time may increase their influence on collective decisions.

Even if Lamont admits that disagreement and even horse-trading may occur, her study brings us closer to an understanding of the many social mechanisms which help enhance a form of practical decision-making that most of the participants find respectable, given the complexity of the task and given the time constraints under which committee work takes place.

Here is an example that resonates with Lamont's work. In a committee that reviewed innovative and cross-disciplinary applications for PhD projects, the secretariat asks two or three panelists to prepare a recommended decision about each application before the meeting. It turns out that panelists who accept a proportion of proposals that is starkly different from the proportion of proposals that are ultimately financed will, unless there is a systematic reason found in the allocation of applications to each panelist, either be overruled very often or will contribute to unfair decisions by promoting too many of "their own" applications. For that reason, the secretariat calculated the initial acceptance rates from each panelist, so that these rates were on the table and could inform the common deliberation. One panelist openly shared in a meeting how he had increased his acceptance rate, so that it would not be unreasonably difficult for a proposal if this particular panelist had taken part in the initial review. The panel collectively calibrated and adjusted the instruments used in quality assessment. The ongoing and reflexive fine-tuning of instruments is a pattern found in other literatures on practice and multiple orders of worth (Stark 2009: 27).

In her study, Lamont finds that the panel participants identify with what they see as the highest standards. Their sense of integrity is essential to the collective belief that the process is fair (Lamont 2009: 136). The same sense of integrity is essential for the ongoing pursuit of the perfection of the collaborative instruments and decision-making processes in use. Even if the participants' sense of a fair process *might* be partly illusory, their investment of their own sense of integrity in the very process contributes to making the practice as good as it can be under the circumstances (which includes huge amounts of paperwork and time pressure during meetings).

Lamont's observation of the importance of a practitioner's sense of integrity resonates with how Schwandt anchors the very theory of practice in the existence of people as moral beings. Practice cannot be separated from how we define ourselves. Faced with the dilemmas and difficulties that define practical situations, people blaze a trail for themselves guided by their sense of the kind of human beings they want to be. Our sense of who we are stands and falls with how we conduct ourselves.

According to the practice perspective, quality problems can come from an insufficient understanding of the situation, from lack of training or experience, from moral failure, or simply from the insurmountable of messiness of the human condition. Problems do not come and go merely because you "choose" a perspective (or not). As German hermeneutic philosophers would say, there is no *überwinden* of such problems, only *verwinden* (Vattimo 2005). The difference is difficult to translate, since both mean "overcome." But überwinden has a sense of something victorious which is not found in verwinden. The meaning is that quality problems cannot be "resolved," but you can "deal" with them in more or less qualified ways, depending on the exercise of practical wisdom.

An advocate of the quality as practice perspective might say that, in a given practical situation, all of the aforementioned quality perspectives are in fact somehow already taken into account. Nobody would deny that political goals deserve respect, that users should be attended to, that competition is sensible (at least up to a point), that some criteria matter, and so on. A practical philosopher might argue that, seen in isolation, each of already-presented perspectives is merely an ideology. All of the perspectives may have some partial thing to say, but the tricky thing is how to interpret its specific meaning in a given situation and which weight each of many concerns should be given in a particular practical situation. That can only be determined after an interpretation of the situation.

A quality problem can be exacerbated, however, if external criteria are imposed on practitioners, forcing them to prioritize only aspects corresponding to these criteria, thereby ignoring the moral complexity of the situation in toto. The whole meaning of the practice perspective rests with the notion that good practice is a response to a situation, so an in-depth understanding of the situation is required to make careful interpretation possible.

Limitations and Ambiguities

This perspective is fine when it comes to understanding a practice that is merely "good" in Dewey's terms. However, the perspective is less helpful when it comes to discriminating between "good practice" and just "practice."

While the strength of the quality as practice perspective is that it questions any pre-given set of criteria as standards of good practice, until the situation at hand is sufficiently understood, the weakness is that, since it tends to see all practice from the "inside" of the situation, it also affords a permissive view on what good practice then might be.

Although philosophically, good practitioners constantly review their own practice, the term "practice" often becomes mobilized in real-life political discourse as a (general) defense against performance management, audit, comparison, in fact against any critical review of a given way of doing things in a given setting.

Although the best proponents of this perspective advocate ongoing self-critical reflection upon practice, the philosophical foundation of this perspective also lends itself to being rhetorically abused to defend all kinds of practices.

This has to do with the inherent link between the practice and the understanding of the situation in which it is embedded. Good practice is relative to a particular understanding of the situation to which it is a response. However, "the situation cannot explain itself in a proposition," as Dewey (1931: 98) explains. It is not and cannot be stated explicitly. Although aspects of it can be highlighted and discussed, the situation in its entirety cannot. Quality is captured only inside a quality script which remains intuitive and therefore not fully articulated.

"Knowing the situation" is an epistemic privilege that allows one to make judgments about what constitutes quality as practice, but reference to a known, but unarticulated "situation" does not always constitute a transparent foundation for democratic reasoning and critical argument.

While situations are at least partly defined by their boundaries in time and space (Stark 2009), analysts who seek to understand good practice too often seem to know how to define the situation at hand. The practical situation is very often defined from the standpoint of a small group of professionals in a "community of practice" or in terms of some sort of locality (e.g. a local school). How can one know that practice is solidary with the local? In school politics, for instance, most analyses of practice examine a situation where local school teachers struggle with national tests and standards that are more or less irrelevant in the local situation. But is the delineation of national school policy—with or without tests—not also a difficult practical question? Is it also not practice to engage in national debates, to develop a cool new computer system for national tests, to write a book for an international audience, or to send a rocket up into space? The recent, broad application of "the practice turn" in social science would evidently answer: Yes, practice manifests in all kinds of situations, in many areas of professional activity, and in many walks of life (Antal et al. 2015; Stark 2009).

Yet, there is a particular pattern in a typical way of situating practice studies on the micro level. It equates "the situation" with "the local situation" (Stake 2004). More often than not, practice is seen as one thing and society as another. As a consequence, society-making is not regarded as practice. Instead, society provides all of the challenges, such as indicators, competition, and globalization, which practice has to struggle with, sometimes juggling multiple "orders of worth" (Stark 2009). More often than not, practice itself is portrayed as heroic against these influences from something "outside" of "the situation." The underlying idea seems to be that practices were better off if society left them alone.

Again, however, this heroic and usually tragic picture of practice rests with an understanding of a "situation" that others in society may not share. Thrownness and "situatedness" are in themselves not enough. Consider an animal trainer in a theme park. It requires many years of training, practice, patience, and courage to train wild animals to perform. However, the overall idea of keeping wild animals in captivity for entertainment purposes no longer fares well in Western culture. The fact that the animal trainer's job requires highly advanced skills and is difficult as seen from "within" has simply lost relevance. It might be a complicated practice, but the rest of society does not recognize it as a good one.

Diane Vaughan's excellent study of the Space Shuttle Challenger disaster is not articulated as a study of practice, but can be read as such. She demonstrates how the disaster resulted not from external pressures to launch the rocket before it was ready or from scrupulous, risk-taking managers. Instead, she shows how ambiguities about safety and early warning signals were overlooked, eliminated, and/or buried in documents. The factors leading to the disaster were in fact normalized in NASA. They were, in my interpretation, part of practice. But neither the term practice nor the situation to which it refers seems to guarantee *good* practice.

The quality as practice perspective has an ambiguous potential to turn in two directions. The first is a conservative one in which "thrownness" means being relegated to a situation that cannot be defined and articulated. Any practice—also "good practice"—rests with this thrownness. The primary rhetorical use of this version of practice is that it provides a defense against the forces of the modern world (e.g. science, globalization, management). When it is criticized, this practice defends itself as rooted in "the nature of teaching" or "the essence of our identity in this community." This view of practice is conservative in its political implications: Existing practices should be protected.

The other direction in which the quality as practice perspective can be taken is one where the situation in toto may be impossible to enunciate, but it remains open for curiosity and questioning. The perspective is helpful in appreciating the difficulties, the many "orders of worth" at play in contemporary society (Stark 2009), but there are no guarantees to be found in any inner essence of either the "situation" or "the practice." There is no original first way in which we find ourselves thrown as human beings. Indeed, school teachers are teachers in a school, but they are also teachers in a society. Practices are essential in the sense of important but not in the sense of something natural and essential inside things and situations themselves. Practices are a way of looking at human activity, be it at any level of analysis you may find relevant. Society-making is also practice, even if it is difficult and incorporates many other practices.

This non-conservative version of practice theory (and of its hermeneutic foundation) is in my view consistent with contributions from Rosanvallon (2009) and Vattimo (2005). Rosanvallon describes democracy as inherently situated and historical. Democratic "learning" can therefore be seen as a form of situated practice that must constantly "invent" itself, as it is not a function of any universal or ahistorical principle. With Vattimo (2005), we learn that there is no ultimate first way of being a human being, so there can be no first-order guarantees from which principles of practice can be derived. As an alternative, Vattimo offers the notion of *pensiero debole*, weak thinking, the purpose of which is to help weaken epistemic privilege and weaken authority. In that sense, Vattimo uses the anti-criteriological principles of the practice perspective to weaken the perspective itself.

Concluding Reflection

The presented perspectives on quality are fundamentally different. The fact that they can be meaningfully identified and separated—without necessarily exhausting the concept—shows that quality as a concept is so rich that it cannot both be grasped in totality and have any degree of specificity at the same time.

Notice how each of the perspectives subscribes to a particular understanding of what "the quality problem" might be. The link between the two is tight. The relevance of a given quality perspective in a situation depends on whether the corresponding quality problem can be found and is of concern to some in the given situation. Therefore, an identification of quality problems may be a fruitful way of finding out why or why not a given quality perspective is relevant in a situation. It would be a shame to work on non-existent problems.

Conversely, once a quality perspective is chosen, it also defines the kinds of problems people may have. The nine perspectives define quality problems in as many ways. So although some may find some problems more pressing in some situations than in others, there is no direct way in which an analysis of reality can inform us about which quality perspective should be applied to which situation. A perspective transports its own quality problems with it that happen to fit miraculously with the perspective. Nevertheless, understanding the problem-perspective dyad brings us closer to what it is that makes various perspectives relevant and what it is that people may disagree about in a given quality situation. In turn, our analysis cannot do what can otherwise be done rhetorically with an unspecific use of the term quality, which is to conceal problems and differences under an ever-positive veil of obscurity. If we refrain from any specificity and use quality in a broad, all-encompassing political rhetoric, quality can "suck up" all of the problems mentioned in the sum of all these perspectives. It is a rhetorical free ride to refer to quality as long as it is unrelated to the specificities of perspectives, situations, and problems.

In addition to the usefulness of an inter-perspective analysis of quality suggested in this chapter, there is also the intra-perspective dimension.

If a perspective is "worked through" with sufficient care, insistence, and meticulousness, it often turns out to be "unstable" or "non-essential." We can "peel the onion" and not get to a core that remains stable. For example, political goals are hazy or shifting. Implicit goals become explicit and change the evaluative framework. Users have autotelic needs and wants separated from the use of things (Bauman 1983), and they do not become happy when they get what they want; or they become happy about something that they were not able to explicate in advance. Users are also sometimes in irrevocable disagreement with each other. Standards are created in the moment of calculation. There is no solid rock underneath them when they change. Practices are sometimes self-reflexive. So, even in a strict logical domain, quality perspectives can be logically separated from each other, but that still does not provide them with an essence which guarantees their stability in use.

There is no guarantee in the empirical world that quality perspectives occur in purely logical, separate forms. They may be appealed to only in the form of hunches, assumptions, or rhetorical moves. To create and hold together alliances, tacit overlaps between some of them may be emphasized, such as "standards" in the interests of "users" or vague goals turned into a notion of comparative "excellence" or the "practice" of being "impact-oriented." Since many of the quality perspectives have an elective affinity with the views of particular stakeholders (e.g. goals with political principals, user needs with users, standards with bureaucrats, practice with professionals), there is likely to be some form of "ambiguous policies" (Baier et al. 1986) or "productive misunderstandings" (Stark 2009) creating overlaps or alliances between various types of quality agents and weaving them into stories of quality (Weick in Dean and Bowen 2000: 163).

Presumably, in the greater socio-historical stream of shifting significations and imaginaries, some perspectives and alliances between perspectives will gain more traction at some points in time than others. In an era of bureaucratization, standards will flourish. In an era of globalization, excellence will be demanded. It has also been suggested in the analysis of the nine perspectives that the codification and ease of operations in time and space is something that helps select some perspectives before others, especially in relation to the production of quality assessments across time and space, beyond singular situations. For example, the expert perspective and the practice perspective by definition score low on codification, and so does the user perspective (unless it is reduced to a few quantifiable dimensions). On the other hand, the standards perspective, the organizational recipe perspective, and the excellence perspective are particular fit to be transformed into procedures which pave the way for management of large-scale quality zones extending through time and space.

Still, given our understanding of the opacity of the concept of quality so far and given the need for alliances and consensus, it would be futile to establish a grandiose hypothesis about any linear development here.

Instead, I will pursue another strategy. A strategy is needed to help explain how quality becomes fixed in particular ways in particular situations. By fixed I do not mean stable forever, I just mean fixed enough for long enough time to make an argument or statement about quality or to carry out some sort of evaluative undertaking. In order to grasp this, I turn to quality measurements and the agencies performing them because they play an important role in stabilizing what would otherwise be elusive, opaque, vague, or multi-dimensional quality.

References

Andresen, Emilie, and Maj Fjordside. 2015. *Uklare Begreber, Store Forventninger og Nye Roller: Et Studie af Hverdagsrehabilitering som et Eksempel på Samskabelse* [Unclear Concepts, Big Expectations and New Roles: A Study of Everyday Rehabilitation as an Example of Cocreation]. Thesis, Department of Political Science, University of Copenhagen.

Antal, Ariane B., Michael Hutter, and David Stark. 2015. *Moments of Valuation: Exploring Sites of Dissonance*. Oxford: Oxford University Press.

Baier, Vicki E., James G. March, and Harald Sætren. 1986. Implementation and Ambiguity. *Scandinavian Journal of Management Studies* 2 (3/4): 179–212.

Bateson, Gregory. 1972. *Steps to an Ecology of Mind*. New York: Ballantine Books.

Bauer, Martin W. 2016. A Word From the Parting Editor, 4760 Pages Down the Line. *Public Understanding of Science* 25 (2): 130–134.

Bauman, Zygmunt. 1983. Industrialism, Consumerism and Power. *Theory, Culture and Society* 1 (3): 32–43.

Bereiter, Carl. 2002. *Education and Mind in the Knowledge Age*. Mahwah: L. Erlbaum Associates.
Bergh, Andreas. 2011. Why Quality in Education – and What Quality? – A Linguistic Analysis of the Concept of Quality in Swedish Government Texts. *Education Inquiry* 2 (4): 709–723.
Beuscart, Jean-Samuel, and Kevin Mellet. 2013. Competing Quality Conventions in the French Online Display Advertising Market. *Journal of Cultural Economy* 6 (4): 402–418.
Biesta, Gert. 2007. Why 'What Works' Won't Work: Evidence-Based Practice and the Democratic Deficit in Educational Research. *Educational Theory* 57 (1): 1–22.
Brown, Wendy. 2015. *Undoing the Demos*. New York: Zone Books.
Brunsson, Nils. 1989. *The Organization of Hypocrisy: Talk, Decisions and Actions in Organizations*. New York: Wiley.
Brunsson, Nils, and Bengt Jacobsson, eds. 2000. *A World of Standards*. Oxford: Oxford University Press.
Chavarro, Diego, Puay Tang, and Ismael Ràfols. 2017. Why Researchers Publish in Non-mainstream Journals: Training, Knowledge Bridging, and Gap Filling. *Research Policy* 46 (9): 1666–1689.
Cheney, George, Jill J. McMillan, and Roy Schwartzman. 1997. Should We Buy the "Student-As-Consumer" Metaphor? *The Montana Professor* 7 (3): 8–11.
Cook, Thomas D., and Donald T. Campbell. 1986. The Causal Assumptions of Quasi-Experimental Practice: The Origins of Quasi-Experimental Practice. *Synthese* 68 (1): 141–180.
Dahlberg, Magnus, and Evert Vedung. 2001. *Demokrati och Brukarutvärdering* [Democracy and User Evaluation]. Lund: Studentlitteratur.
Dean, James W., Jr., and David E. Bowen. 2000. Management Theory and Total Quality. In *The Quality Movement & Organization Theory*, ed. R.E. Cole and W.R. Scott, 3–21. Thousand Oaks: Sage.
Dewey, John. 1931. *Philosophy and Civilization*. New York: G. P. Putnam's Sons.
DiMaggio, Paul, and Walter Powell. 1983. The Iron Cage Revisited: Institutional Isomorphism and Collective Rationality in Organizational Fields. *American Sociological Review* 48 (6): 147–160.
Dörner, Dietrich. 1996. *The Logic of Failure: Recognizing and Avoiding Error in Complex Situations*. Cambridge, MA: Perseus Books.
Droitcour, Judith A., and Mary G. Kovar. 2008. Multiple Threats to the Validity of Randomized Studies. In *Fundamental Issues on Evaluation*, ed. N.L. Smith and P.R. Brandon. New York: The Guilford Press.

Eisner, Elliot W. 1976. Educational Connoisseurship and Criticism: Their Form and Functions in Educational Evaluation. *Journal of Aesthetic Education* 10 (3/4): 135–150.

———. 2003. Educational Connoisseurship and Educational Criticism: An Arts-Based Approach to Educational Evaluation. In *International Handbook of Educational Evaluation*, ed. T. Kellaghan, D.L. Stufflebeam, and L.A. Wingate. Dordrecht: Kluwer Academic Publishers.

Espeland, Wendy N., and Michael Sauder. 2007. Rankings and Reactivity: How Public Measures Recreate Social Worlds. *American Journal of Sociology* 113 (1): 1–40.

Fischer, Frank. 2003. *Reframing Public Policy: Discursive Politics and Deliberative Practices*. Oxford: Oxford University Press.

Fountain, Jane E. 2001. Paradoxes of Public Sector Customer Service. *Governance* 14 (1): 55–73.

Funnell, Sue C., and Patricia J. Rogers. 2011. *Purposeful Program Theory: Effective Use of Theories of Change and Logic Models*. San Francisco: Jossey-Bass.

Furusten, Staffan. 2000. The Knowledge Base of Standards. In *A World of Standards*, ed. N. Brunsson and B. Jacobsson. Oxford: Oxford University Press.

Furubo, Jan-Eric, Ray C. Rist, and Rolf Sandahl. 2002. *International Atlas of Evaluation*. New Brunswick: Transaction Publishers.

Galbraith, Jay R. 1983. Strategy and Organization Planning. *Human Resource Management* 22 (1–2): 63–77.

Gawande, Atul. 2014. *Being Mortal, Medicine and What Matters in the End*. New York: Metropolitan Books.

Hallström, Kristina T. 2000. Organizing the Process of Standardization. In *A World of Standards*, ed. N. Brunsson and B. Jacobsson. Oxford: Oxford University Press.

Harvey, Lee, and Diana Green. 1993. Defining Quality. *Assessment and Evaluation in Higher Education* 18 (1): 9–34.

Harvey, Lee, and Bjørn Stensaker. 2008. Quality Culture: Understandings, Boundaries and Linkages. *European Journal of Education* 43 (4): 427–442.

Hermann, Stefan. 2007. *Magt og Oplysning. Folkeskolen 1950–2006* [Power and Enlightenment. The Public School 1950–2006]. Copenhagen: Unge Pædagoger.

Husz, Orsi. 2012. The Morality of Quality: Assimilating Material Mass Culture in Twentieth-Century Sweden. *Journal of Modern European History* 10 (2): 152–181.

Julnes, George, ed. 2012. *Promoting Value in the Public Interest: Informing Policies for Judging Value in Evaluation. New Directions for Evaluation, No. 133*. San Francisco: Jossey-Bass.

Kreutzmann, Gladys. 1994. *Börn og Unges Anbringelser uden for Hjemmet* [Children and Young People's Placements Outside the Home]. Nuuk: Direktoratet for Sociale Anliggender og Arbejdsmarked.

Lamont, Michèle. 2009. *How Professors Think: Inside the Curious World of Academic Judgment*. Cambridge, MA: Harvard University Press.

Latour, Bruno. 1987. *Science in Action: How to Follow Scientists and Engineers through Society*. Stony Stratford: Open University Press.

———. 2004. Why Has Critique Run Out of Steam? From Matters of Fact to Matters of Concern. *Critical Inquiry* 30 (2): 225–248.

Mathison, Sandra. 1991. Role Conflicts for Internal Evaluators. *Evaluation and Program Planning* 14 (3): 173–179.

———. 2011. Internal Evaluation, Historically Speaking. *New Directions for Evaluation* 132: 13–23.

Meyer, John W. 2008. Building Education for a World Society. In *Changing Knowledge and Education*, ed. M.A. Pereyra, 31–49. Frankfurt am Main: Peter Lang.

Meyer, John W., and Brian Rowan. 1977. Institutionalized Organizations: Formal Structure as Myth and Ceremony. *American Journal of Sociology* 83: 340–363.

Meyer, John W., John Boli, and George M. Thomas. 1994. Ontology and Rationalization in the Western Cultural Account. In *Institutional Environments and Organizations*, ed. W.R. Scott and J.W. Meyer, 9–27. Thousand Oaks: Sage.

Noordegraf, Mirko. 2016. Reconfiguring Professional Work. Changing Forms of Professionalism in Public Services. *Administration and Society* 48 (7): 783–810.

Olsen, Niklas. 2016. Velfærdsstatens krise og neoliberalismens indtog i Danmark i 1970'erne [The Crisis of the Welfare State and the Arrival of Neoliberalism in Denmark in the 1970s]. *Slagmark* 74 (Fall): 119–138.

Øvretveit, John. 2005. Public Service Quality Improvement. In *The Oxford Handbook of Public Management*, ed. E. Ferlie, L.E. Lynn Jr., and C. Pollitt. New York: Oxford University Press.

Pawson, Ray, and Nick Tilley. 1997. *Realistic Evaluation*. London: Sage.

Pflueger, Dane. 2016. Knowing Patients: The Customer Survey and the Changing Margins of Accounting in Healthcare. *Accounting, Organizations and Society* 53: 17–33.

Polanyi, Michael. 1966. *The Tacit Dimension*. Chicago: The University of Chicago Press.

Power, Michael. 1996. Making Things Auditable. *Accounting, Organizations and Society* 21 (2/3): 289–315.

———. 1997. *The Audit Society*. Oxford: Oxford University Press.

Prewitt, Kenneth, Thomas A. Schwandt, and Miron L. Straf. 2012. *Using Science as Evidence in Public Policy*. Washington, DC: National Academies Press.

Reeves, Carol A., and David A. Bednar. 1994. Defining Quality: Alternatives and Implications. *Academy of Management Review* 19 (3): 419–445.

Roberts, John. 2018. Managing Only with Transparency: The Strategic Functions of Ignorance. *Critical Perspectives on Accounting* 55: 53–60.

Rosanvallon, Pierre. 2009. *Demokratin som Problem* [Democracy as the Problem]. Hägersten: TankeKraft Förlag.

Røvik, Kjell A. 2005. *Moderne Organisasjoner: Trender i Organisasjonstenkningen ved Tusenårsskiftet* [Modern Organizations: Trends in Organizational Thinking at the Millennium]. Bergen: Fagbokforlaget.

Sahlins, Marshall. 1976. *Culture and Practical Reason*. Chicago: Aldine.

Schwandt, Thomas A. 2002. *Evaluation Practice Reconsidered*. New York: Peter Lang.

Schwandt, Thomas A., and Holli Burgon. 2006. Evaluation and the Study of Lived Experience. In *The SAGE Handbook of Evaluation*, ed. I.F. Shaw, J.C. Greene, and M.M. Mark, 99–118. London: Sage.

Sennett, Richard. 2008. *The Craftsman*. London: Penguin Books.

Sismondo, Sergio. 2008. Science and Technology Studies and an Engaged Program. In *The Handbook of Science and Technology Studies*, ed. E.J. Hackett, O. Amsterdamska, M. Lynch, and J. Wajcman, 13–31. Cambridge, MA: The MIT Press.

Sower, Victor E., and Frank K. Fair. 2005. There Is More to Quality than Continuous Improvement: Listening to Plato. *QMJ* 12 (1): 8–20.

Sørensen, Eva M., and Søren K. Foged. 2015. Mål- og Resultatstyring i Kommunerne Efter Krisen [Target and Performance Management in the Municipalities After the Crisis]. *Økonomi og Politik* 88 (1): 46–56.

Stake, Robert E. 2004. *Standard-Based and Responsive Evaluation*. Thousand Oaks: Sage.

Stark, David. 2009. *The Sense of Dissonance, Accounts of Worth in Economic Life*. Princeton: Princeton University Press.

Stern, Elliot, Nicoletta Stame, John Mayne, Kim Forss, Rick Davies, and Barbara Befani. 2012. *Broadening the Range of Designs and Methods for Impact*

Evaluations: Report of a Study Commissioned by the Department for International Development, DFID Working Paper 38. London: Department for International Development.

Stilgoe, Jack, Richard Owen, and Phil Macnaghten. 2013. Developing a Framework for Responsible Innovation. *Research Policy* 42: 1568–1580.

Strang, David, and John W. Meyer. 1994. Institutional Conditions for Diffusion. In *Institutional Environments and Organizations*, ed. W.R. Scott and J.W. Meyer, 100–112. Thousand Oaks: Sage.

Vattimo, Gianni. 2005. *Nihilisme og Emancipation. Etik, Politik, Ret* [Nihilsm and Emancipation. Ethics, Politics, and Law]. Aarhus: Aarhus University Press.

Vedung, Evert. 1997. *Public Policy and Program Evaluation*. New Brunswick: Transaction.

Wallenburg, Iris, Julia Quartz, and Roland Bal. 2016. Making Hospitals Governable: Performativity and Institutional Work in Ranking Practices. *Administration & Society*: 1–27.

Weick, Karl E. 2000. Quality Improvement: A Sensemaking Perspective. In *The Quality Movement and Organization Theory*, ed. R.E. Cole and W.R. Scott, 155–172. Thousand Oaks: Sage.

Weick, Karl E., Kathleen M. Sutcliffe, and David Obstfeld. 2005. Organizing and the Process of Sense-making. *Organization Science* 16 (4): 409–421.

Wimbush, Erica, Steve Montague, and Tamara Mulherin. 2012. Applications of Contribution Analysis to Outcome Planning and Impact Evaluation. *Evaluation* 18 (3): 310–329.

Young, Joni J. 2006. Making Up Users. *Accounting, Organizations and Society* 31 (6): 579–600.

4

Quality Inscriptions: Their Makers and Their Consequences

The previous chapter made clear that the concept of quality itself is spacious enough to embrace a wide variety of perspectives. Furthermore, within a given perspective, no one can guarantee that (the social construction of) quality remains stable and fixed.

In order to determine what quality might mean more specifically in specific contexts, this chapter is concerned with how quality inscription takes place, who makes such inscriptions, and what the consequences of quality inscriptions are. This topic is not peripheral. In education policy, for example, the mechanisms used to secure quality assurance and evaluation have been more in focus than quality itself (Kaukko et al. 2018: 180).

By quality inscription I mean a form of codified documentation of quality. Inscription devices comprise methodological, statistical, organizational, and practical tools that render visible and transform otherwise complex, ambiguous realities into figures, scales, indicators, numbers, or categories. Without quality inscriptions, it would not be possible to produce comparisons, ratings, or rankings (Dahler-Larsen 2014).

An inscription turns "pieces of matter into written documents" (Latour and Woolgar 1986: 51). "Inscription" means that a particular interpretation of the quality of a quality object finds a solid form so that

P. Dahler-Larsen, *Quality*, https://doi.org/10.1007/978-3-030-10392-7_4

it can travel in time and space. More often than not, codification implies quantification using scales, rankings, and so forth; in principle, however, inscription can assume any form or shape that maintains and stabilizes some discernable traces of the quality object. The inscription is presented as if it "is" the object. The point is not a philosophical one about whether the object that is referred to "really" "exists" in some ontological way. It is just enough to note that there would be no contact with the object in the way it is defined through the inscription were it not for the inscription itself. An inscription helps produce "the occasional conviction of others that something is a fact" (Latour and Woolgar 1986: 105). Many inscriptions are less successful. Quality inscriptions are statements the further fate of which are in the hands of others (Orlikowski and Scott 2008). They are performative acts which can fail (Butler 2010).

Nevertheless, quality inscriptions often play an important role in defining quality in practice. We have seen in historical and conceptual analyses that quality is radically polysemic. The measurement of quality therefore plays an important role in providing quality with specific meaning and direction in a given situation. Measurement requires a machinery for inscription. Inscriptions carry an imprint referring back to the actors who made them. Remember that quality perspectives are linked to understandings of problems. In turn, since problems and frames are important political devices (Stone 2012), quality inscriptions can be more politically significant than they appear. The definition of quality that an inscription offers is a social factor in itself (Koselleck 2011). Quality inscriptions can be used to make particular appeals to people to act in particular ways and to enact the quality object in particular ways. We will return to constitutive effects of quality inscriptions later in this chapter.

Inscriptions and Organizational Hinterlands

Inscriptions are only possible in particular social contexts. Three observations allow us to move theoretically closer to an understanding of how inscription takes place and who has the capacity to make inscriptions.

The first observation is that the codification of inscriptions requires infrastructure and machinery. For example, sending out a digital survey that measures customer satisfaction requires computers, digital contact with respondents through mailing lists or webpages, computerized technology to manage and analyze survey responses, and so forth. Infrastructure and machinery are also necessary to make results available to the potential users of the quality information. The availability of computers and the Internet have played a decisive role for the production and dissemination of evaluative data about quality. In any specific situation, computers, programs, networks, capabilities, and competencies need to fit together in a specific manner in order to produce a particular inscription. As Latour (1987) explains, what is needed from a center of calculation is not some extraordinary or extraterrestrial cognitive capacity—it is instead a practical and operational way of compressing large amounts of data into concentrated inscriptions. The center of calculation thus avoids drowning in data. Similarly, data must be compressed, transported, and presented to relevant audiences in digestible form.

The second observation: Once the demands on the infrastructure become sufficiently complex, organization becomes necessary. For example, the production of internationally comparative test results as an indicator of school quality requires a highly complex machinery that depends on expertise, technology, and political support. Tests must be developed by experts, translated, and calibrated. To produce comparative results, the organization must have legitimate access to schools in many countries. The test machinery must not only reach out to the individual students in many countries but must also do so in a manner that accounts for the factors influencing the comparability of the data, including controls for cultural bias across nations. Technology must be developed and alliances built with experts and hundreds of local, political, and administrative gatekeepers. There must also be infrastructure (data presentation formats, media, networks with governments) that allows a producer of quality inscriptions to spread the use of data into the relevant quality zone. By quality zone I mean the time and space in which the quality inscription is meant to be relevant. In Programme for International Students Assessment (PISA), the quality zone is the global system of competing school systems. The scale of this quality zone is indicative of the scale of the organizational apparatus needed.

Few organizations other than the OECD will be able to produce results that are as successful as PISA assessments in all these aspects. Because of the high threshold of organizational requirements to produce and diffuse such inscriptions, it is almost impossible to develop and implement a viable alternative to PISA.

The third observation is that although some form of independence from the production of the quality object itself can be a key ingredient in trustworthy quality measurement, independence is always relative. There is no such thing as total independence of everything else in this world. Here, the notion of relevance structure mentioned in the introduction is a helpful reminder. A relevance structure is a particular way of being engaged in the world. Organizations also have relevance structures. Organizations already carry an "imprint" of how they are anchored institutionally (Scott 1992). Institutional anchoring relates to money, support, expectations, sanctions, and ways of thinking.

Again, the example with the OECD and PISA studies is illustrative. The OECD is an international organization promoting economic development. The relevance structure and favorite mentality that permeate the OECD are economic ones. When the OECD engages in measuring quality in schools, then, the larger framework in which they define quality is embedded in an economic way of thinking. In an OECD perspective on school quality, the national school systems are conceived of as competitors in a global marketplace. So while the quality assessment may be "independent" (in the sense of being made "at a distance"), it is not independent from a very particular kind of relevance structure and institutional commitment.

In a similar vein, a concept of "good governance" was coined by the World Bank in the late 1980s. The Bank did not have legal capacity to interfere directly in member countries' internal affairs. Although "good" can mean many things, in the case at hand "good governance" in fact embodied an economist view with a focus on market-led steering (at the expense of other values such as democracy, environment, and social cohesion) (Erkkilä and Piironen 2014: 349). This view resonated with the dominant philosophy in the World Bank as well as with economist ideology at the time.

Studies in the sociology of knowledge have shown that the production of a particular knowledge requires a large set of connections between multiple elements in a whole "hinterland" of constructions undergirding innovation (Bijker and Law 1992). To understand how an organization produces quality inscriptions, a useful key is an analysis of the organizational hinterland.

The hinterland ties the organization to the world in particular ways while simultaneously allowing the organization to act in a specific manner. The hinterland may include an ideology, a self-understanding, alliances, expectations, and promises that induce the organization to inscribe quality some ways and not in others. And not to forget: resources.

Making a quality inscription requires a technical infrastructure and organizational machinery that are usually costly. Seen from the perspective of the organization producing the inscriptions, it is important that these costs do not become a burden on itself. It therefore either has to receive generous external support or enroll "free" contributions from partners in the organizational hinterland. Common ways of doing so are to use inputs that employees have to provide during normal work hours (documentation of public services) or ask consumers to provide ratings (consumer reviews).

Consequently, even if quality machineries are expensive to run, some of their costs are (1) external to the inscribing organization, (2) not monetarized, and therefore (3) not visible. But resource dependencies remain. It is therefore beneficial for quality-inscribing organizations to command or recruit others to work for them or, alternatively, find financial models that are profitable and do not disturb the alleged integrity of the quality inscriptions. This can be difficult.

No example illustrates this point better than the discussion on credit rating agencies (CRAs) following the 2008 financial crisis. A CRA is a company that assesses the debt instruments (bonds and other securities) issued by firms or governments and assigns "credit ratings" to these instruments based on the likelihood that debt will be repaid (Rom 2009: 640).

While you might be tempted to believe that credit ratings merely have to do with creditworthiness, according to the terminology circulated among specialists, CRAs in fact gauge the "quality of the underlying asset" (White 2012: 105) or "financial quality of the securities" (Duffhues and Weterings 2011: 342). Credit ratings are, thus, inscriptions of *quality*. Investors use them to gauge the quality of the financial entities in which they invest (Rom 2009: 640).

While the dominant CRAs use a variety of rankings comprising categories (e.g. AAA or A1+), the critical distinction is whether or not a particular entity is "investment grade." Many bonds categorized as "investment grade" by the CRAs were proven by the 2008 financial crisis to be "junk bonds." The realization of this fact, which occurred too late and on a massive scale, led to a "cliff effect."

Credit ratings have been used for more than a century. One of the first known examples is Moody (still in business), which rated the bonds used to finance railroads. This was an "investor-pays" business model, meaning that potential investors could purchase a copy of Moody's publication before deciding in which railroad bonds to invest.

After the crisis in the 1930s, credit ratings were used in the public regulation of banks. In 1936, a source mentions that US banks should not invest in something "speculative," but should base their investments on "recognized rating manuals" (White 2012). Similar regulation was extended to pension funds in the mid-1970s. Some financial institutions have bylaw restrictions commanding them to react to credit ratings on an ongoing basis when composing their portfolios (Scalet and Kelly 2012: 479).

In the late 1960s and early 1970s, the CRA business model changed from an investor-pays model to an issuer-pays model (Scalet and Kelly 2012). One contributing factor, which illustrates the rule of the *pudenda origo* (lowly origins) of social change, is that the emergence of cheap photocopying rendered it too difficult to make a sufficient number of potential investors pay for publications with credit ratings (White 2012: 99). Furthermore, bond issuers themselves became increasingly interested in their own ratings, partly because they were subject to regulation (White 2012).

The issuer-pays business model had severe consequences. When an issuer of a financial entity decides to choose a CRA, it can play rating agencies against each other. While several ratings agencies might be consulted, only the most favorable rating is published. Conversely, CRAs also have commercial interests. They can offer consulting services to issuers who want to know how to achieve the best ratings possible. After selling these consulting services, the CRAs can then sell a rating. A CRA is subject to conflicting interests when assessing the quality of a financial entity, which it has helped develop (Rom 2009; Scalet and Kelly 2012: 482). Objectivity flies out the window if the payment received by the CRA in fact depends on the rating. Altogether, these mechanisms pushed "CRAs to offer favorable ratings in the interests of their own profits" (Scalet and Kelly 2012: 482).

Until the 2008 financial crisis, numerous complex financial products were sold that consisted of inferior securities packaged in ways that were not very transparent. At the same time, CRAs produced many more credit ratings without increasing their staff correspondingly, and some of their ratings were based on procedures lacking in transparency. They also made out-of-model adjustments (Rom 2009: 647). In retrospect, CRAs were also criticized for not monitoring the rated assets properly and responding too late to market tendencies.

According to the CRAs, however, not all fluctuations should be reflected in changed ratings. The CRAs wanted to "rate through the circle" so that temporary ups and downs would not lead to continuous changes in ratings. For that reason, downgrades occur infrequently (Rom 2009: 645). On the other hand, when it becomes clearly visible that a rating requires revision, it may come so late that a "cliff effect" occurs, as in 2008.

While incompetence, greed, over-optimism, lack of proper procedure, and the increasing complexity of the financial products all might have contributed to the disaster (Rom 2009), it is instructive to study the consequences of the issuer-pays business model. This model created a particular set of dependencies in the organizational hinterland of CRAs, which seriously damaged the solidity of their quality inscriptions.

This observation justifies two related questions, the first relating to whether the criticism of CRAs is not too easy: Will not all assessments of the quality of financial assets be tentative? And would we not be dissatisfied if procedures were followed slavishly—and also if they were not?

Whether or not it is true that CRAs are too reluctant to lower existing credit ratings, the CRAs learned from the disaster and changed their practices after 2008. When they in fact performed a "less expected downgrade" (of Austria, France, and Italy in 2012) (Eijffinger 2012: 212), were these countries not dissatisfied then? After all, the assessments of creditworthiness are just that: assessments. They are more or less tentative. And will all such assessments not make some happy and some unhappy, regardless of the exact quality of the assessment? Is it too much to expect perfection in credit ratings?

The next, related question goes one step further. Why focus so much on the (lack of) perfection in credit ratings? If people (including especially investors) are so unhappy with credit ratings, why not simply ignore them? Is it not somewhat pathological to blame the CRA when someone's investments lose value? Should investors not know that they are taking a risk? Should they take more responsibility for their investments?

The question is asked not for rhetorical reasons but for theoretical ones. What is missed in how the question is asked is the public and institutional function of credit ratings. Credit ratings cannot be ignored because they play a functional role in relation to the buying and selling of financial entities. Regardless of whether one "believes" in their consistency with "real" creditworthiness, creditworthiness refers to payments, which will or might be made in the future, so it is unknowable until it becomes inscribed. Once inscribed, however, it becomes known. Until payment is actually made, a credit rating is the best proxy available for that payment. On that basis, economic life is regulated. When banks and pension funds can(not) buy or sell particular bonds because of the credit rating, these ratings have a real function that cannot be ignored. This might be called "over-reliance," but "creditworthiness statements have attained the force of law" (Eijffinger 2012: 913).

Advanced discussions on how to improve the regulation of CRAs must therefore consider the complexity and paradox in the social function of credit ratings. For example, the certification of CRAs (to improve the credit ratings' trustworthiness) may increase reliance on CRAs, which may also exacerbate cliff effects. The engagement of public authorities in the rating of credit may lead the public supervisor to be held accountable (Eijffinger 2012: 915). As an alternative, some dream of several new CRAs other than the three dominant ones that have existed since 2000

(White 2012), but entry into this market is difficult for newcomers. And can newcomers be trusted?

Credit ratings are institutional mechanisms. They are social constructions of reality. People "invest" their hopes, anger, and arguments in the "quality" of the credit ratings not because they have an interest in the inherent quality of the financial entities but because the credit ratings are already linked cognitively and institutionally to expectations, prices, interest rates, and therefore to the buying and selling of assets.

Thus, it is important to understand organizational hinterlands of quality-inscribing organizations because they make an imprint on how quality inscriptions are made. Next, quality inscriptions and their consequences are more closely linked than conventional terminology suggests. It is reduction to assume that first a good quality inscription is made that is true to reality and then the quality inscription has some real effects, but only if the inscription is valid. "Valid" or not, the inscription works in the moment of its inception. Our example shows how social ties and connections with a quality inscription—the "investment" in it, if you will—have already been made. Consequences are already linked closely to the inscription and are just waiting for its enunciation.

A reality-to-become is, thus, *part* of the organizational hinterland. No claim is made that there is only one such possible reality. The point is merely to warn against a theoretical model affording anyone to stop time as quality inscriptions are made and then to start time again when one is ready to accept their consequences. A vocabulary must be developed to describe how quality inscriptions help create reality through connections and associations (Latour 2005). Some of these are already packaged. In the case of CRAs, expectations from sellers and buyers and authority-imposed regulations are already part of the landscape in which credit ratings operate based on a particular business model. It is a set-up ripe with consequences.

For example, when South African Minister of Finance Pravin Gordhan presented his budget for next year, he was under pressure. Everybody wants him to do more than he can. In what appears to be a clever political move, he presents his budget with a lions-against-buffalo metaphor (if lions cooperate, they can kill the biggest buffalo). He manages to raise income taxes and taxes on cigarettes, beer, wine, and alcohol while keeping his deficit under control and setting a little money aside for education, old age grants, and social grants. All this, he claims, pays due diligence to the credit ratings of South African bonds (Cape Times, Feb. 23, 2017). The next day, the Fitch CRA declared that "the budget showed deficit reduction remained an important policy aim, but political and social pressures would test government commitment to fiscal consolidation" and, furthermore, that "the main challenge to fiscal consolidation comes from factional tensions in the African National Congress (ANC) which are diverting political energy from economic reform" (Cape Times, Feb. 24, 2017).

The situation is not one where credit ratings are produced and later have consequences; they are already inside South African politics. They are involved and involving. Minister Gordhan has already taken them into account as he prepares his budget.

In other words, a quality inscription is constructed in a particular manner due to its particular hinterland, which at the same time paves the way for a set of consequences. The next section is devoted to what I call the constitutive effects of quality inscriptions. By constitutive, I mean how a description helps construct, form, and shape the reality it claims to describe. As already suggested, the constructed/constructing aspects of quality inscriptions are closely intertwined.

Constitutive Effects of Quality Inscriptions

Remember that the inscription presents the inscription of the object as if it were the object itself, so it is fair to claim that the inscription has constituted the object (as it appears as that particular kind of object). An inscription also performs a "call" for someone to act upon the inscription and to do work on the quality object. In the case with CRAs, notice how closely these aspects are related. Once a certain credit rating drops, the act of "selling" is sometimes almost automatically triggered, at least it might be, when the credit-rated entity is subject to regulation. Notice also that a self-fulfilling prophecy might unfold: The market value of the entity decreases as people want to sell it. The rating is more than a description. It is an interference.

The consequences of the interference are potentialities that may be enacted more or less depending on circumstances. "Constitutive effects" is my term for how a quality inscription influences reality while it claims to describe it.

In my earlier work (Dahler-Larsen 2013), I have suggested that constitutive effects can be observed in different domains, such as

- the content of some object or practice,
- the timing of activities related to that object or practice,
- the social relations of those involved,
- the broader worldview in which the object or practice is situated.

For example, testing in schools leads to "teaching to the test" and a revision of the curriculum (content). It helps organize the timing of pedagogical activities (especially up to a test), it influences social relations (e.g. when teachers or schools compare test results), and it constitutes a particular view of schools and education as sites for performance.

One of the key mechanisms that helps enforce constitutive effects is simply that human attention is limited. When a particular form of quality inscription is encoded into an organizational procedure, that procedure likely has an impact on how people enact the shaping of a particular social order because the procedure "steals" attention away from other potential ways of seeing the world (Dahler-Larsen 2013). The notion of quality itself also guides the orientation of people in a particular direction since it is often connected with a self-evident notion of "good" or "better." It is usually not necessary to question whether grade A++ is better than A+ or whether a higher rank is better than a lower one. Evidently, the pressure to act upon a given quality inscription varies from one situation to another and can only be determined empirically. However, there is a link between the notion of quality itself, its organizational life, and its constitutive consequences.

In the following, I wish to inquire into constitutive processes in further detail. (A quantified inscription will be used as particularly typical and illustrative, but a quality inscription in qualitative form would be within reach with a slight change of argumentation). In the following, I explain the mechanisms of constitutive effects in terms of seven processes that are both logical and social: categorization, abstraction, commensuration, connection, interpellation, temporalization, and fixation.

Categorization

Quality inscriptions define categories to which quality objects belong, the aspects of the quality object that are worth evaluating, and the labels signifying varying degrees of goodness.

Any quantification rests on a fundamental categorization of what is being tallied, including individual and collective identities to which numbers can be ascribed (Porter 1995: 42) as well as all kinds of quality objects and their properties. The practice of counting is embedded in or dependent on a specific kind of categorization. Sometimes it is the counting itself that mobilizes categorization. Consider, for example, quotas for people of particular ethnic backgrounds in particular social positions. Quotas may be seen as a helpful way of alleviating former inequalities in some countries. As Neville Alexander (2013) points out, however, such arrangements conserve the ethnic or racial categories of the past. The act of counting and distributing people according to ethnic categories maintains and stabilizes the categorization system.

Categorizations are cultural and institutional products, but more than one relevance structure can be at play among those who apply them to practical purposes. A focus on some aspect of the quality object as the defining aspect is needed; in the terminology of Schutz (1975), a typification. It is the "typicality" of something that connects the object and the broader category. Schutz explains that the same object can be typified in different ways, a phenomenon referred to as indexicality (Schwandt 2000). Ambiguous situations are those where typifications do not give themselves. Nevertheless, categorizations have performative implications; in a very fundamental sense, categorizations help get things done.

For example, if a quality education of carpenters requires students to spend 12 weeks at a carpenter's workshop, it is necessary to define such a workshop. And if there are not enough carpenters who accept apprentices, the educational institution will have to provide a workshop itself, even if it may be problematic to categorize it as "a carpenter's workshop."

It will be tempting to do so, however, if the school thereby solves a quality problem for itself and its students.

It makes a difference whether or not an object is constituted as a quality object. The aspects of life that are seen as relevant for an assessment of "quality of life" are those that somehow should be attended to, reflected upon, and changed, if necessary. Other aspects of life may be seen as not relevant, or unchangeable.

To qualitize a phenomenon is to make it subject to distinctions. Hochschild (2004) reports on a survey in which a manager's family members are asked to rate how the manager functions as a private person. While the survey makes family life "a quality object" that the managers in focus must consider, it also makes it an object of rational management practice, as the "relevance structure" of the company where the managers are employed and their ability to perform there has motivated, informed, and structured the survey.

Categorization also applies to a quality object "in the capacity of" a particular property or its "belonging to" a group of phenomena of particular ideological or practical interest. For example, when a social service is understood in terms of categories such as inputs, processes, outputs, and outcomes, then the placement of what constitutes quality in an object within those categories makes a difference, as these categories already signify specific social ideologies and purposes.

For example, consider an ideology that identifies quality in public management with an outcome-oriented approach. Once care for the elderly becomes seen as a quality object, caretakers are compelled to define intended outcomes, such as an increased "ability of the elderly to do their own daily chores," "increased quality of life," and so on. These outcomes are inherently difficult to achieve, as the situation of elderly individuals deteriorates predictably. Those who take care of the terminally ill often experience tension between a philosophy of caring and the "outcomes" consistent with a utilitarian ethic. The problem here, then, is not only the categorization of something as a quality object but the simultaneous incorporation of the quality object into a very particular regime of quality measurement which thereby subjects it to a particular form of social control where only "outcomes" are given attention and priority.

To insist that the "outcomes" of services are defining for quality is to combine quality with a particular ideology of management and steering. Perhaps surprisingly, however, the very definition of "outcome" is socially flexible, to put it mildly. Although some tend to think that the definitions of inputs, processes, outputs, and outcomes are cast in stone, the practical handling of quality objects under evaluation suggests otherwise. Bureaucratic processes can be treated as "outcomes" if the purpose is a more efficient implementation of legal requirements. Incomes can be categorized as outcomes when external funding is used as a proxy for research quality. Even in an instruction booklet used to educate evaluators, where the example was a family trip with an outcome called "strengthened family bonds," travel as an activity was nowhere to be found and the output was called "tickets" (W.K. Kellogg Foundation 2004).

What needs to be understood about the categories of inputs, processes, outputs, and outcomes is not how particular phenomena are sorted "correctly" but rather, in constitutive terms, what is produced through this categorization, the difference it makes for an object to be described in terms of its "outcome," and the differences the particular mentality of categorization engrained in this exercise make for the world.

* * *

The perils of categorization can be complicated and dynamic. How should research production be measured? In Denmark, this problem is taken care of by a national bibliometric research indicator system Bibliometrisk Forskningsindikator (Bibliometric Research Indicator) (BFI). It was introduced to measure research production so that research funds could be reallocated depending on research production. The BFI is constructed according to a Norwegian model designating two levels of publications: Level 1 is comprehensive and inclusive, where the only requirement is that the journal (or publisher) uses peer review and can be found on a recognized list of serious outlets. Level 2, which comprises no more than 20% of the publication outlets in each sub-discipline, is the finer category and gives more points. Groups of recognized scholars in each sub-discipline decide the allocation of outlets into each of these groups.

The purpose of the two-tiered system is to prevent the type of simple, constitutive effects found earlier in Australia (Butler 2003), where the number of publications was used as an indicator, which led to increased quantity but lower quality (measured as the number of articles in prestigious journals). All in all, then, the BFI is introduced as a measure of research quantity which is allegedly inclusive and fair and corrects sufficiently for research quality.

To avoid the unintended redistribution of funds, the indicators are normalized so that funds are only redistributed across universities, not across fields (e.g. natural sciences, humanities).

The Ministry of Research, which reviews the bibliometric registrations leading to the BFI, has found that "too many" publications "primarily from Danish publishers" are registered as "research," whereas an analysis they have had carried out casts "doubt" on the scientific nature of these publications.

As criteria relevant for sorting a publication as a research publication, guidelines describe "categories of publications," peer review, the use of scientific method, the contribution of substantially new knowledge, and the intended target groups of the publication. The underlying agenda seems to be that before these guidelines existed, too many researchers have registered too many dubious products simply to earn bibliometric points. Moreover, perhaps too many of the academic groups involved in defining lists of journals have included too many journals at level 1 that are not seriously academic. The motivation to do so is that the higher the number of publications in level 1, the more can be admitted into level 2, which is the prestigious one. The rule that makes this unfortunately link between the two categories is that only 20% can be allocated to level 2. Therefore, a higher denominator allows for a higher numerator.

In terms of categorization, the notion of "new knowledge" or "original work" is not always easy to apply. When new empirical data are reported, this categorization may be easy to make. But there are sometimes conceptual or methodological problems standing in the way of scientific progress, and a researcher very often considers the development of a field, discusses the obstacles that need to be overcome, and proposes some ways forward in the way to think about key issues. All of this may constitute a contribution to the field, but the "new knowledge" criterion cannot always be applied in a very exact manner. When it is good, even a fairly pedestrian introductory book to a field organizes what is known about a field in particular original, and hopefully clear manner. Only neo-positivists distinguish sharply between knowledge and how we think about it. When we struggle with how to organize what is known, we can also contribute to new knowledge. If the "new knowledge" criterion is strictly applied, review articles that synthesize what is known in a field would be disqualified. But some review articles are in fact among the most useful and most cited articles.

Another criterion is the use of the publication in relation to intended target groups. Especially in the social sciences, research on a contemporary topic can be relevant among practitioners, policy-makers, journalists, academics in think-tanks, key people in trade unions and the public administration, consultants, and others. The fact that a book contributes to the "dissemination" of knowledge does not take the research out of the book. It can still be based on scientific method, including critical thinking, and still be peer-reviewed.

In small countries there may be, say, five researchers who are interested in a book because it relates closely to their own research, while there may be 500 or 5000 practitioners among the readers. If you consider the actual function of the book, it is in purely quantitative terms more dissemination of research than it is a contribution to research, not taking into account the uncomfortable little fact that, in some areas of knowledge, think-tanks, consultants, international organizations, and others contribute substantially to the production of new knowledge production regardless of whether they are technically called researchers (Gibbons et al. 1994; Prewitt et al. 2012). Identifying research as something that is directed at university-based researchers is therefore somewhat old-fashioned. It assumes an old, linear model in which research is aimed at researchers in their own circles. Furthermore, one could conceive of one's role as a researcher as one that writes for society, not for researchers.

Equally problematic is the use of research publications in teaching. Clearly, such usage does not take the research element out of the text. This is obvious when research articles are included in the teaching material for graduate courses. Books can also be used. These are often written in a research context. The counterargument made in the guidelines is that textbooks are something else. Their main purpose is teaching. Nonetheless, the guidelines make a concession. If a "textbook" contains a substantial element of new knowledge (not merely a summary of what is already known in a field), then it can be categorized as research on an exceptional basis. So if a researcher writes a book that is likely to be used in teaching, then the categorization of it as "teaching material" becomes fuzzy if new data are inserted which add flesh and blood to the phenomena discussed in the book.

If a book is categorized as "dissemination," there is no category for describing it as peer-reviewed. The webpage designer crafting the software used for documentation of research had imagined that research publications and teaching publications could be peer-reviewed, but not "dissemination" texts. Nevertheless, many books categorized as "dissemination" have in fact gone through peer review, and peer review is in fact one of the criteria in the guidelines.

Finally, the guidelines mention that one can make a judgment about the "primary," "intended" purpose of the text.

As a result of these ambiguities in categorization, a researcher may still find that he or she places one chapter in a book in one category, while another researcher at another university puts his or her chapter in the same book in another category.

Recently, a new problematic categorization has been added to registrations of research activity, this time regarding oral presentations. Researchers are asked to categorize whether a presentation is "internationally recognized," "nationally recognized," or "locally recognized." Geographical locations are hereby conflated with social recognition, to the extent that the three levels of recognition are understood to be hierarchically ordered. One categorization is assumed to be aligned with another one, although they are logically clearly different.

The measurement process sets a whole range of practices in motion aimed at categorizing stuff that then becomes measured as "research" and "research products," which give "bibliometric points" and some degree of "recognition."

In retrospect, the quagmire of categorization is set in motion by the BFI itself and other practices of counting. BFI has rendered the registration a contested issue in itself now that registrations are visible and some of them have financial consequences. Consequently, there is now suspicion that some registrations are "faulty," implicitly because there is a financial incentive to "upgrade" publications. The link between registrations and money streams turns "faulty" registrations into a more serious problem. A dynamic set of rules is therefore needed to control and correct registrations on an ongoing basis. In that sense, however, *the quality inscription system has created and intensified problems with the categorization of research publications, not resolved them.*

In the words of Kaltenbrunner and de Rijcke (2017: 1): "Quantitative indicators to measure publication activity do not automatically resolve discussions about the nature of academic performance, but relocate them to an administrative setting characterized by specific rules of engagement" as individuals "continue to pursue conflicting normative and epistemic agendas."

Before BFI and other counting practices existed, categorization of research activity and products was much less of a problem. One of the primary constitutive functions of a quality inscription machinery might therefore be to produce the categorizations on which it builds. In a world full of ambiguity, categorization processes are openly controversial or tacitly fuzzy.

Abstraction

Consider a course evaluation system at a business school. It may include dimensions such as content, theory/practice balance, coherence, structure/format, level of student activity, team atmosphere, communication on digital website, and student learning in terms of new perspectives, better understanding, and use in practice.

It does not matter which subject is taught. A course on "Methods in social science" is compared without further reservations to the one on "Hospital management." Some might argue that it is unfair to compare "relevance for my practice as a manager" across these various subjects. But comparison presupposes abstraction.

In fact, abstraction is fundamental for particular codifications of knowledge. Reading requires an abstraction from what letters otherwise look like. The art of calculation implies abstraction from the substance of what is being counted. Modernity is characterized by a vast increase in the abstraction of measures (Nisbet 1966). While pre-modern measures were often anthropocentric (the distance of 3 ft) or highly contextual (a day's journey), modern measures are abstract and only connected to physical objects through highly mathematical and scientific formulas. Originally, a meter was 1/10,000,000 of a quarter of the circumference of the globe as measured by Méchain and Delambre (Alder 2002). Now, according to Wikipedia, it is defined by the General Conference on Weights and Measures as the distance traveled by light in a vacuum in 1/299,792,458 of a second. The point is that metrics become increasingly abstracted from properties that make intuitive and experiential sense to us.

To avoid excessively easy criticism of all measurement, it is worth noting that many measures were developed out of a need not only for coordination (think: train timetables) but also for fairness and justice. For example, market transactions are perceived as more fair and transparent when all parties know which quantity is delivered and how to resolve conflicts over this should they occur. Kula (1996) shows how it became difficult to coordinate action, trade, and commerce over distance when measures were defined differently in different locations.

An interest in objectivity has played an important role in the history of measurement (Porter 1995), although research also shows that what passes as objective measurement of complex phenomena is sometimes a result of a pedestrian compromise between a variety of social forces (Desrosières 2002).

* * *

Modern society is organized on the basis of fundamental measuring devices regarding volume, distance, time, and money. Monetarization means the translation of substantively and experientially different phenomena into things that are comparable on the same scale and therefore exchangeable. The abstraction inherent in these processes is sometimes debatable. This becomes especially pertinent when abstraction means ignoring the specificities of the situation that, for some, is inherently part of the definition of quality.

For example, in education international comparison often brings with it the assumption that everyone is striving for the same goals and adhering to only one definition of quality (Meyer 2008). This weakens the classical canons celebrated by the traditional humanities, as they are tied to literature, language, and history in their specificity (Meyer 2008: 42). International comparative studies of education sometimes ignore these purposes of education.

A fundamental question in comparative statistics is whether it is possible to ensure that a phenomenon under measurement actually means the same thing to people in different countries. Here, native English speakers should be reminded that terms equivalent to "achievement" and "performance" do not exist in many other languages. On the other hand, other languages also hold certain key terms central to educational thinking (e.g. *Bildung*) that might not be directly translatable into English. If we respect the historical, contextual, and situated productions of meaning in education (Nóvoa and Yariv-Mashal 2003), it is impossible to believe that the establishment of any comparative quality inscription device (whether articulated in English or not) takes place without considerable abstraction from national and local specificities.

A loss of meaning can only be registered from some perspectives, not from others. If one meaning system (A) is in a position to demand that another meaning system (B) presents its statements in such a manner that they can be understood from A's perspective, that is, although well-intended, equivalent to establishing power over B when B is not in position to demand the same thing from A (Becker 1996). Perhaps the issue—whether indicators mean the same to people in different national contexts—is not that relevant in practice. Perhaps it matters less which specific meanings from national and local contexts are ignored or glossed over. What matters more is that another transportable meaning system is produced from which these specific differences do not count if they cannot be translated into this "global" vocabulary. This functional superiority of a global inscription device may be more important than its (perceived) lack of methodological validity.

One of the main accomplishments of a successful global inscription device might be that it produces a common set of categories; a joint, imagined educational space within which educational policies and activities can take place (Nóvoa and Yariv-Mashal 2003; Ozga et al. 2011). From that perspective, it is highly advantageous that a vocabulary is established that makes it possible to talk effectively about educational issues in a general way. It may be the very construction of such a common language that constitutes success for a global inscription device. If that holds true, then criticism of a quality description device for having low validity (meaning: it does not correctly describe the reality it claims to measure) is based on an inadequate understanding of the performative and constitutive capacities of such a device. To say that it incorrectly represents reality may be to miss how it, at least partially, defines anew what it claims to measure.[1]

At the same time, the abstract, "common" language makes invisible and irrelevant the loss of meaning that cannot be articulated in that language. A common space defined by a given quality regime comes at the price of abstraction from various contextual conditions inside that space, but from the perspective of the quality inscription which defines the established quality zone, these contextual differences become invisible and not relevant.

In an international study (Ozga et al. 2011), survey data was used to capture how teachers perceive the usefulness of international comparisons (e.g. PISA) as well as their perceptions of school quality. Danish teachers in particular found these international comparisons to be of little use for developing education quality. They were the only national group of teachers who held more negative than positive views about international comparison. At the same time, their understanding of quality in education differed starkly from those of teachers in other countries. Considering various dimensions of quality, the Danish teachers ranked "student skills" lower than teachers in any other country and placed greater emphasis on "active involvement of students" and enabling students to become "responsible citizens." The study shows that resistance toward international comparison cannot necessarily be explained (away) as resistance toward change or as a conventional defense of professional interests. Instead, negative views on international comparison are stron-

[1] The above section is a rephrased passage from Dahler-Larsen (2013).

gest among those who define educational quality in ways that differ from what is typical in other nations. International comparison is made possible through a common form of metrics that implies abstraction from variations in local definitions of value and purpose. This does not mean, of course, that a comparison is based on a "golden standard" or an "average" of all of the countries compared. An "ethnocentric" or "colonial" standard defined by one or a few countries or a messy compromise might as well be defining for the alleged "international" perspective. The point is, however, that comparison requires abstraction from variations in situated definitions of purpose. Resistance toward international comparison is not randomly distributed. In the example above, resistance made particular sense for those whose national definition of quality was distinctly different from the definitions in other countries.

Any abstracted, cross-national comparison of educational quality (e.g. PISA) requires an enormous apparatus in order to make inscriptions. Testing systems must be in place in many countries, as must the expertise and rules that regulate how testing is performed. Only then can countries be compared. It is difficult to establish an alternative to PISA, as it would also have to enroll a large number of countries. In that sense, PISA also "makes itself necessary." While PISA creates a new and common imaginary space in which policy-making can take place, only PISA is in a position to provide the data describing how each country is located in the common quality zone which comes out of the operations. Since this statistical universe is constructed out of comparative data from an increasing number of countries, producing an alternative to PISA would be a very demanding task (Dahler-Larsen 2014). A competitor would have to provide an extensive quality inscription machinery as well as mobilizing a large number of countries, because the selling point is the comparative data.

PISA is imprinted with the economic ideology of the OECD, and its epistemic force is sustained through the power of that organization to construct the infrastructure necessary to support it. This infrastructure would be practically impossible to construct for anyone else. Notice the link between the epistemic effect of abstraction and the hinterland of the organization producing it.

In a similar vein, the notion of excellence in research sometimes requires an abstraction from the diversity of purposes of research. The excellence perspective on quality, for example, ideally assumes that there is only one quality zone in the world, which is equivalent to assuming that all research has the same goal. Nevertheless, research may focus not only on so-called world class research, but also on improving local living conditions, solving problems with stakeholders, enlightening a national population, giving advice to policy-makers, enhancing public debate, challenging totalitarian regimes, and/or raising the knowledge level in teaching (Chavarro et al. 2017). Somehow, these various understandings of purposes, which may be more or less tied to local situations, tend to disappear from the radar screen when excellence is defined (abstracted from local contexts) in terms of global competitiveness.

* * *

Much has been said and written about how monetarization and marketization contribute to the structuring and restructuring of modern life (Hardt and Negri 2001). Abstraction is crucial to both of these processes. A diversity of things are measured on the same numerical scales so that they can be exchanged, bought, and sold.

Some see discourse on quality as fundamentally antithetical to the world of money and quantification. With an appeal to the classical quality/quantity distinction, and with the investment of the hope the quality signifies something more human and sensible than the ugly quantified world, it is not difficult to choose a side to sympathize with. However, it is hereby ignored how clever capitalist and bureaucratic organizations are in incorporating humanistic critique (Boltanski and Chiapello 2007).

More specifically, it is ignored how contemporary quality inscriptions operate with the same kind of abstractions which money do. Quality inscriptions, as we know them, do not "oppose" such abstraction-based quantification of the world; instead, they actually extend it with other means into new territories. Quality inscriptions can reach into areas of life that have yet to be monetarized but make them subject to similar processes of abstraction and quantification. *Quality does what money can-*

not do. Quality goes further. It encompasses family life as a part of management. It captures not credit but the symbol of credit*worthiness*. It reaches into ten aspects of teaching (see the example from course evaluation). Quality inscriptions make the rating and ranking of different phenomena possible. They do so by ignoring (i.e. abstracting from) aspects that would otherwise be considered personal, existential, or situation-relevant. Quality inscriptions turn a wide range of quality objects into elements in quality zones extending in time and space so that these elements can be made visible, audited, documented, compared, managed, or exchanged. The latter allows for a market-like structuration of social relations. A social transformation in the direction of market-like economization can be done without monetization (Brown 2015: 31). *By carrying out this transformation not in the name of money, but in the name of quality, opposition may be reduced, and the transformation may be more easily expanded into social domains, which would be otherwise difficult to colonize.*

Commensuration

Commensuration is the process by which parts of a phenomenon or parts of different phenomena are cut out and defined as corresponding to the same unit of measurement. Commensuration takes place through the use of scales.

Different scales have different properties. For example, ordinal scales imply ranking without the definition of any numerical distance between the steps. Interval scales describe distances between scores in meaningful ways but they have no zero and do not allow for multiplication and division (the air today may be a number of degrees warmer than another day, but not twice as hot). Ratio scales with a defined zero point afford numerical manipulations on scores such as multiplication and division. It is good practice in the social sciences to measure a phenomenon on a scale with properties that are consistent with the properties of the phenomenon; no more, no less.

In the light of a constitutive perspective, the reverse is often the case. An object is imbued with the qualities of the scale used in the inscription.

Sometimes categories that are technically speaking steps on an ordinal scale are labeled with numbers and then these numbers are used for calculation as if it originated from an interval or ratio scale. Sometimes phenomena are simply institutionally defined numerical characteristics. The Danish education system uses a grading scale that includes zero and five steps defined by positive numbers (02, 04, 7, 10, and 12) and one step with a negative numerical value (−3). The logical meaning of a performance with a negative numerical value is mystifying. How can anybody perform in a way which is worse than nothing? Once the average of all grades is calculated, however, it works well, arithmetically as well as practically.

Once a given scale is institutionalized, it simply defines various objects as commensurable. For example, commensurability is achieved when different types of publications are given points so that they can be reported on the same scale. Commensurability makes comparison possible between materially different kinds of quality objects or objects found in different contexts.

Commensurability is also a bridge from the past to the future. For example, experiences that resulted in a particular rating or ranking last year can be linked with expectations about what should be done next year. It is not always necessary to connect the two by means of an explicit, formal theory (Brunsson and Jacobsson 2000). The quality inscription is the tool connecting the two. The quality inscription brings the past and future "closer" to each other. A teacher who sees the evaluation of this year's course, can "commensurate" his or her experience with an anticipation of the next; one score is an occasion to start thinking about how to improve the next one. Commensuration makes the appropriation of the future possible. *Commensuration makes the future available as calculative space*. Commensuration is a form of social imaginary (Castoriadis 1997).

The opportunity for movement is regulated by the scale itself and its properties. Standards are often fixed in terms of a given point on a scale. If these standards function as minimum standards (i.e. everybody must pass the defined threshold), there is likely to be intense social activity related to scores around that point on the scale. When maximum standards are imagined (more is just better—we cannot be too awesome), then many scales have no upper limit. This means that there is no end to how one can perform. Commensuration makes the future open for endless growth, a social imaginary very typical of modernity. When managers say, for instance, that "performance is very clearly defined" in their organization with reference to particular quality indicators, they sometimes forget to mention that expectations for performance are not really fenced in when indicator scores have no upper limits. In practice, it is often not too difficult to accept an obligation to produce 3% more next year than this year. It is a small percentage, but increasing the number of products 3% annually for 24 years means doubling the production. As the future becomes a dynamic quality zone where one is committed to exponential growth, severe consequences may occur such as exhaustion and depletion of resources.

Connection

Quality inscriptions make connections between things and people as well as between people. *The mathematical properties of quality inscriptions represent social relations.* Scales and commensuration embody imaginaries of how people are connected and positioned.

An ordinal scale resembles the structure of a social hierarchy. The improvement of scores is equivalent to social climbing. What is new in ranking as compared to traditional social hierarchies is that the allocation of positions is neither inherited nor prescribed; rather, it is achieved anew every time a new version of the quality inscription is issued. Quality rankings are also different from conventional social classes in the sense that solidarity is not expected between members of the same status (Nisbet 1966). People go in and out of relative positions. Everybody competes with everybody on an ongoing basis. Quality rankings resonate with a notion of social status where one's position is insecure and even marginal changes in relative status can be measured precisely.

Ordinal scales sometimes have a special golden top category consisting of "the excellent," the access to which may be somehow privileged or restricted. This makes it particularly clear that rankings are positional goods. The excellent may be defined explicitly as "superior" to others, or numerical restrictions may say that only *x* percent be ranked "excellent." Sometimes there are hidden or not-so-hidden social factors (money, infrastructure, language, location) rendering some structurally inclined to become ranked as excellent, and not others.

If one or a few categories are particularly attractive as a positional social good, then we can expect congestion at their entrance. Some will question entry criteria and find them too easy or too difficult. In Denmark, some researchers found it was "too easy" to get published in (some of the journals in) Category 2 in the bibliometric indicator system. They wanted a tighter definition and a new, more exclusive third category. The value of a positional good increases if access to it is restricted. Although dreams of becoming a member of a higher category may be an important social driver in a status society, many will tacitly know that they will never reach the "excellent" category at the top of the hierarchy. Nevertheless, they have to make a plan or a strategy that illustrates their willingness to fight for rising status. Such a strategy or plan is a clear sign of individual and organizational rationality (Meyer et al. 1987). *What a functionally successful ranking system produces is not a lot of winners but very few winners and a lot of people willing to fight or appearing to be willing to fight to become winners, even though many of them are realistic enough to know that it is never going to happen.*

Other quality inscriptions focus less on access to the top of a ranking system but place greater emphasis on variation on average scores (remember that, by calculation, average scores can become standards in themselves). This form of arithmetic includes everybody, at every position on a ranking scale. Most people will have an interest in not being below-average; at a very quick glance, the average becomes a landmark that easily allows one to know where to find "good" and "bad." Many will probably have scores around the average, so it is a safe place to be socially situated. While above average is good, below is not so good, especially if you are so far below that you belong to a very small group. Quality inscriptions that report scores and averages resonate with a social imaginary metaphorically described as a herd of animals; you do not want to be alone so that you can be singled out as prey when the herd moves forward. But there is some safety in the middle of the crowd.

Maybe all quality inscriptions do not fit clearly with either the "winner" or "herd" metaphors. Nevertheless, there is an elective affinity between the use of metrics and the imagination of the social order. Quality inscriptions influence how people position themselves in relation to each other. Sometimes, the connection between them is made only through the quality inscription.

Let us extend this type of thinking to broader sets of relations. How are different types of actors connected? Let us consider how a teacher at a business school is connected with "the evaluation unit" which takes care of student surveys. This is an interesting relation, because it only exists on this particular occasion, but the unit produces a quality inscription that makes all of the following connections. The unit sends an e-mail with the survey results which goes to the teacher and to management. The teacher knows that management might also see the evaluative data, and they probably know that the teacher knows that.

Student questionnaires reconnect the teacher with the students in a funny way, because they sometimes say things in their questionnaires that they would not say to the teacher directly. This particular quality inscription "positions" and "enrolls" them (i.e. assigns them a role) so that they speak as anonymous consumers of teaching. In that capacity, they sometimes air frustrations in the survey that are directed toward program managers rather than teachers.

As described above, the student satisfaction survey also reconnects the teacher to her fellow teachers in the same program. They are positioned in the same quality zone. Contrary to practice in many other settings, the evaluation unit circulates course ratings with the individual names of all of the teachers. This allows each teacher to meet the statistical representation of all other teachers, so that if any two of them meet in person one day, their statistical representations are part of the encounter. Perhaps more importantly, each teacher is well aware of whether he/she is above, below, or around average.

Finally, the quality inscription links teachers to the overall quality system at the business school, which in turn is embedded in a larger set of procedures that grants it accreditation as an institution. Someone else takes care of these connections, but they influence teachers in turn because the kind of surveys described in the example are necessary for the accreditation system.

Allow a final example: Comparisons of airport quality. Who is going to choose an airport because of its relative quality? If one wants to get from A to B, it would make little sense first to fly to remote locations just to get to an airport of high quality. So why compare airport quality? Some conference organizers market their conferences in relation to reputable airports. If people are already airborne, then it makes sense to let airports compete over which is best when it comes to hosting conferences and the like. When conference organizers seek to attract attendees, perhaps inscriptions of airport quality matter.

The literature about isomorphism in organizational fields (DiMaggio and Powell 1983) would suggest that airport managers compete among themselves about who enjoys the most prestige based on such quality ratings. This would have little to do with how passengers experience airports, but it is important to management to be seen as rational, modern, and legitimate by other managers, and presumable it is important for airport managers to be well positioned within the quality zone consisting of airports competing worldwide.

Airport quality inscriptions may not be primarily for people who have a home in a particular place and are in need of an airport. Nevertheless, such inscriptions are relevant and do create connections, perhaps between airport managers, and between conference managers and conference attendees.

By making otherwise uneven things commensurable and connecting things and people across time and space, quality inscriptions make new perspectives possible from which quality can be defined, made visible, compared, and managed.

Interpellation

When people are connected through quality inscriptions, they are connected and related in particular capacities as individuals or organizations. Interpellation is the process whereby someone is called to speak or act in a particular capacity. Hey, you! Actors are enrolled, meaning that their involvement is carved out as corresponding to particular roles. While "role" may have connotations of something arbitrary and self-chosen (like hats you put on or take off), at better conceptual parallel is Marx's term *character mask* (borrowed from a metaphor from classical drama, where actors wore masks that defined their character). In modern times, a character mask is a particular function primarily defined in relation to market transactions.

Building on this idea, quality inscriptions appeal to fundamental functions in relation quality: Those who produce quality objects, those who use them, and those who produce the quality inscription which holds this configuration together. There is a set of masks corresponding to each of the functions in a larger quality configuration. For example, producers are responsible for quality objects. Through interpellation, they can be reminded of this responsibility.

Producers of quality objects are differentiated in a number of functions corresponding to layers and functions in organizations. While some professionals are often responsible for direct, first-hand contact with users, the organizational mediators and "quality specialists" are responsible for the coordination and evaluation of these services. Furthermore, there are managers with separate strategic responsibilities. They might be accountable toward external auditors or quality inspectors in separate agencies. Organizational recipes and quality inscriptions are important as tools for communication between these agents. Because of hierarchies, differentiation and complexity in organizations, however, it is not always easy to identify "the producer" in an unequivocal way, especially if the product is risky for some. Different layers of an organization may try to take responsibility for quality management or parts hereof, while the responsibility for quality itself (and risk) maybe pushed around between several organizations or parts hereof (Rothstein et al. 2006).

On their side, users of quality objects are also interpellated. They are not just natural persons; they are defined in terms of specific social and organizational matrixes that change over time (Pflueger 2016). Users are constituted in ways that are incorporated in the design of quality inscriptions. For example, a user is often interpellated as one who makes sovereign choices (the customer is king), but only a few products are presented as the options of choice. In that sense, there is a close affinity between the situation of the customer as king and the placement of the user in a very definite and regulated position in a social order (Bauman 1983). Elevation of the consumer often goes hand in hand with the degradation of the citizen (Fountain 2001) and the undermining of democratic responsibilities, or at least with the reduction of user preferences into a few manageable dimensions.

The producers of quality inscriptions may be situated inside or outside of the organization producing the quality object. They may be financed by different partners in the quality configuration (the network of roles and relations involved in quality), they may have more or less institutional permanence, they may be backed by expertise, and they may speak more or less on behalf of well-identified actors in specific locations in the quality configuration (e.g. "consumers" or "producers").

Most observers find that the social positions of those producing quality inscriptions have been strengthened in recent years. The trend is against calling them in on an ad-hoc basis (like old-school evaluators). Instead, they should produce ongoing streams of evaluative information. They should be institutionalized as a high-level organizational function (Läubli Loud and Mayne 2013) and/or differentiate themselves into an autonomous Luhmannian system in society, wherein chains of organizations bestow each other with legitimacy through quality inscriptions, and those at the end of such chains authorize each other (Lindeberg 2007). This development toward the "autonomization" of the quality-inscribing institutions is followed by and contributes to the production of new, related roles. These include educators, experts, and consultants who are interpellated in various complex combinations as quality inscribers and advisers to quality inscribers.

An example illustrates this complexity. The inspection of the quality of foster homes in Denmark has been delegated to five municipalities, which are responsible for inspecting all of the other municipalities. The inspectors inspect each other. A ministerial agency for social services was asked to help develop principles for the inspection to secure uniformity on the national level. They developed a quality handbook and a set of guidelines for inspectors. They also trained inspectors and cultivated their sense of good practice through quality audits. They devised a statistical system to monitor what was registered in inspection reports.

There was also an initiative to develop a risk-based algorithm so that foster homes likely to deliver poor quality would be inspected more often and more intensely. It was difficult to determine which data should be used and which voices would be seen as relevant for providing reliable input into this algorithm (insofar as it should also be justifiable as a legal administrative perspective). With the introduction of a "risk manager," a person playing that role would be held accountable for that.

A whistleblower arrangement was put in place, allowing children and others to warn the authorities anonymously if something suspicious was going on at a foster home. This amounts to an interpellation of a social role as "the anonymous unidentified observer" to be active in quality assurance.

The agency also established an expert advisory group to follow the process and advise on how to improve the quality of the inspection of the quality system. The advisory group made interpellations such as the following: "It would be a good idea if you, as an agency, thought about whether you could ask the municipalities to ask the inspectors to document whether they systematically remember to ask the foster homes to document the following and then ask the municipalities to coordinate the resulting data with the risk management people."

There was a mushrooming of social roles with highly differentiated responsibilities in relation to the many quality inscriptions. Although more than a bit of political blame avoidance is presumably also at play here, the larger point is not to suggest a conspiracy theory; rather, the point is to illustrate how a complex quality configuration produces multiple forms of quality inscriptions layered on top of each other and how it makes correspondingly complex interpellations possible.

Add to the complexity of roles a dynamic development of the quality configuration. Quality agents who fill up the interpellated spaces come and go. Although each of the partners involved in this lengthy process may have done their best to live up to a notion of accountability, the sum of all of these small and partial accountabilities do not add up to a unified evaluative grip on the entire process.

The emergence of new, multiple, and fragmented roles in relation to quality inscriptions has implications for an understanding of both accountability and trust. While quality inscriptions are often officially justified as tools that help enhance accountability and solve problems of mistrust among agents, their actual functions in the midst of a complex configuration of actors may be quite different. As the complexity of this configuration increases, so do the number of interpellated types of actors and the relations between them. For example, the exact accountability of an expert who advises an agency that produces a handbook which guides local quality managers in working with professionals in foster homes is often not clearly defined. The dynamic effects of numerous interconnected interpellations may be quite different from the official rhetoric about quality and accountability. It is not discussed whether an *n*th layer of accountability mechanisms adds to the overall accountability of the entire quality system.

As several quality roles interact with each other in a larger configuration, all "enforcing" themselves and "interpellating" others, mistrust might be produced as much as trust. Accountability might not be clarified, but fragmented and confused. This is not necessarily dysfunctional in a complex system dealing with complex and dynamic matters, but it is not consistent with an official ideology where quality inscriptions make things transparent and accountability clear.

Temporalization

Quality inscriptions are temporal events and take place at particular moments in time. If people take a periodical nature of quality inscriptions into account, their actions will reflect these rhythms. Similar behavioral patterns are known from budgets. Especially near the end of a given period immediately before the next deadline, people will orient their behavior toward phenomena occurring in time to have an impact on the upcoming quality inscription.

The ideal today, however, is online information. Consequently, particular peaks in behavior immediately before deadlines will become superfluous. Instead, people will be reminded about the omnipresent nature of quality inscription.

Quality inscriptions often use time itself as an indicator of an aspect of quality. In situations where the appropriate service is difficult to specify because it depends on interaction and context (e.g. health care, social services), the timing of delivery becomes an important proxy variable. In modern culture, time is often an abstract and general medium (like money) into which other phenomena can be commensurated. So timeliness itself becomes a quality criterion.

This creates tension as different quality objects across time, space, and substance are characterized by different eigentimes. The eigentime is the inherent temporal logic characterizing development and change in an object (regardless of the external views upon it), such as the growth and reproduction cycles of biological organisms (Gläser and Laudel 2015: 1210).

Students learn at different speeds. Some musical instruments are more difficult to learn to play than others. Some complex projects require more time for practical work, internal learning, and coordination than do others.

Having in mind the eigentime of various forms of research, one of the criticisms of the regimes measuring research quality is that they tend to favor "safe" research projects with short time horizons. This is the response to how such regimes "compress time" in their ongoing registration practices in combination with the time required to make funding decisions and promotion decisions.

Quality inscriptions sometimes appropriate or even accelerate time by means of the well-known scheme of inputs, processes, outputs, and outcomes. Plans for having a quality object that extends through these categories all the way to intended outcomes and thus into the future are seen as rational and sensible; in other words, the more an evaluative view has appropriated the future, the more respectable it is. When focusing on outcomes, the producers of quality objects are thus encouraged to already conquer the future as they engage with their quality object. Time is accelerated as they are evaluated on the basis of their construction of a future that is not yet present.

To the extent that quality inscriptions connect and relate the producers of quality objects to one another, quality inscriptions "enhance time." One's movement in time is relative to the movements of the others. In that sense, in a competitive perspective, if you do not move while others move forward, you are not standing still—you are in fact moving backwards. In practice, this effect is facilitated through benchmarking and constant comparison.

By reminding producers and consumers of their relative timing, quality inscriptions reach across space, enhancing social contingency and a fluid modernity (Bauman 2000). They accelerate time. Our contemporary culture emphasizes "the newest," "breakthroughs," "speed-dating," "emerging markets," and "innovation." In an era of decreasing institutional stability and the increasing fluidity of individual life plans and careers (Beck 2002), quality inscriptions may contribute to an acceleration of social time through a self-fulfilling mechanism. While the number of options available for the individual increases, the proportion of options which are possible in this world but which cannot be chosen by that individual increases even more (Rosa 2003: 14). The acceleration of life in both objective and subjective terms follows. We attempt to live "twice as fast." This is our culture's self-created functional equivalent to religious ideas of "eternal life" (Rosa 2003: 13). While theories of social acceleration have been applied to contemporary life in general, there are also specific analyses related to particular sectors and institutions. For an analysis of how social acceleration permeates contemporary life in research, see Vostal (2016).

The social acceleration of contemporary time can be understood in relation to Koselleck's theory of experience and expectation. Social acceleration is an increase in the decay rates of the reliability of experiences (Rosa 2003: 7) and the constant re-instantiation of expectations.

Intuition and documented quality inscriptions are not coordinated in time. Quality inscriptions sometimes render definitions of the "quality" of an object visible and tangible at a faster speed than intuition would allow. For example, while a teacher struggles to make sense of the experience gained from an ongoing course, the results of a mid-term online student evaluation of the course has already been shared with managers, coordinators, and teachers, so they already have official status as an "organizationally valid" inscription. Reflections have to "catch up" with the official inscription.

Perhaps the most important contribution made by quality inscriptions to social acceleration is how they inspire ambitions and expectations, using connections, commensuration, and competition as vehicles. Quality inscriptions bring the potential future closer by facilitating the enunciation of expectations. Even expectations that have not been met anywhere are stimulated by the use of scales. Scales, mathematics, and social expectations are related. The meaning of a variable is that scores vary or can be made to vary. Scales stimulate social imaginaries of calculative spaces in which the future is already made ready for operations. Users can "demand more." Producers can seek to "score even better next time." If not, competitors are already "doing better."

Acceleration occurs when the space we call the present—which is the space between the experiences of the past and the expectations for the future—is condensed. Quality inscriptions contribute to this process by hollowing out the present and redefining it as a moment in which one is already working toward a more attractive score in a quality inscription in the future.

Inscriptions of quality facilitate a process in contemporary society that neatly corresponds to Koselleck's description of how modernity infuses concepts with a particular form of social productivity. Concepts characteristic of modernity transport expectations about a new social order (think: progress, change, crisis, democracy, revolution, participation, equality, liberty. And now: quality). This section has shown how Koselleck's theory of how concepts create expectations can be supplemented by a theory of how quality inscriptions and scales do the same.

Fixation

Fixation refers to the pinning down of an otherwise broad concept into a specific sense. In some theories, a similar phenomenon is referred to as "stabilization," which sounds like something durable over time. Fixation is not necessarily durable over time. A concept of quality has to be fixed just long enough to do some constitutive work, not longer. If that work can be achieved better by shifting fixations, we should understand how that is possible, not how the concept is maintained over time. What is often intended with the term stabilization, however, and which is meaningful enough, is that there are forces helping to support and solidify a specific version of a particular concept so that it can do its work. Our theory about this kind of support for constitutive effects must include temporalization and acceleration, however, so I therefore prefer fixation over stabilization as the key concept.

Fixation takes place through all of the associations and connections that the concept (in a particular version) makes between a given hinterland and an emerging social order. Here, things become "fixed." Fixation is keeping a concept in place while at the same time "fixing" a social arrangement.

Indicator fixation is a mechanism that helps us understand what is going on. Once the quality of a phenomenon is expressed through an indicator, practices turn toward what is seen as important in the light of the indicator (Dahler-Larsen 2013; Munro 2004). This phenomenon is described well in the literature under headlines such as performance paradox (van Thiel and Leeuw 2002), tunnel vision, creaming, and so forth (Lilford et al. 2004).

In my earlier work, I have suggested a distinction between trivial and advance indicator fixation. In a trivial situation, practices are simply diverted from an original or intended definition of quality because the indicator lacks validity (Dahler-Larsen 2008). The problem here is imperfect measurement of a well-defined idea.

In the advanced version, however, the indicator helps define what it claims to measure. No original or underlying version of quality is compromised. Advanced measure fixation is a relevant concept when "underlying and original intentions" are either theoretically or empirically insufficient, inadequate, invisible, or non-existent. The advanced measure fixation is the most subtle and interesting way in which a quality inscription defines quality in a quality object. It is advanced because it is immune to a critique saying the true and original meaning of the concept under measurement has not been captured. When the concept under measurement is vague, open, or multidimensional, so much greater is the power of the inscription to define what the concept should mean. Quality inscriptions are often good examples advanced measure fixation because, as it has been shown, the concept of quality itself is so open for interpretation.

The best way to understand fixation is through the embeddedness of a quality inscription within a larger quality configuration and the associations and networks that define it. Expressed in processual terminology, we have seen how categorization, abstraction, connection, interpellation, and temporalization are all able to contribute to a given fixation of quality at a particular moment.

Infrastructures, technologies, and forms and shapes of inscription play crucial roles here, which is much in line with what is suggested by Actor Network Theory (ANT) (Latour 2005). The way a quality object (in terms of its transformations and traces) is mediated by infrastructure and transported through the quality configuration helps define quality.

David Byrne (2012) gives a powerful example of how technology helps "fix" a particular notion of quality. An ear trained to listen to live music will appreciate it as it sounds on the spot. The diffusion of cheap digital recording technology has changed the encoding of music. People get used to hearing music where the timing is determined by a machine. Singing out of tune is automatically corrected by electronic filters. As people grow used to hearing digitally produced music, their implicit expectations change. They have difficulty listening to live music, which now sounds imperfect, if not outright faulty. In order not to fail in the ears of the audience, live concerts are therefore increasingly resembling studio productions. Even live concerts are now played by musicians who hear a predetermined, computerized number of beats per minute in their headphones. "Standards are raised" is a description of this trend. Unless one keeps an ear trained to appreciate and celebrate the virtues of handmade music.

The term "lock-in" can be used to describe how a particular notion of quality tends to become self-affirming, making producers who do not comply look incompetent, making users expect what is usually delivered, and making alternative notions of quality invisible or forgotten.

* * *

This chapter ends with an example summarizing the constitutive effects of quality inscriptions upon modern life. It deals with quality of life itself.

Many socio-political and metrological forces come together in the measurement of the quality of life. One of the most interesting contributions was made in the 1990s with the concept of quality-adjusted life years (QALYs). The QALY concept was developed in medicine to help make decisions regarding health interventions (Bache and Reardon 2016: 101). Survival rates were too simple. They did not take into account that some patients would survive but still have a relatively miserable life (suffering from missing limbs, depression, or living with the side effects of invasive treatments). QALY compensates for this. Instead of a binary analysis (life/death), new sliding scales emerged (Davies 2015: 127). QALY offered an abstract definition of a life year with perfect quality against which various degrees of deteriorating life quality could be compared. Estimates of these varying degrees—and their corresponding economic value—first came from hypothetical questions to patients, such as "How much would you be willing to pay to not lose your right arm?" Quantifications of quality of life also came from assessments of a patient's ability to function in five domains: mobility, discomfort, self-care, anxiety/depression, and usual activities (Bache and Reardon 2016: 101). Given a need for "broader conceptions of well-being" and an appreciation of data based on people's experiences rather than hypothetical preferences, recent developments seek a compromise between subjective measures and the five functional domains mentioned earlier (Bache and Reardon 2016: 101). This move also allowed for the further integration of mental health and subjective notions of a good life into quality of life assessments.

Still, the overarching mission regarding QALY is to help make decisions about medical intervention. In combination with data about the cost of such interventions and the monetarized value of QALYs, rational decisions can be made.

In a broader perspective, quality of life indicators constitute targets for policy-making (Bache and Reardon 2016: 114). Once acceptable indicators of quality of life have been established, it becomes meaningful to ask how policies can be redesigned to help maximize quality of life. The quality inscriptions thereby constitute new political objectives. A critical counterargument is, evidently, that existing conventional economic measures (e.g. GDP growth) continue to dominate political discourse and that politics is far too messy to reorient itself toward new alternative indicators in any consistent way (Bache and Reardon 2016: 133). However, that counterargument takes little away from the constitutive power of indicators. Once indicators such as quality of life indicators have achieved a certain level of acceptability and visibility, they will be used as arguments for changing the orientations of people and potentially of policies. The fact that they do not work "perfectly" from the beginning may actually help sustain ongoing justifications for doing more. Relevance and social consequences do not hinge on perfect implementation. "Imperfect" implementation can be used as an argument in favor of paying more attention to the issue represented by the indicator. To establish with certainty whether an indicator has failed is an empirical question, and one which requires attention to more than one dimension.

Quality of life indicators are sometimes presented in a very positive and progressive light as alternatives to the dominant economistic indicators in modern society and as indicative of an important cultural turn in favor of post-materialist values. However, quality of life indicators have more in common with economistic indicators than what is officially acknowledged. As with QALYs, quality indicators sometimes pave the way for the monetarization of new domains of life. Even without direct monetarization, inscriptions of quality of life share important characteristics with economistic measures. They cut social life into little pieces based on abstraction, commensuration, and connection. They render the incomparable comparable. Quality indicators are functionally superior for some aspects of life, as they can go even further than monetarization. Quality inscriptions extend measurement, abstraction, quantification, componentiality, and calculability into "life" in toto, including areas of life such as emotional well-being.

Like money, quality inscriptions make as many aspects of life as they can interchangeable through quantification and they *ignore or weaken those manifestations of life that have no exchange value because they do not lend themselves to inscriptions fit for circulation*. It is an important constitutive effect in itself. The very fact that we live in an era where it has become possible to conceive of such a notion as "quality of life" testifies to the emergence of a social order that has made that kind of constitution possible through peculiar shifts in social imaginaries.

According to Davies (2015), "the happiness industry" is a conglomerate of new alliances between medicine and economics, between technocracy and neoliberalism. The discourse on quality creates not quality but rather a *lack* of quality that is everywhere in need of intervention and treatment. In Davies' analysis, one of the constitutive effects of the quality of life discourse is an increased use of anti-depressants in what he calls the competitive-depressive society.

* * *

To sum up, no matter how much we dig into the concept of quality itself, it will not reveal any specific inner meaning. Its meanings, always situated, are produced through processes of categorization, abstraction, connection, interpellation, and temporalization, all of which contribute to a given fixation of quality at a moment in time. The potential consequences in terms of constitutive effects of quality inscriptions are wide-ranging.

Notice, however, terms such as "contribute" and "potential." How can we understand the extent to which constitute effects are enacted in practice? The next chapter offers qualitization as a perspective on this issue. Qualitization as an active speech act that seeks to set such effects in motion by using quality inscriptions to appeal to a whole configuration of agents.

References

Alder, Ken. 2002. *The Measure of All Things: The Seven-Year Odyssey and Hidden Error that Transformed the World*. New York: The Free Press.

Alexander, Neville. 2013. *Thoughts on the New South Africa*. Pretoria: Jacana.

Bache, Ian, and Louise Reardon. 2016. *The Politics and Policy of Wellbeing*. Cheltenham: Edward Elgar.

Bauman, Zygmunt. 1983. Industrialism, Consumerism and Power. *Theory, Culture and Society* 1 (3): 32–43.

———. 2000. *Liquid Modernity*. Cambridge: Polity Press.

Beck, Ulrich. 2002. *Fagre Nye Arbejdsverden* [Schöne neue Arbeitswelt]. Copenhagen: Hans Reitzel.

Becker, Howard S. 1996. The Epistemology of Qualitative Research. In *Essays on Ethnography and Human Development*, ed. R. Jessor, A. Colby, and R. Schweder. Chicago: University of Chicago Press.

Bijker, Wiebe E., and John Law. 1992. *Shaping Technology/Building Society: Studies in Sociotechnical Change*. Cambridge: The MIT Press.

Boltanski, Luc, and Eve Chiapello. 2007. *The New Spirit of Capitalism*. London: Verso.

Brown, Wendy. 2015. *Undoing the Demos*. New York: Zone Books.

Brunsson, Nils, and Bengt Jacobsson, eds. 2000. *A World of Standards*. Oxford: Oxford University Press.

Butler, Linda. 2003. Explaining Australia's Increased Share of ISI Publications: The Effects of a Funding Formula Based on Publication Counts. *Research Policy* 34: 565–574.

Butler, Judith. 2010. Performative Agency. *Journal of Cultural Economy* 3 (2): 147–161.

Byrne, David. 2012. How Music Works. *Smithsonian* 43 (6): 24–26, 29.

Cape Times, Feb 23 2017. Cape Town: Cape Town Independent News & Media PLC.

Cape Times, Feb 24 2017. Cape Town: Cape Town Independent News & Media PLC.

Castoriadis, Cornelius. 1997. *World in Fragments: Writings on Politics, Society, Psychoanalysis, and the Imagination*. Stanford: Stanford University Press.

Chavarro, Diego, Puay Tang, and Ismael Ràfols. 2017. Why Researchers Publish in Non-mainstream Journals: Training, Knowledge Bridging, and Gap Filling. *Research Policy* 46 (9): 1666–1689.

Dahler-Larsen, Peter. 2008. *Kvalitetens Beskaffenhed* [The Nature of Quality]. Odense: University Press of Southern Denmark.

———. 2013. Constitutive Effects of Performance Indicators: Getting Beyond Unintended Consequences. *Public Management Review* 16 (7): 969–986.

———. 2014. Global Inscription Devices and the Politics of Education. *Knowledge Cultures* 2 (4): 90–109.

Davies, William. 2015. *The Happiness Industry: How the Government and Big Business Sold Us Well-Being*. London: Verso.

Desrosières, Alain. 2002. *The Politics of Large Numbers: A History of Statistical Reasoning*. Cambridge: Harvard University Press.

DiMaggio, Paul, and Walter Powell. 1983. The Iron Cage Revisited: Institutional Isomorphism and Collective Rationality in Organizational Fields. *American Sociological Review* 48 (6): 147–160.

Duffhues, Piet, and Wim Weterings. 2011. The Quality of Credit Ratings and Liability: The Dutch View. *International Journal of Disclosure and Governance* 8 (4): 1–21.

Eijffinger, Sylvester C.W. 2012. Rating Agencies: Role and Influence of Their Sovereign Credit Risk Assessment in the Eurozone. *Journal of Common Market Studies* 50 (6): 912–921.

Erkkilä, Tero, and Ossi Piironen. 2014. (De)politicizing Good Governance: The World Bank Institute, the OECD and the Politics of Governance Indicators. *Innovation: The European Journal of Social Science Research* 27 (4): 344–360.
Fountain, Jane E. 2001. Paradoxes of Public Sector Customer Service. *Governance* 14 (1): 55–73.
Gibbons, Michael, Camille Limoges, Helga Nowotny, Simon Schwartzman, Peter Scott, and Martin Trow. 1994. *The New Production of Knowledge. The Dynamics of Science and Research in Contemporary Societies*. London: Sage.
Gläser, Jochen, and Grit Laudel. 2015. A Bibliometric Reconstruction of Research Trails for Qualitative Investigations of Scientific Innovations. *Historical Social Research – Historische Sozialforschung* 40: 299–330.
Hardt, Michael, and Antonio Negri. 2001. *Empire*. Cambridge, MA: Harvard University Press.
Hochschild, Arlie. 2004. Gennem Sprækker i Tidsfælden [Through Cracks in the Time Bind]. In *Arbejdssamfundet* [The Labour Society], ed. M. Hviid and J. Tonbo, 109–131. Copenhagen: Hans Reitzels.
Kaltenbrunner, Wolfgang, and Sarah de Ricjke. 2017. Quantifying 'Output' for Evaluation: Administrative Knowledge Politics and Changing Epistemic Cultures in Dutch Law Faculties. *Science and Public Policy* 44 (2): 284–293.
Kauko, Jaakko, Risto Rinne, and Tuomas Takala. 2018. *Politics of Quality in Education. A Comparative Study of Brazil, China, and Russia*. New York: Routledge.
W.K. Kellogg Foundation. 2004. *Logic Model Development Guide*. Battle Creek: W.K. Kellogg Foundation.
Koselleck, Reinhart. 2011. Introduction and Prefaces to the Geschichtliche Grundbegriffe. *Contributions to the History of Concepts* 6 (1): 1–37.
Kula, Witold. 1996. *Measures and Men*. Princeton: Princeton University Press.
Latour, Bruno. 1987. *Science in Action: How to Follow Scientists and Engineers through Society*. Stony Stratford: Open University Press.
———. 2005. *Reassembling the Social: An Introduction to Actor–Network-Theory*. New York: Oxford University Press.
Latour, Bruno, and Steve Woolgar. 1986. *Laboratory Life, the Construction of Scientific Facts*. Princeton: Princeton University Press.
Läubli Loud, Marlène, and John Mayne. 2013. *Enhancing Evaluation Use: Insights from Internal Evaluation Units*. Thousand Oaks: Sage.
Lilford, Richard, Mohammad A. Mohammad, David Spiegelhalter, and Richard Thomson. 2004. Use and Misuse of Process and Outcome Data in Managing Performance of Acute Medical Care: Avoiding Institutional Stigma. *The Lancet* 363: 1147–1154.

Lindeberg, Tobias. 2007. *Evaluative Technologies: Quality and the Multiplicity of Performance*. Copenhagen: Copenhagen Business School.
Meyer, John W. 2008. Building Education for a World Society. In *Changing Knowledge and Education*, ed. M.A. Pereyra, 31–49. Frankfurt am Main: Peter Lang.
Meyer, John W., John Boli, and George M. Thomas. 1987. Ontology and Rationalization in the Western Cultural Account. In *Institutional Structure: Constituting State, Society, and the Individual*, ed. G.M. Thomas, J.W. Meyer, F.O. Ramirez, and J. Boli, 12–37. Newbury Park: Sage.
Munro, Eileen. 2004. The Impact of Audit on Social Work Practice. *British Journal of Social Work* 34: 1075–1095.
Nisbet, Robert. 1966. *The Sociological Tradition*. London: Heinemann.
Nóvoa, Antonio, and Tali Yariv-Mashal. 2003. Comparative Research in Education: A Mode of Governance or a Historical Journey. *Comparative Education* 39 (4): 423–438.
Orlikowski, Wanda J., and Susan V. Scott. 2008. Sociomateriality: Challenging the Separation of Technology, Work and Organization. *The Academy of Management Annals* 2 (1): 433–474.
Ozga, Jenny, Peter Dahler-Larsen, Christina Segerholm, and Hannu Simola. 2011. *Fabricating Quality in Education: Data and Governance in Europe*. London: Routledge.
Pflueger, Dane. 2016. Knowing Patients: The Customer Survey and the Changing Margins of Accounting in Healthcare. *Accounting, Organizations and Society* 53: 17–33.
Porter, Theodore M. 1995. *Trust in Numbers: The Pursuit of Objectivity in Science and Public Life*. Princeton: Princeton University Press.
Prewitt, Kenneth, Thomas A. Schwandt, and Miron L. Straf. 2012. *Using Science as Evidence in Public Policy*. Washington, DC: National Academies Press.
Rom, Mark C. 2009. The Credit Rating Agencies and the Subprime Mess: Greedy, Ignorant, and Stressed? *Public Administration Review*: 640–650.
Rosa, Hartmut. 2003. Social Acceleration: Ethical and Political Consequences of a Desynchronized High–Speed Society. *Constellations* 10 (1): 3–33.
Rothstein, Henry, Michael Huber, and George Gaskell. 2006. A Theory of Risk Colonization: The Spiralling Regulatory Logics of Societal and Institutional Risk. *Economy and Society* 35 (1): 91–112.
Scalet, Steven, and Thomas F. Kelly. 2012. The Ethics of Credit Rating Agencies: What Happened and the Way Forward. *J Bus Ethics* 111: 477–490.
Schutz, Alfred. 1975. *Hverdagslivets Sociologi* [The Sociology of Everyday Life]. Copenhagen: Hans Reitzel.

Schwandt, Thomas A. 2000. Three Epistemological Stances for Qualitative Inquiry: Interpretivism, Hermeuneutics, and Social Constructivism. In *Handbook of Qualitative Methods*, ed. N.K. Denzin and Y.S. Lincoln, 189–210. Thousand Oaks: Sage.

Scott, W. Richard. 1992. *Organizations. Rational, Natural and Open Systems*. Englewood Cliffs: Prentice-Hall.

Stone, Deborah. 2012. *Policy Paradox*. 3rd ed. New York: Norton.

van Thiel, Sandra, and Frans L. Leeuw. 2002. The Performance Paradox in the Public Sector. *Public Performance and Management Review* 25 (3): 267–281.

Vostal, Filip. 2016. *Accelerating Academia, the Changing Structure of Academic Time*. New York: Palgrave Macmillan.

White, Lawrence J. 2012. Credit Rating Agencies: An Overview. *The Annual Review of Financial Economics* 5: 1–22.

5

Qualitization and Models of Qualitization

Given the broad and vague character of the concept of quality, and given the relativity of quality perspectives, the concept itself does not prescribe how it is going to be used. It does not set itself in motion. Let us look at *how* it happens.

A metaphor: Even if there is disagreement about whether the family should watch TV, what is on TV, and what should be seen, the one family member who has the remote control regulates *how* it is chosen whether to turn on the TV and eventually what to see.

The enunciation of quality in specific instances can be conceived as a speech act called "qualitization." Not merely a description of a quality object, qualitization is an act that makes promises or raises expectations about actors and actions in relation to something defined, performed, and constituted as "quality." Qualitization sets the concept of quality in motion in a rhetorical, relational, practical, and social sense.

Qualitization can be carried out in different ways. This chapter describes three models of qualitization: the metrological, deliberative, and configurative model. Each of them incorporates different assumptions and practices regarding qualitization. Each of the three models describes styles of measurement and related social practices, but also to some extent normative and prescriptive models of how this *should* be done properly.

P. Dahler-Larsen, *Quality*, https://doi.org/10.1007/978-3-030-10392-7_5

So, when people disagree in practice about *how* the concept of quality should be put to work in real life, this chapter offers a way of understanding what their differences are about. This is important to understand because even if differences in the very meaning of quality may remain unreconciled, once qualitization takes place, quality is set in practical motion in particular ways.

Qualitization

My notion of qualitization is inspired by Säljö (2002), Weick (1995), and Dewey (1931), all of whom suggest that our epistemologies assume too often that the world consists of physical entities that we can identify with nouns. We should instead be paying more attention to verbs and social processes. As the preceding chapters have shown, quality is not a thing with an internal, essential substance. Instead, it is a concept the meaning of which is derived from the social use made of it in specific contexts. Qualitization deals not only with measurement of quality but also with various assumptions about what makes measurement trustworthy, and even more importantly, what consequences should the resulting notion of quality have for various categories of people. Qualitization not only defines how to get to quality inscriptions but also why people should respect them and act upon them.

My delineation of the term "qualitization" is in debt to my brilliant colleague Ole Wæver, who has coined the term "securitization" to denote how security issues are invoked by means of a speech act with a particular rhetorical and semiotic structure. This structure comprises elements such as a referent object, an existential threat, securitizing actors, functional actors, and so forth (Buzan et al. 1998). Whether the statement about a security threat will be taken as valid in a broader, social context can only be known later. Even if the success of the speech act depends on the social reactions and chain reactions of the audiences (Buzan et al. 1998: 31), the appeal made in the speech act is as real as it gets. Securitization is a speech act that expresses a proposal about a social construction of security. The outcome of that speech act cannot be determined by the act itself, but it does set things in motion.

A similar logic is now applied to how statements about quality are produced and made relevant through a speech act in a specific context. The inspiration from securitization theory is clear, although the idea is taken in different directions. The conceptualization of the structure of the qualitizing speech act is more loose and less mature than the securitizing one Wæver successfully identified. On the other hand, whereas securitization can occur within a given rhetorical and semiotic structure without appeals to the word security itself, my approach is to follow only the very term quality itself, given my semasiological strategy.

Let us first consider an example of qualitization:

A quality situation occurs when the teaching of students is described through a quality machinery such as web-based questionnaires. The underlying quality perspective is that the quality of teaching depends on student satisfaction. An exact form of quality inscription is sent to all teachers (in the form of a score sheet). The quality office is the inscriptor. The quality object has to do with how the teacher has designed and taught the course. This quality object is situated in a quality zone consisting of all teachers in the same institution. The quality problem for one teacher has to do with the relative score of this person in relation to others, but there is only a real problem if the score is low. Most of the time, however, it is enough to keep an eye on quality. The responsibilization of the teachers is one of the important consequences of qualitization.

Experienced teachers do most of the quality work ahead of time, which includes elaborate course descriptions, defining objectives clearly, and relying on a variety of teaching forms with interaction between theory and practice. It also includes setting a tone toward students, which is conducive to student satisfaction. If the latter continues to be low over several semesters, managers will have to deal with it as a quality problem. Different quality agents will then be mobilized (later on maybe a stress coach, an IT consultant, a pedagogical specialist, or a colleague, depending on the nature and dynamics of the problem).

Notice here how a fairly simple and somewhat random definition of a "quality situation" connects with a broad set of actors and expands into a web-like quality configuration. The consequences of qualitization are up to the "contractions" and movements in this wider web. Seeing qualitization as an element in an ongoing process of social construction is not the same as declaring it to be fictitious. It is as real as it can get, but the first enunciation of a quality inscription is not much more than an invitation to structure reality in a particular way. One could also imagine variations and reinterpretations of key elements: the course evaluation is part of quality assurance systems which guarantees the school a place in the national quality zone for educational institutions. The quality object can be debated: Does it also include time for preparation, student behavior, and classroom facilities?

A definition of the initial quality situation is merely an example. Others could have offered alternative definitions, which could have mobilized different elements in alternative networks. One form of qualitization can be nested into another one, for example, when systematic student satisfaction surveys become part of an accreditation regime for the whole educational system. In that case, the responsibilization of teachers turns teachers into self-investors and service-providers meshed with the morality of the state and the health of the economy (Brown 2015: 84). An accreditation also includes responsibilization of managers, deans, and so on. Qualitization as such does not assume one known and defined situation.

* * *

In a schematic and ideal-typical way, qualitization can be defined as follows.

Qualitization is a speech act combining some or all of the following rhetorical moves:

- *It mobilizes the notion of quality and thereby a taken-for-granted notion of the good and*
- *defines a situation as a quality situation by means of*
- *a quality recipe and/or quality perspective*
- *and a quality machinery*
- *in the production of a quality inscription*
- *enunciated by an inscriptor*
- *about a quality object*

- *placed in a quality zone*
- *and thereby presents a quality problem,*
- *which calls for a quality agent*
- *situated in a particular quality configuration*
- *to take responsibility for quality work.*

The notion of qualitization thus brings together components in our analysis in this book so far. Qualitization culminates in a call, request, or demand. Qualitization works by implication. Among these implications are that people should respect a definition of quality or a decision about the definition of quality for particular reasons or that someone should take responsibility for securing the quality of something for someone else. This quality work can include any kind of choice, action, improvement, learning, and so on that relates to a quality object and responds to the call stated in qualitization.

Qualitization is an analytical framework describing how an appeal to quality seeks to become translated into social reality. Not all elements of qualitization need to be empirically manifest and clearly enunciated in any given instance. The proposed analytical framework allows for various combinations.

The conceptual framework presented here does not assume the "clarity" of a situation, "sincerity" of an inscriptor, "reliability" of the quality inscription, or a consistent "value system" of a quality agent as necessary conditions for a functional appeal to get quality work started. Someone may be "inspired" to do quality work or even "forced" to do so as a result of, say, a power differential between an inscriptor and a quality agent in a particular quality configuration that leaves one with little choice (Moe 2005). Pressure on a quality agent may be exerted using a variety of links and associations. The effects of qualitization may be achieved through assumptions, norms, nudging, incentives, social pressure, or taken-for-grantedness. They do not necessarily result from a quality agent's conviction or alignment with particular values. Positive reactions among quality agents may be enhanced if they are sympathetic with the underlying quality perspective and other characteristics of a quality inscription, but sympathy is not a precondition for action. Reactions may include debating or challenging a given quality inscription or inscriptor, appealing to alternative quality perspectives, or producing new inscriptions. One qualitization may thus lead to another.

Note that qualitization can be enacted by an official quality inscriptor, but also by others.

When qualitization takes place through a network, it is possible to produce both situations and effects across quality zones distributed over time and space. There is no limit as long as a qualitization process brings a sufficient number of the elements described above together into an active configuration.

Here, "bring together" means connect over time and space, often through quality machineries, infrastructures, and technology. Qualitization does not require face-to-face meetings between quality agents. On the contrary, the separation in time and space of, say, the quality inscriptor from other quality agents may be an important productive social factor in itself. It may put the quality inscriptor in position to use data collected from others over long distances. It may make the inscriptor more independent of or unknown to the quality agent. It may protect the qualitizer at distance from social critique. And it may relieve the quality inscriptor of responsibility for the consequences of qualitization.

All in all, the proposed analytical scheme suggests that qualitization takes place through an interaction of elements. The emphasis on particular elements may differ, their combinations may differ, the degree of explication of each element differs, and so may the outcomes of the exact configuration established through qualitization. The minimal definition of qualitization is merely that an appeal to a particular notion of quality becomes enunciated and set in motion socially through an appeal to some or all of the elements described above. One can imagine that with more elements, more combinations, and more extension in time and space, the qualitization process becomes more far-reaching.

On that basis, I wish to outline three models regarding *how* qualitization takes place as part of social life: the metrological, deliberative, and configurative models.

The metrological, deliberative, and configurative models describe practices of qualitization which involve habits, propensities, inclinations, and ways of performing. Remember that qualitization is an active speech act.

Each of the three places a particular emphasis on selected elements (or selected combinations of elements) in the qualitization process. Each of them has more elective affinity with particular quality perspectives than others. The three models also have normative and prescriptive capacities, although perhaps not in the same proportion. They stipulate different aspects of qualitization as key parts of a legitimate and trustworthy process. Advocates of the metrological, deliberative, and configurative models do not necessarily see themselves as actively and explicitly involved in "qualitization." Qualitization is an analytical construct which allows a comparison between these three models. Each of these models is open or closed regarding particular aspects of the qualitization process. While the metrological model and the deliberative model each have a fairly narrow focus, the configurative model claims that many elements and a broad set of actors and machineries are in play in the qualitization process.

Each of these models offers entry points into the problematique of socio-political implications of quality. The configurative model offers the most new and radical view on the production of constitutive effects, but let us look at each model in turn.

The Metrological Model

Metrology is the art and science of measurement. In the metrological model, the uncomplicated existence of an object under measurement is taken for granted. The quality object is given. The problem is how to measure it or, in the terminology of this book, how to produce a proper quality inscription. The assumption is that measurement can be improved to accomplish continuously better approximations of a correct representation of the object.

The main role of the quality inscription is to be genuinely informative. It can therefore offer support to decision-making about a quality object. However, the metrological model is defined on the basis of its emphasis on measurement. The metrological style of qualitization sees correct decisions (and eventually other elements) in qualitization as a function of good measurement. Imagine a situation where there is a choice between three quality objects but the exact quality of each of these objects is unknown. Once the metrology delivers a trustworthy quality inscription encompassing all of the three objects in commensurable terms, the decision about which to choose becomes self-evident. While the metrological style enrolls a decision-maker, it also prepares the decision so much that if the quality situation is streamlined and the quality object is properly metrologically inscribed, a robot could make the decision, provided that the robot were able to express its preferences and criteria for quality.

A variation of the metrological models says that you should measure different aspects of quality in quality objects depending on the purpose at hand, so that not all decisions should be based on the same measurement. Again, however, this modification merely adapts metrology to different types of decisions. Once the purpose of decision-making is set and objects are given, the only tricky part left is that which is handled by metrology itself.

The metrological model describes no other role or function for quality inscriptions than this informative support for important decisions. If the metrology is optimal, there are no side effects or problematic overflows.

As a corollary, a maximum effort must be ensured to secure optimal measurement. The metrological model therefore enrolls metrological expertise as a privileged type of knowledge. For example, bibliometricians are used in research evaluation. In turn, they emphasize how their expertise is a precondition for the production of trustworthy bibliometric data.

The metrological model supports the ongoing refinement of indicators and measures. This includes the refinement of validity and reliability. The metrological model often prescribes rules for the verification of data, such as the refinement and calibration of instruments and verification of measurements by people involved in the production of quality objects before the finalization of the quality inscription. Purification and refinement are key elements in establishing trustworthy measurement (Latour 1987; Porter 1994).

Technical expertise and refinement of metrological equipment help provide authority and trustworthiness to the kind of qualitization which is guided by the metrological model.

As part of the development of metrological knowledge, metrological specialists often consider how different indicators describe different aspects of quality objects. Metrologists do not interpret this plurality as having to do with any opacity of the object under measurement. Instead, they propose that different indicators are relevant for different types of decisions and perhaps in a broader perspective for forms of use beyond decisions; however, a particular temporal and logical order of things is in place in the metrological model: There are purposes and there are objects. Then comes the proper measurement to support the right social actors with well-defined purposes about the best available information about the objects to be acted upon in relation to those purposes.

In order to ensure that metrics are not used in ways that threaten their validity, metrological specialists sometimes try to educate decision-makers about which measures should be used for which purposes. Metrologists insist that decision-makers should keep their purposes clearly defined so that measures can be used properly in relation to them.

The model does not mention that measurements influence the interpretation of opaque objects or that inscriptions influence the people who engage with them or the definition of situations in which they find themselves. When these effects occur, advocates of the metrological model do not see these effects as problematic if only the correct quality measures are in place (Kelman and Friedman 2009). Then people are welcome to react to them.

Therefore, there is a tendency among metrologists not to theorize or worry about social implications of qualitization. The main focus is on measurement itself. When that is perfected, the social consequences of measurement are negligible or unproblematic. Good metrology guarantees good qualitization, if you will.

The discussion between Moed (2018) and Wouters (2018) regarding bibliometrics is particularly illustrative of controversy regarding the assumptions of metrology. Moed (2018) argues that it is not a problem if researchers react to bibliometric measures if only the measurement is properly carried out. He also argues that different measures can serve different evaluative purposes. Alternatively, from a critical view it is argued that evaluation and decision-making happens all the time and in many social settings, and there is more than anecdotal evidence of constitutive effects (Wouters 2018). The social use of bibliometrics cannot be turned on and off at the discretion of the metrologist. Measurement does not work in isolation. It is therefore not responsible to produce quality inscriptions and not be concerned about their practical consequences. The critics say that a purely metrological ambition to be empirical and value-free is indicative of "the failure of a paradigm" (Wouters 2018).

A final example illustrating the metrological perspective and its critics is related to tests in schools. Some psychometricians focus only on the technical quality of tests based on criteria such as precision and reliability. They may admit that there can be "unintended" effects of testing, but they argue that the more precise and reliable the tests, the more negligible are their unintended consequences. Others argue not only that measurement itself is less important than psychometricians argue. (The consequences for pedagogy and for school climate deserve more attention.) What is worse is that psychometricians misspecify the link between the technical aspects of tests and these social consequences. If precise measurement is made sacrosanct, psychometricians will recommend adaptive tests, which happen to operate on the basis of complex algorithms. The test items themselves become practically invisible for teachers and the rules for calculating test scores incomprehensible. Furthermore, with adaptive testing, even the most clever children will walk away from the test situation feeling they were unable to answer about 50% of the test items correctly, because that is how adaptive tests operate. In other words, the desire for precise measurement leads to alienation of teachers and children vis-à-vis the test.

Critics argue that the focus on measurement characteristic of metrological model is sometimes a disadvantage in a broader social perspective.

The Deliberative Model

According to the deliberative model, quality cannot be defined without discussion. Deliberation is a process whereby people with different experiences and viewpoints exchange views on a quality object. This interaction produces knowledge that is more than simply a sum of individual viewpoints. It is a potential social transformation. If deliberation is free from domination of any particular, socially privileged actors, if actors are oriented toward attending to each other's views, and if they are willing to revise their views in the light of inputs from others, the transformative potential of deliberation can be realized. A domination-free social context is therefore a precondition for good deliberation (Habermas 1991; House and Howe 2000).

Philosophically, the absence of power allows reason and deliberation to flourish; people bring their different experiences and viewpoints to the table. Deliberation can enrich understandings of quality, and an exchange of views under controlled rules leads to a richer and finer collective understanding of quality.

For example, commissioners, architects, constructors, and the users of buildings have different perspectives on what constitutes quality in the situation, partly because they attend to different constraints and challenges in that situation (e.g. esthetics, budgets, infrastructure, users). The assumption in the deliberative model is that an appreciation and attunement to the views of others contributes to the refinement of an understanding of quality.

In the deliberate style of qualitization, there is a close link between participation, knowledge, and legitimate decisions. Participation guarantees the best possible understanding of quality. It also makes decision-making legitimate for both social and epistemic reasons. Deliberation is a good way to identify complex quality, but it is also the best way to ensure that a quality decision and other kinds of quality work are consistent with the best available and most carefully calibrated versions of social norms and values.

In recent years, the advocates of the deliberative ideal have cultivated their interest in the real social conditions under which deliberation takes place. In Science and Technology Studies (STS) studies, many have advocated formats involving not only political elites and experts but wider groups of stakeholders and citizens (Hackett et al. (eds.) 2008). The same is true for responsible innovation (Stilgoe et al. 2013).

The prescriptions emanating from the deliberative style of qualitization are clear. Create forums for deliberation. Keep rules which enhance rational, learning-oriented, and power-reducing deliberation. Expand the number and variety of stakeholders who can participate. When asked about their aspirations, advocates of the deliberative model often say, "I wish more stakeholders could be included."

In spirit, the deliberative model is "open" and "inclusive." However, its openness is restricted to types of statements produced in compliance with the procedural rules of the deliberative ideal. Philosophically, that raises the question of how to determine (before seeing the situation and before anyone has spoken) that this should be the preferred procedural model (Schwandt 1994). In fact, the model permits someone to say, "Sorry, the statement you just made falls outside of the boundaries of the deliberative model." As Vattimo (2005) explains, however, the metaphysical justification for that particular model is assumed *before* anyone has spoken. In real-life situations in history, politics, and society, someone has always spoken earlier. There is already a social life in process. The deliberative model discriminates between acceptable and unacceptable interventions seen from the perspective of the model. However, that distinction is only acceptable insofar as the model has already been metaphysically taken for granted.

It is easy for advocates of the deliberative school of thought because the deliberative model assumes the availability of virtually unlimited time (Palonen 2002: 100).

As mentioned earlier, Lamont (2009) provides a fine example of how deliberation takes place under practical circumstances, involving real people who make difficult decisions under time pressure. Her empirical focus is on how professors make funding decisions in panels. Their practice is complicated because there are partly different understandings of what constitutes good research in the various fields and subfields. As part of their deliberation, they exercise "cognitive contextualization," meaning that they change the weight attached to various criteria depending on the field or discipline of the proposal under review (Lamont 2009: 106).

Panelists who push their own field too much lose credibility (Lamont 2009: 137). Conversely, someone who is known for serious contributions and well-calibrated judgments across fields and subfields gains influence over time. The interaction between experts takes place with reference to highly advanced academic norms specific to disciplines and subdisciplines, but Lamont also demonstrates the importance of tact, dialogue, and courtesy. In sum, her account shows the importance of sociality for deliberation, but the sociality she finds in real life is different from the heavenly absence of power and domination defining the

Habermasian deliberative ideal. In Lamont's analysis, people have emotions and relations. They exercise strategic voting and horse-trading, but they also cultivate and celebrate social behaviors and mechanisms which enhance good deliberation.

However, one cannot only question the philosophical foundations of the model (which Vattimo does), one must also discuss how much the model contributes to an understanding of what actually goes on in all of the situations where deliberation is far from perfect or even lacking from decision-making. The deliberative ideal can be used as a *critical standard* against which decision-making can be assessed in practice. In practice, people express resentment and anger over decisions made without consultation, over new realities installed behind their backs. This is also true for new forms of quality measurement. "We never had time to sit down and discuss this before it was implemented" is a frequently heard statement in everyday language articulating such a reaction. The same is true for the overflows and constitutive effects following from quality measurements.

Advocates of the deliberative paradigm assume that when something happens which is not properly discussed, it lacks legitimacy. A parallel assumption is that only a good deliberation can guarantee the legitimacy of qualitization processes. Presumably, this is also true regarding constitutive effects. While they may occur, the only way to keep them under control is to subject them to common deliberation.

When the deliberate model is used as a critical standard, what it means in practice is that there was not enough time for deliberation, the deliberation was not good enough, or it failed to include enough participants. A critical voice might ask, however, what if there is more time set aside for deliberation, and everybody is included? Do we really mean that in the meantime, there is no pressure to act? And will all collective action not still be bedeviled by normative tensions and uncomfortable side effects? As Harry Boyte (2011) argues, perhaps deliberation is philosophically conceived too much like a university seminar, while the collective obligation to construct a common world (with all its ambiguity and tension) cannot be set aside just because more time and space is required for proper deliberation. Perhaps the deliberative model works better as a critical standard than as a model for collective construction of reality.

The deliberative paradigm ignores the many ways in which action-already-taking-place is by definition shaping the collective political order. The deliberative model cherishes an ideal; it also strongly ignores or condemns ways of creating realities that are not enacted in accordance with that ideal. To curse such situations is not to understand them. From the perspective of the deliberative model, curses are often cast upon the types of social change induced by the third and final model, the configurative one.

The Configurative Model

The configurative model describes how quality inscriptions transported over time and space help reconfigure a social order. It describes qualitization performed through networks, connections, and associations without presupposing the proper measurement of the quality of quality objects. There is also no assumption about deliberation over the meanings of quality. In these two ways, the configurative style differs starkly from the metrological and deliberative models, respectively. The configurative model does not assume that there is any legitimate overarching principle in the way qualitization takes place, such as the respect for expertise in the metrological model or the equal rights to participate in the deliberative model.

The configurative model operates through quality inscriptions that interfere with people's lives through the connectivity of elements. I have called it the configurative model because it operates by bringing elements together in a *quality configuration*. Infrastructure such as manuals, guidelines, computers, and reporting mechanisms are crucial. Infrastructures make it possible for metrics to circulate through time and space, from the global to the corporeal (Beer 2016, Ch. 3), thereby accelerating the immediacy of quality inscriptions for more people in more situations. Circulation is critical because it does not only help spread metrics in time and space, it also helps spread the values which were encoded into the production of metrics. This is particularly critical since circulation is often not controlled collectively by people who become involved in a quality configuration. Instead, it is circulation which creates the configuration. Thus, the configurative style of qualitization makes evaluative judgments circulate ahead of the ability to discuss them deliberately and control them through collective decision-making. It can also circulate quality inscriptions that are poorly crafted in metrological terms. That does not take much away from the practical function of the inscription.

It was suggested earlier that when quality inscriptions constitute a quality object that they claim to describe, they fix or stabilize a definition of quality by means of processes such as categorization, abstraction, connection, interpellation, and temporalization. The outcome of such processes in the form of constitutive effects hinges on the connectivity and interaction in a network or configuration. It is not necessary that all of the agents in the configuration act collectively as a community. On the contrary, they may not even know each other. The effects of qualitization are produced "between them" as a result of bringing the elements together into an operational quality configuration. The best metaphor for what produces effects of quality inscriptions is not the power of an antecedent "causal factor," but the interaction which comes from already "being inside" the configuration and influencing its elements. The production of responsibilization is a key element. For example, school teachers in a country are held responsible for the international ranking of their pupils in an international comparison once it is made public. A complex configuration of computers, test machineries, politicians, and media is in play, but there was never an initial meeting where international quality inscriptors met with school teachers and discussed how to make quality inscriptions and how to use them.

There is no lengthy historical tradition of such large-scale quality configurations and networks across time and space (e.g. in a global context) and therefore no lengthy historical tradition of studying them. There is something socio-historically new at play, which is potential long-distance production of constitutive effects which are neither under control of metrologists nor subject to common deliberation. There is much we do not know about constitutive processes. Constitutive processes should not be forced into theoretical distinctions of yesterday. The particular force of constitutive processes may in fact rest with their capacity to transgress conventional distinctions and instead operate under the radar defined by traditional concepts. It would be wrong to assume that all constitutive effects are produced in one way only.

Constitutive Effects of the Configurative Model of Qualitization

Well-known schools of thought have traditionally set the tone for the major part of studies of consequences of evaluative regimes, quality inscriptions, and the like. One is the neo-institutional sociology of organizations which suggest that organizations are able to decouple the innate values and core operations of the organization from what is shown to outsiders (Meyer and Rowan 1977). Evaluation can be mere window-dressing. Another school of thought delivers a Foucault-inspired critique of neoliberal steering techniques. It suggests that evaluative regimes colonize organizational practices and undermine professional autonomy. Since what is studied is "governing at a distance," it is assumed that when new technologies for steering are installed, they also succeed in governing (Shore and Wright 2015).

Somewhere in between these extreme positions, a number of scholars admit that there are non-linear consequences of performance measures, quality control, and so on, but these consequences are unintended, as they flow from imperfect measurement and from how people under measurement are gaming with the measures (Smith 1995; van Thiel and Leeuw 2002). A number of studies in recent years have added much complexity and nuance to our understanding of the effects of quality inscriptions.

Very good studies exemplifying the power of constitutive effects are provided by Espeland and Sauder (2007) and Sauder and Espeland (2009). They describe how law school rankings exert influence on the management practices in these schools. Although not articulated explicitly in the terminology of "qualitization," "connections," and "configurations," their study makes perfect sense in this terminology. Through surveillance and normalization, the constitutive effects of ranking "clinch" particular management practices because the rankings influence alumni and student perceptions—and thereby money streams. These connections are enforced by a self-fulfilling logic. Some people actually believe that rankings reflect "genuine quality." Many merely react to the reactions of others (e.g. changes in reputation). As a consequence, streams of teachers and students are directed in ways that help confirm the patterns already suggested by the rankings (regardless of the validity of the rankings) (Espeland and Sauder 2007). When that mechanism becomes real, then those who speak up against rankings speak up against reality. The study exemplifies a kind of institutional "lock-in" that helps stabilize the constitutive effects of rankings. The institutional lock-in is a result of the social construction of a configuration of rankings, alumni reactions, money streams, imaginations, and management reactions.

In a similar vein, notice in another example cited earlier how credit ratings, budgets, policies, media, politicians, and a credit rating agency came together into one configuration, which influenced the budget for 2018 in South Africa. In both cases, bringing together diverse elements into a quality configuration is crucial for making the configuration operational in practice.

While these observations clearly suggest that constitutive effects do exist, a number of relatively new studies helps us understand the anatomy of constitutive effects even better. These studies were made possible by five theoretical advances. These are "departure from intentions," "departure from value consistency," "discovery of multiplicity," "discovery of the affective dimension," "discovery of ambiguous involvement," and "institutional lock-in." In the following, I will explain how each of these is consistent with the configurative model.

Departure from Intentions

Espeland and Sauder (2007) claim that there are both intended and unintended effects of quality inscriptions. It seems they are trying to transgress the distinction. If effects come out on both sides of the distinction, how useful is the distinction?

Definitions of unintended consequences rest upon the delineation of some original intention behind a quality inscription (Dahler-Larsen 2013). In addition to being difficult to identify and determine empirically, such original intentions might also be lost in history and translation. As the distance between the production of an inscription and its consequences extends through many associations in such a network, new actors are enrolled. Can new intentions not be invented as the network extends across time and space? Should an emerging configuration of interests not be seen as more relevant than one "original" intention? The combination of elements in a quality configuration might also lead to consequences that best deserve to be understood as real consequences in themselves, not merely as distorted shadows of earlier, now opaque, intentions. A paradigm which commits itself to the notion of unintended consequences assumes that original inventors of tools such as quality inscriptions have a privileged position regarding the definition of correct use of their tools. In quality configurations which create themselves anew across time and place, this assumption may be futile.

New actors become involved as the network expands. They deal with the demand to qualitize in their own way. For example, an agency responsible for measuring school quality may provide a ranking of schools based on student performance (grades and tests) after control for the socio-economic background and the ethnic compositions of parents across school districts. In the sake of transparency, they also publish raw grades and test results. Some parents use the latter data to make school choices, because the level of students matter to them, regardless of whether the numbers are due to the activities of the school itself or social background factors. A good result is a good result. At the same time, some parents protest against having social background factors published, because they think that they can be good people and live in a good neighborhood even if there are many, say, single mothers. As people engage with the ranking of schools, they attach their own agendas to the project.

There is one more, even deeper, theoretical reason to be skeptical about "original" intentions as the yardstick for the evaluation of the consequences of qualitization. The notion of intentions rests on an actor-oriented view of the social world. However, qualitization is the appeal to a combination of elements in a network that defines the actors as much as they define the network. Actors are interpellated or "summoned" in very particular capacities as quality agents, such as "evaluators," "users," "experts," and so forth. Some are even expert "advisors" of agencies, which hire consultants to produce inscriptions or teachers of such consultants and the like. Without quality configurations invoked by qualitization, these roles or categories of actors would be difficult to imagine. The constitutive effects of qualitization thus extend across the usual distinctions between "actors" and "structures" (Boedker and Chua 2013; Feldman and Orlikowski 2011). The notion of "original intentions" hinges on a moral model of individual agency which is perhaps becoming increasingly obsolete.

Departure from Value Consistency

The neo-institutional hypothesis mentioned above predicts that organizations will decouple their production core from evaluation procedures, if the evaluation regimes represent values which are not compatible with the organization's own core values. The configurationist paradigm suggests otherwise. It does not assume that the functions of quality inscriptions depend on any acceptance of how they inscribe quality. Quality inscriptions can work with the full spectrum of institutional "pillars" (Scott 1992), ranging from the normative, the cognitive, and the regulative to the affective registers. As a corollary, they can work through force, through economic incentives, through norms and convictions, sometimes even internalized to a degree that some describe as the "happy slave syndrome" (Boedker and Chua 2013: 264).

Given the many roads that quality inscriptions possibly take through the social landscape, they sometimes lead to controversy. Some researchers even suggest studying the social life of inscriptions using the controversies they elicit as an analytical entry point (Venturini 2010). While such a strategy possibly produces insights, controversy is not necessarily overt. Resistance to particular quality inscriptions is sometimes exerted through dodgy registration practices or hesitation to facilitate the streams of information otherwise characterizing a quality configuration (not filling in surveys, not sending documents, not reacting to reminders). These slow forms of resistance should not be analytically underestimated and may account for much of what is otherwise observed as "implementation problems" with quality reforms, a very common phenomenon (Øvretveit 2005).

Sometimes professionals recognize that a particular quality inscription machinery is becoming part of reality even if it is more or less inconsistent with their professional values. Reality does not always reflect norms. Facticity is also a way of shaping reality (Mortensen 2004). A quality inscription helps define an inescapable organizational reality, for example, when it is linked to the resources necessary for the survival of the organization. One example was found in a study of upper secondary school teachers. Although they were critical about student satisfaction surveys, they considered using data from student satisfaction surveys on the school's website in order to attract more students next year and thereby perhaps avoid downsizing the number of teachers at the school (Dahler-Larsen and Pihl-Thingvad 2014).

In a fine, large-scale study of the impact of bibliometric measures upon researchers in Denmark, it was found that implementation of a new registration system did not depend on a normative match between the system and the core values of the adopting institutions (Mouritzen et al. 2018: 304). Instead, a group of managers used the new system to change norms and values in some universities. Once the new system is implemented, at least those who receive a new and better status may actually believe in the appropriateness and fairness of the shift in values (Dahler-Larsen 2013). Some may jump onboard later even if they did not know that a new form of quality inscription would have such a wonderful effect, so they could not say in advance that they would support it. They can only support it in retrospect.

One fundamental reason why it is theoretically unsatisfactory—and often unproductive—to focus on whether professionals and other key quality agents *normatively accept a given quality inscription in principle* is that they are usually not faced with it in principle but in practice. In practice, they do not struggle with the "principles" inherent in a quality configuration. They may know neither who made the inscription nor the exact circumstances under which it was made. Teachers might not remember or understand the role of the OECD in making the inscriptions of school quality known from Programme for International Students Assessment (PISA).

A further reason why a general position on values may not be the best key to an understanding of the constitutive consequences of quality inscriptions is that a given quality agent sees the social relevance of an inscription not in the light of principles but in light of the score already received. Where you stand in relation to principles depends on where you are positioned in relation to scores. Some research managers "use" university rankings only if they are favorable for their university. If not, they remain silent. That is not a result of a "value-based" position vis-à-vis the quality inscription. It is pragmatic use that is best explained by the score, whatever it happens to be. The position taken is not based on a metaphysical commitment to values but on a situated calibration of pros and cons in a strategic situation embedded in a given social context with a particular form a qualitization at play together with last, but not least, a particular score.

The key to understanding the configurative model is that it operates without an assumption of value consensus or consent. Values and consent may well be mobilized, but the model works by bringing partners into an active quality configuration whether they agree or not. The fact that some level of interpretive flexibility (or value disagreement) is possible around a social construction so that it mobilizes diverse actors (Pinch and Bijker 1984) may in fact increase its use and its circulation rather than the opposite.

Many quality inscriptions are produced at a distance and travel quickly. There is no chance to form a consensus before new things are implemented. Quality configurations operate in a way which is starkly different to the process suggested by, for example, a deliberative model. Based on the deliberative model, it is still possible to criticize the introduction of the new system on the basis that it was never properly discussed among all relevant stakeholders, but the deliberative model does not control reality. Something even more problematic than the lack of discussion is at stake. It would not necessarily help to bring all stakeholders together to coordinate their convictions, because professionals like the ones in the examples above do not base their action on conviction. Their motivations to act arise out of management pressure, the desire for new status, a desire to save or promote their school, the simple factuality of the quality measurement system, and presumably a number of other explicit or implicit factors at play in the quality configurations in which they find themselves. They seem more susceptible to a hundred forms of nudging and twenty forms of pressure rather than one strong and stable conviction. In that sense, their actions mirror the characteristics of the quality configurations in which they find themselves.

Discovery of the Affective Dimension

Quality inscriptions do not work through "hard" institutional sanctions alone, then, but also through flows of emotional energy (Boedker and Chua 2013). Conventional theoretical ideas such as neo-institutional "decoupling" or "unintended consequences" are unable to account for the strong emotional reactions, which quality inscriptions trigger among professionals (Jensen 2011: 79). For example, a good score may create excitement, pride, and a sense of personal worth. Bad or uncertain scores may promote anxiety, fear, or resentment. Emotions bring with them particular dispositions for actions. Emotions are productive, not least under social conditions of unclarity. Emotions may be one of the currencies that are circulated by the style of qualitization consistent with the configurative model. Qualitizations may work because they trigger anger, pride, sadness, resentment, or an aggressive will to win.

For example, teachers struggle with uncertainties in performance measurement, the meaningfulness of feedback from students, and with varying individual/collective attributions. As teachers typically use themselves in the process of teaching, they become involved as "workable objects" that are continuously subject to improvement along dimensions not yet described. Quality inscriptions relocate tensions and frictions so that struggles about performance and its interpretation are internalized by the teachers as struggling performers (Englund and Frostenson 2017).

A study of teachers involved in language courses for immigrants found that a new test system for course participants (which was used not only to measure their proficiency level but also as a performance indicator which influenced school budgets) had an impact on teacher's sense of professionalism. While teachers usually exposed themselves to heartbreaking stories among the participants (some of whom were refugees who had experienced torture), the new test system made teachers focus more directly on measurable outcomes of teaching. The teachers developed a sense of professionalism, where a certain level of emotional detachment from heartbreaking stories was an integrated part (Dahler-Larsen and Pihl-Thingvad 2014).

A study looking at the relation between performance indicators and stress across professional groups found that stress was most intense among those who held strong professional values and who found that the performance criteria they were subjected to were internally inconsistent as well as inconsistent with professional values. The indicators did not produce the kind of clarity one could expect if they were to reduce stress (Dahler-Larsen and Pihl-Thingvad 2014).

Another study found that the degree of implementation of a new bibliometric system among researchers was negatively correlated with the perceived quality of the psycho-social work environment (Mouritzen et al. 2018: 143). Degree of implementation included not only whether the bibliometric points earned influenced reallocation of financial funds across departments, but also, for example, whether researchers kept copy of the rules of the bibliometric categorizations in their own computer, and whether they personally remembered the number of bibliometric points they have scored in a given time period. These factors neatly exemplify the *variety* of ways in which professionals deal with quality inscriptions.

Reactions to quality assessments of research among research are sometimes stronger than what would be predicted based on dimensions such as financial rewards and career opportunities. Also when financial incentives are absent, weak, or indirect, quality inscriptions may incite very strong reactions among professionals (Dahler-Larsen 2013). This is the case among researchers whose self-esteem is at stake, for example. Fochler and de Rijcke (2017) show that researchers participate actively in the use of indicators of quality, sometimes also for the purpose of self-promotion. The affective registers of quality inscriptions are multiple. Quality inscriptions can be ways to keep certain affective reactions under control, but quality inscriptions can also in themselves be used for self-promotion and/or produce a climate of anxiety.

Discovery of Multiplicity

Practitioners are often subject to more than one type of quality inscription, more than one type of performance measurement, audit, evaluation, and so on. Multiple quality inscriptions are to be expected when several quality configurations operate in the same social territory.

Stark (2009), with his description of multiple orders of worth, illustrates how actors sometimes creatively deal with several value systems and multiple quality criteria at the same time. They create their own devices, which allow them to deal with complex situations under time pressure.

Pollock et al. (2018) also suggests that multiplicity allows for a creative combination of several devices, especially when rankers and quality inscriptors can be influenced by the people, who are otherwise subjected to measurement. Theoretically, this situation paves the way for a "reflexive transformation" of quality regimes rather than "reactive conformance." This use of this option requires not only the multiplicity of inscriptions, as Pollock et al. point out, but also a certain position of power as well as resources, which allow for discretion and maneuvering. Not all people under measurement are in such a position.

Likewise, Callon et al. (2002: 213) suggest that quality can be negotiated in "hybrid forums capable of holding debates on the organization of markets." Not all enjoy such privileges. There might be a slight bias in studies of multiple forms of qualitization toward privileged groups, who have more influence and a bias toward positive evaluation of "positive friction" rather than confusion and frustration. Even so, the discovery of multiplicity in qualitizations constitutes an important corrective to studies, which simplistically assume that only one quality inscription rules in each situation.

Discovery of Ambiguous Involvement

Power (1996) posits a model of reflexivity (inspired by Ulrich Beck) against a model of the audit society where inspections (what we here call "quality inscriptions") are institutionalized. He argues that the models of (flexible) reflexivity often underestimate the institutional power that backs up (rigid) quality regimes.

Perhaps the two can operate simultaneously and in tension. Institutionalized regimes of quality inscription can be powerful while at the same time installing uncertainty, contingency, and (some kinds of) reflexivity. All that is needed is, for example, an inconsistency between multiple, simultaneously institutionalized regimes (e.g. a national definition of policy objectives in schools versus an international comparison of "school quality"). Once there is sufficient discrepancy between the demands of an institutionalized quality regime and the demands of various concrete situations in which practitioners find themselves, they will have to reflect upon which principles reign and what must be done in the uncertain space between the different orders of worth. In other words, there is no great theoretical distance between the exercise of power and a widespread sense of uncertainty; they might work together more than one might immediately expect. Reflexivity is not the same as freedom, especially if there are many conflicting criteria and demands at play, if resources are scarce and the institutional room for maneuvering is narrow.

Maybe power works by creating difficult situations and raising expectations to unknown and uncertain levels. If there is any complaint, power answers: I really have nothing to do with this. In fact, the situation is really up to you. All that is needed is to locate the subject into a quality configuration that makes the performing quality agent face this difficult situation and ask the subject to use reflexivity to deal with it.

Roberts (2018) describes a management mechanism that places a heavy burden of ambiguity on the shoulders of subordinates in organizations. That mechanism is managing *only* with transparency. The idea here is that managers install particular quality inscriptions and deal with only that part of reality, which becomes transparent through these inscriptions. Whether there are conflicting demands, and whether there is friction between quality inscriptions and reality, or between quality inscriptions and organizational norms, is really left up to others in the organization. Subordinates are thereby ambiguously involved in the dealing with quality inscriptions. They find themselves in a strategic landscape, which is difficult to navigate and where quality inscriptions cannot be circumvented.

In a study of upper secondary teachers, I found considerable ambiguity toward the use of quality indicators of their schools (e.g. student satisfaction scores). Although they disagreed with the meaningfulness of student satisfaction scores as an indicator of education quality, they definitely found a good or increasing score useful for marketing purposes. They were, thus, faced with the strategic dilemma of whether a poor indicator should be used for a constructive purpose (Dahler-Larsen 2016). If more students were attracted to the school, they could help save the jobs of, say, two of their colleagues.

These findings are consistent with other findings of ambiguity, opacity, unclarity, and bricolage regarding the translation of quality inscriptions into practices (Dambrin and Robson 2011). They are also consistent with Wallenburg et al. (2016: 12), who find "ambivalence" in the sense that rankings are both "irrelevant, inescapable, and influential at the same time."

Quality inscriptions do not need to be metrologically well designed nor well implemented in order to have constitutive functions. Much in contradistinction to the expectations of the metrological paradigm, Dambrin and Robson (2011) describe how a performance system with very "weak traces" of the object it claims to measure nevertheless helps reshape people's professional identities. They found that a number of checks and balances were put in place and that professionals largely accepted a situation where bonuses were paid out on the basis of an incomprehensible system of performance measurement that was, logically, very poorly related to actual performance. They conclude that inscriptions with weak references to quality objects and with poor normative foundation can also be performative. The enabling character of inscription devices does not necessarily depend on their metrological solidity. Not *necessarily*, although there can be other situations where constant contestation triggers metrological improvements and where certain levels of metrological sophistication (Cohen 2006; Porter 1995) and purification (Latour 1987) are necessary for the social accept of the metrics. Again, the key lies in the social and infrastructural network, not in the measured object itself.

Broken or half-cooked inscriptions may even increase commitment (Dambrin and Robson 2011). Opacity can lead to trust, and thereby also to use. Ambiguity can be extremely socially productive. For example, if the rules of the game change regularly (Dambrin and Robson 2011: 440), all of these "imperfect" "implementations" of different systems of quality inscription may present a way of keeping quality agents on their toes. The configurative paradigm portrays unclarity as "productive" insofar as it triggers various forms of actions and maneuvering. Anticipation of even potential use of quality inscriptions in the future can make people prepare themselves for the situation, thus in effect helping to create a new reality mirroring what the quality inscription seeks to accomplish.

Jensen (2011) described how groups of researchers were involved in the construction of a new bibliometric research evaluation system, which many of them criticized intensely, yet they feared that without their input, the system might be even worse. The system was changed several times, and as a result of their ambiguous involvement, no one was quite sure of what was going on (Jensen 2011). Controversy is not necessarily "bad," as it may lead to the refinement of the quality inscription and to expanded forms of involvement (Arnaboldi and Azzone 2010), but ambiguity increases when it is difficult to predict where the quality system is going. Nevertheless, uncertainty is productive.

The concept of *overflow* (Callon 1998) can be applied in an understanding of the non-linear ways in which various actors at different levels respond to quality inscriptions.

A variety of outcomes in the plural are produced through the dispersed reactivity of the actors involved (Espeland and Sauder 2007: 6). Even when official quality inscription practices are circumvented, new practices are installed. For example, when nurses are expected to register patients' pain scores, some circumvented the system by filling in pain scores without asking patients on the grounds that it would be ridiculous and unprofessional to ask patients about their pain (Wallenburg et al. 2016: 14). This practice did not prevent the scores from being registered and circulated as if nothing was wrong.

Consider also a practice referred to as "buffering." Buffering occurs when managers decide that some scores should only be kept at an institutional level, departmental level, or group level, thus protecting individuals from individual scores (Fochler and de Rijcke 2017). The bibliometric scores at a university department offer an example. Buffering is sometimes seen as an act of care for individual researchers. However, individuals who assume that they produce high scores on the indicator in question might feel that they are making an above-average contribution to the collective pool of recognition attributed to the department. For them, buffering is unfair.

One of the common responses to buffering among these researchers is that they contact their department head or dean to present metrics showing individual achievements and scores. When indicators are publicly available or can be calculated by individuals (which a massive set of data now can), buffering is circumvented, even if managers did not originally intend to use bibliometric data at the individual level. Once individual researchers become active elements in a qualitizing configuration, these "original" intentions are no longer active players. It does not matter that managers have not designed a so-called incentive structure related to individual researchers, because these individual take initiatives themselves.

Researchers are both colleagues and competitors, and the practice of buffering may test their solidarity when some feel they work harder than others and are not recognized enough. If favorable quality inscriptions are available at the individual level, then why not use them. Again, this practice is in contrast to the metrological paradigm, which assumes that purposes rest calmly until purposes and data are neatly coordinated. It is also in contrast to the deliberative model, since no collective discussion takes place before individual action. The configurative model instead suggests that people improvise and make up new purposes if inscriptions are available. Competition can be "pushed downwards" regardless of whether it was intended (Jensen 2011).

Institutional Lock-In

Perhaps paradoxically, quality configurations create ambiguity which requires an answer, which happens to be provided by the configuration itself. This happens, for example, when professionals are asked to document practices which are difficult to measure, and they ask an evaluation machinery to provide lengthy and detailed descriptions of how to do so.

While multiplicity and ambiguity should be acknowledged, quality configurations sometimes become self-fulfilling prophecies, which are institutionally locked-in.

Some actors amplify the constitutive effects of quality inscriptions. Local facilitators or "experts" occasionally use quality inscriptions to enact the imagined reality they desire. For example, when bibliometric measurements define research quality, some self-appointed local "wise men" claim to know what is required to publish in the most prestigious journals. They then train younger scholars according to these ideals even if there is no strong theory explaining why the proposed publication strategy (in terms of research themes, methodologies, and preferred outlets) works better than another and why it should continue to work in the future. A publication strategy aimed at particular journals does not secure publication. In fact, contributions submitted to an excessively prestigious journal may be rejected. Nevertheless, the advice given has had a constitutive influence on research themes, methodologies, and on the notion of what constitutes good research. Through the influence of the local intermediaries, these effects may be much stronger than one might expect based on the quality inscription itself, in case a bibliometric indicator. Again, it is not the indicator as such which does the job. It is its representation and active mobilization inside a quality configuration.

The same is true when local managers enforce particular quality inscriptions through incentives and promotion procedures resulting in an amplification of the constitutive effects stronger than otherwise anticipated.

In some situations, even a contested quality configuration produces inscriptions (e.g. test results in schools) which happen to correlate with some desired outcomes (e.g. final exam results). Even if the test results might be contested, their "predictive value" in relation to outcomes becomes an argument in favor of further institutionalization of the tests.

In some situations, a quality configuration comprises one element which is held in place even if it is clear to everybody who has firsthand knowledge about that element that it cannot be trusted. For example, the response rate in student surveys may be so low that local decision-makers in an educational institution refuse to use them. However, as long as these student surveys are an integral part of a larger accreditation regime, there is no institutional room for discussing them openly. The consequences that would be unleashed by failed accreditation would be too serious. The regime is thus self-sustaining despite its lack of local meaningfulness.

A final, and perhaps most subtle way in which self-perpetuation happens, is related to evaluation of quality inscription systems. An example is an evaluation of a bibliometric system claiming to measure the quantity and quality of research publications. An evaluative finding might be that the amount of quality publications has increased since the introduction of the quality inscription. This effect is unsurprising insofar as the indicator itself has reminded researchers about how their products are measured. During the evaluation, an increase in "quality publications" is measured along dimensions that are defined in the quality inscription, which is itself under evaluation. The definition of quality is thus used once more as the basis for the evaluation of an indicator based on the same definition. The strange form of reflexivity involved here is self-fulling. It does not question the underlying definition of quality. It is not able to reflect upon the value framework which undergirds the quality inscription itself. It only approves of it by once again measuring the movements of a number of objects on scales already defined by the same inscription.

How and whether the given quality inscription stands for quality as such is not problematized. An assessment of the goodness *of* a quality inscription is recirculated *in* the quality inscription to confirm the quality of the quality inscription. A functional moral approval takes place without an explicit judgment. Consequently, the "quality" of the "quality inscription" is confirmed. Its constitutive effect is to consolidate other constitutive effects. It simply proves the merits of a scale in terms of the ability of the scale itself to make objects move along the scale. That is enough to make it a "good" scale. In contemporary terms: Our quality system works. A triumph of performativity.

Despite the ambiguity, multiplicity, and complexity in the operations of quality configurations, they sometimes have the capacity to defend themselves and become more or less self-confirming and self-sustaining.

A Reflection on Moral Judgment

If the above analysis is correct, quality configurations set in motion values, emotions, multiple orders of worth, and ambiguous involvements. Conventional theoretical models are surprisingly primitive in describing the complexities of moral judgment in and of these processes. If quality inscriptions lead to *colonization*, who can doubt that this is not a good thing? If actors are involved in *gaming*, do we not already know their moral quality? When effects are deemed *perverse* or *pathological*, conventional paradigms have already made an early moral judgment. From an analytical viewpoint, it would be better to develop approaches, which do not have such premature, built-in normative biases.

Moreover, moral judgments operate not only as analytical devices but also as active players in quality configurations. For example, managers admit that perhaps quality inscriptions have a few unintended consequences, but the very term unintended works as an assurance that the intentions of managers are good and pure. A clever counter-argument is attributed to the Norwegian historian Anders Johansen talking about a quality indicator: "To relate it to what might follow in practice is a complete misunderstanding….. If people would only learn to ignore the consequences, they would realize that the arrangement is unproblematic" (cited in Jensen 2011: 80).

Sometimes new quality inscription devices are introduced by managers or by quality inscriptors with a reassuring sentence stating that "we are sure that you professionals will maintain a high professional standard and maintain your own good sense of practice while you implement this new quality assurance system." Subordinates are then left in a moral quagmire if they report troublesome constitutive effects of the quality system, because these problems will be taken as evidence of transgressions of their own ethics (Bruno et al. 2014: 206). In a similar vein, professionals are sometimes blamed for tinkering with quality data in their own interest. Perhaps professionals could also be motivated to do so by concerns for their patients, their professional group, their school or other factors (Wallenburg et al. 2016: 12). On their side, professionals can of course also use moral arguments about themselves, about managers, and about quality inscriptions in their argumentation. These arguments, too, can circulate in quality configurations as active players in the formation of stories about heroes and villains, who all claim, from their perspective, that quality is on their side.

The configurative paradigm does not have a strong normative benchmark against which it passes unequivocal moral judgment. It does not have something similar to the metrological insistence on proper measurement or the deliberative insistence on explicit and open collective debate. The configurative perspective does not make direct moral judgments, but it plays with moral judgments and sets them in motion, through responsibilization and counter-responsibilization. These judgments are, in turn, active players in the mobilization of support to some alliances, viewpoints, and positions rather than others. They contribute to the creation of some effects rather than others as well as they regulate the possibility to report on these effects.

Summing Up

Constitutive effects produced according to the configurative style of qualitization do not necessarily have to be unintended, they may or may not work through incentives, they may or may not entice controversy, and they assume neither consensus nor conviction. The configurative style of qualitization works by bringing the elements of a quality configuration together and making them interact. The configurative style of qualitization structures or reconfigures social reality through a multiplicity of connections and pressures into which the actions and reactions of actors are inherently involved and embedded. They do so in a liquid way that allows them to "flow" or "stream" through the cracks between conventional conceptual categories.

Add to this the present positive connotations of quality. Not being in favor of that which can always be presented as the good—no matter what form and shape its inscriptions come in—is not a comfortable position. Critics also run the risk of an ad hominem argument: The reason why you are critical toward this particular quality inscription is that you are unable to deliver quality yourself. The struggles which take place in and around quality configurations are about "quality," but since the concept itself has almost no content and definitely no opposition, and everybody claims to have quality on their side, the concept itself is not a useful key to understanding why quality and the constitutive effects of quality inscriptions become contested.

Nevertheless, constitutive effects do exist. Unless we bury our head in the sand, we should be able to make sense out of the many studies which provide examples. According to the configurative model presented here, the production of constitutive effects of quality inscriptions does not require that objects are measured properly; that effects are intended; nor deliberation about the meaning of quality and the consequences of inscribing quality in one way rather than another. Constitutive effects are produced before, under, over, between, and outside of these categories.

For the advocates of democratic regulation of quality matters in the res publica, however, the above analysis of constitutive effects raises concern. Are constitutive effects also produced before, under, over, between, or outside of forms of democratic control? Does the configurative style of qualitization make *quality without democracy* possible?

References

Arnaboldi, Michela, and Giovanni Azzone. 2010. Constructing Performance Measurement in the Public Sector. *Critical Perspectives on Accounting* 21 (4): 266–282.

Beer, David. 2016. *Metric Power*. London: Palgrave Macmillan.

Boedker, Christina, and Wai Chua. 2013. Accounting as an Affective Technology: A Study of Circulation, Agency and Entrancement. *Accounting, Organizations and Society* 38 (4): 245–267.

Boyte, Harry. 2011. Constructive Politics as Public Work: Organizing the Literature. *Political Theory* 39 (5): 630–660.

Brown, Wendy. 2015. *Undoing the Demos*. New York: Zone Books.

Bruno, Isabelle, Emmanuel Didier, and Tommaso Vitale. 2014. Statactivism. Forms of Action between Disclosure and Affirmation. *Partecipazione e Conflitto* 7 (2): 198–220.

Buzan, Barry, Ole Wæver, and Jaap de Wilde. 1998. *Security: A New Framework for Analysis*. Boulder: Lynne Rienner.

Callon, Michel. 1998. An Essay on Framing and Overflowing: Economic Externalities Revisited by Sociology. In *The Laws of the Markets*, ed. M. Callon, 244–269. Oxford: Blackwell.

Callon, Michel, Cécile Méadel, and Vololona Rabeharisoa. 2002. The Economy of Qualities. *Economy and Society* 31 (2): 194–217.

Cohen, Bernard I. 2006. *The Triumph of Numbers: How Counting Shaped Modern Life*. New York: W. W. Norton.

Dahler-Larsen, Peter. 2013. Constitutive Effects of Performance Indicators: Getting Beyond Unintended Consequences. *Public Management Review* 16 (7): 969–986.

———. 2016. Tæller Vi Det Der Tæller. Målstyring og Standardisering i Arbejdslivet [Do We Count What Counts? Management by Objectives and Standardization in Working Life]. In *Moderne Arbejdsliv*, ed. M.F. Andersen and L. Tanggard, 109–132. Copenhagen: Klim.

Dahler-Larsen, Peter, and Signe Pihl-Thingvad. 2014. *Resultatmålinger og Stress* [Performance Measurement and Stress]. Odense: University Press of Southern Denmark.

Dambrin, Claire, and Keith Robson. 2011. Tracing Performance in the Pharmaceutical Industry: Ambivalence, Opacity and the Performativity of Flawed Measures. *Accounting, Organizations and Society* 36 (7): 428–455.

Dewey, John. 1931. *Philosophy and Civilization*. New York: G. P. Putnam's Sons.

Englund, Hans, and Magnus Frostenson. 2017. Managing Performance Evaluation Uncertainties in Schools: When Teachers Become Struggling Performers. *European Educational Research Journal* (online): 1–22.

Espeland, Wendy N., and Michael Sauder. 2007. Rankings and Reactivity: How Public Measures Recreate Social Worlds. *American Journal of Sociology* 113 (1): 1–40.

Feldman, Martha A., and Wanda Orlikowski. 2011. Theorizing Practice and Practicing Theory. *Organization Science* 22 (5): 1240–1253.

Fochler, Maximilian, and Sarah de Rijcke. 2017. Implicated in the Indicator Game? An Experimental Debate. *Engaging Science, Technology, and Society* 3: 21–40.

Habermas, Jürgen. 1991. *The Structural Transformation of the Public Sphere: An Inquiry into a Category of Bourgeois Society*. Cambridge, MA: The MIT Press.

Hackett, Edward J., Olga Amsterdamska, Michael Lynch, and Judy Wajcman. 2008. *The Handbook of Science and Technology Studies*. Cambridge, MA: The MIT Press.

House, Ernest R., and Kenneth R. Howe. 2000. Deliberative Democratic Evaluation. *New Directions for Evaluation* 85: 3–12.

Jensen, Casper Bruun. 2011. Making Lists, Enlisting Scientists: The Bibliometric Indicator, Uncertainty and Emergent Agency. *Science Studies* 24 (2): 64–84.

Kelman, Steven, and John N. Friedman. 2009. Performance Improvement and Performance Dysfunction: An Empirical Examination of Distortionary Impacts of the Emergency Room Wait-Time Target in the English National Health Service. *Journal of Public Administration Research and Theory* 19 (4): 917–946.

Lamont, Michèle. 2009. *How Professors Think: Inside the Curious World of Academic Judgment*. Cambridge, MA: Harvard University Press.

Latour, Bruno. 1987. *Science in Action: How to Follow Scientists and Engineers through Society*. Stony Stratford: Open University Press.

Meyer, John W., and Brian Rowan. 1977. Institutionalized Organizations: Formal Structure as Myth and Ceremony. *American Journal of Sociology* 83: 340–363.

Moe, Terry M. 2005. Power and Political Institutions. *Perspectives on Politics* 3 (2): 215–233.

Moed, Henk. 2018. Towards a Multi-Paradigmatic, Value Free Informetrics: A Reply to Paul Wouters' Book Review "The Failure of a Paradigm". *Journal of Informetrics*. https://doi.org/10.1016/j.joi.2018.03.003.

Mortensen, Nils. 2004. *Det Paradoksale Samfund* [The Paradoxical Society]. Copenhagen: Hans Reitzel.

Mouritzen, P.E., Niels Opstrup, and Pernille Bak Pedersen. 2018. *En fremmed kommer til byen. Ti år med den bibliometriske forskningsindikator* [*A Stranger Comes to Town. Ten Years with the Bibliometric Research Indicator*]. Odense: University of Southern Denmark Press.

Øvretveit, John. 2005. Public Service Quality Improvement. In *The Oxford Handbook of Public Management*, ed. E. Ferlie, L.E. Lynn Jr., and C. Pollitt. New York: Oxford University Press.

Palonen, Kari. 2002. The History of Concepts as a Style of Political Theorizing: Quentin Skinner's and Reinhart Koselleck's Subversion of Normative Political Theory. *European Journal of Political Theory* 1 (1): 91–106.

Pinch, Trevor J., and Wiebe E. Bijker. 1984. The Social Construction of Facts and Artefacts: Or How the Sociology of Science and the Sociology of Technology Might Benefit Each Other. *Social Studies of Science* 14 (3): 399–441.

Pollock, Neil, Luciana D'Adderio, Robin Williams, and Ludovic Leforestier. 2018. Conforming or Transforming? How Organizations Respond to Multiple Rankings. *Accounting, Organizations and Society* 64: 55–68.

Porter, Theodore M. 1994. Making Things Quantitative. *Science in Context* 7 (3): 389–407.

———. 1995. *Trust in Numbers: The Pursuit of Objectivity in Science and Public Life*. Princeton: Princeton University Press.

Power, Michael. 1996. Making Things Auditable. *Accounting, Organizations and Society* 21 (2/3): 289–315.

Roberts, John. 2018. Managing Only with Transparency: The Strategic Functions of Ignorance. *Critical Perspectives on Accounting* 55: 53–60.

Säljö, Roger. 2002. My Brain's Running Slow Today. *Studies in Philosophy and Education* 21: 389–405.

Sauder, Michael, and Wendy N. Espeland. 2009. The Discipline of Rankings: Tight Coupling and Organizational Change. *American Sociological Review* 74 (1): 63–82.

Schwandt, Thomas A. 1994. Constructivist, Interpretivist Approaches to Human Inquiry. In *Handbook of Qualitative Research*, ed. N. Denzin and Y. Lincoln, 118–137. Thousand Oaks: Sage.

Scott, W. Richard. 1992. *Organizations. Rational, Natural and Open Systems*. Englewood Cliffs: Prentice-Hall.

Shore, Cris, and Susan Wright. 2015. Governing by Numbers: Audit Culture, Rankings and the New World Order. *Social Anthropology* 23 (1): 22–28.

Smith, Peter. 1995. On the Unintended Consequences of Publishing Performance Data in the Public Sector. *International Journal of Public Administration* 18 (2–3): 277–310.

Stark, David. 2009. *The Sense of Dissonance, Accounts of Worth in Economic Life*. Princeton: Princeton University Press.

Stilgoe, Jack, Richard Owen, and Phil Macnaghten. 2013. Developing a Framework for Responsible Innovation. *Research Policy* 42: 1568–1580.

van Thiel, Sandra, and Frans L. Leeuw. 2002. The Performance Paradox in the Public Sector. *Public Performance and Management Review* 25 (3): 267–281.

Vattimo, Gianni. 2005. *Nihilisme og Emancipation. Etik, Politik, Ret* [Nihilsm and Emancipation. Ethics, Politics, and Law]. Aarhus: Aarhus University Press.

Venturini, Tommaso. 2010. Diving in Magma: How to Explore Controversies with Actor–Network Theory. *Public Understanding of Science* 19 (3): 258–273.

Wallenburg, Iris, Julia Quartz, and Roland Bal. 2016. Making Hospitals Governable: Performativity and Institutional Work in Ranking Practices. *Administration & Society*: 1–27.

Weick, Karl E. 1995. *Sensemaking in Organizations*. Thousand Oaks: Sage.

Wouters, Paul. 2018. Book Review: The Failure of a Paradigm. Henk F. Moed. Applied Evaluative Informetrics. *Journal of Informetrics* 12 (2): 534–540.

6

Quality Without Democracy

This chapter analyzes the sociopolitical implications of quality. My assertion is that *we live in times where quality without democracy is becoming increasingly pertinent.*

Let it first be said that qualitization without democracy in *some* contexts and with *some* objects is not a problem. Remember, however, that the quality discourse has invaded the public arena. It encompasses the *res publica*. It describes hospitals, schools, health care, research, infrastructure, governance, our definition of the good life, and almost all other domains of public interest. In some situations, evaluative assessments of individuals can merely be added up. In other situation, a formula for collective judgment is required (Julnes 2012).

The latter is the case for res publica, which is why democracy is important in relation to qualitization. A society that is unable to tackle the problems of the res publica in a way where these problems are understood as inherently *democratic* may in fact lose the capacity to deal with its own matters and take its own destiny in its own hands (Rosanvallon 2009). When the practice of evaluation was invented, it saw itself as embedded in a democratic policy (Dahler-Larsen 2006; Vedung 1997). Evaluation was conceived as an instrument serving the larger purpose of the collective mastery of political existence. Brown (2015: 221) claims that we live in

P. Dahler-Larsen, *Quality*, https://doi.org/10.1007/978-3-030-10392-7_6

times where this very idea is being abandoned. Therefore, quality without democracy is concerning.

In order to identify which forms of qualitization perhaps take place outside of democratic contexts, let me outline two well-known types of legitimate democracy: "government" and "governance." I will describe these two regimes, use them as yardsticks, and then discuss where the metrological, deliberative, and configurative models of qualitization fit. The purpose is not to give "correct" descriptions of government and governance, but merely to establish two democratic yardsticks against which present forms of qualitization can be assessed.

I intend to show that configurative forms of qualitization are particularly problematic in a democratic perspective because they produce constitutive effects that are capable of escaping both of the sets of criteria for democratic legitimacy offered by these two ideal democratic regimes.

Government and Governance

In a system of legitimate democracy called "government," all power comes from the people. Elections and representation secure legitimate government. All legitimate decisions are made within a parliamentary chain of control, meaning that all actions by professionals take place within the limits of what managers ask them to do, and everything that managers do takes place within the limits of what is defined by government.

Regulation takes place with reference to law. The law is hard in the sense that it is backed by sanctions that only the state can impose. Monitoring at various levels secures the integrity of the parliamentary chain of control. The regulators are well defined. Only those regulators (e.g. auditors or inspectors) who are mandated by official legislation and are part of the official government structure (or work on a contract with government) have a legitimate role to play. In that sense, there is a clear distinction between what is legitimate and what not.

Any evaluative approach to public interventions follows the same lines: Evaluation begins with a determination of official political goals. These goals constitute the basis for evaluative criteria. For an exemplary spokesman of this approach, see Vedung (1997).

There is also a role for deliberation. The opposition, a free press, and citizens in general have the right to discuss openly all of the decisions and policies enacted by the government. They also have the right to discuss whether an alternative government would be better. Deliberation is a necessary supplement to democratic institutions. Free press, active intellectuals, and lively public debate are preconditions for the kind of deliberation necessary to keep government on its toes.

Now let us turn to the governance model. Here, deliberation is not a supplement but rather a primary principle. The modes of regulation are soft laws (guidelines, recommendations, agreements) together with indicators, standards, and benchmarks. None of these principles are binding. They are renegotiated and calibrated through dialogue. A great variety of public and private actors participate in governance and maintain their autonomy and identity while so doing.

Governance networks "aim to mobilize the knowledge, resources and energies of free and responsible citizens, civil society organizations, local public agencies and private firms aiming to govern themselves on the basis of narratives, objectives, standards and benchmarks" (Sørensen and Torfing 2009: 238).

By mobilizing these diverse resources, by securing commitment to collective endeavors as well as continued coordination, governance networks have strong functional advantages compared to governments, especially when issues are complex, and social and political environments are dynamic.

The legitimacy of their collective endeavor, however, hinges on ongoing deliberation. In the absence of hard law, the acceptability of governance as a democratic principle rests on the active consent of the participants. In addition, the continued deliberation in the governance network helps channel all of the relevant knowledge and experiences held by network members into collective decisions. It also secures a maximum degree of cooperation needed for the smooth implementation of the chosen solutions, at least in principle (Sørensen and Torfing 2009).

Also the evaluation of governance activities and outcomes adheres to the principle of deliberation. Evaluation questions and evaluative criteria are determined through a process that is both participatory and reflexive. It takes into account criteria both internal and external to the network itself. That requires an evaluation report which is "written democratically" and open to scrutiny. Even more importantly, the evaluation process itself is an exercise in deliberation. For an exemplary spokesman of this approach to evaluation, see Kushner (2017).

Some are skeptical about such networks, particularly because they include self-selected groups of stakeholders at the expense of non-privileged members of society. The lack of inclusiveness in networks thus poses a problem. Others find networks to be sites of democratic discussion and inter-discourse contestation (Sørensen and Torfing 2009). It is exactly the deliberation that enables the inclusion of the governance network in a typology of *ideal* models of *legitimate* democracy. The ideal types in Table 6.1, however, describe regimes of democracy at their best. Their philosophical underpinnings, their normative overtones (Sørensen and Torfing 2009), and the connection between them in real polities could be discussed further. However, it suffices to reiterate only one point in the simple typology offered here: Deliberation plays a key role in both ideal forms of democracy. Although the role of deliberation is not the same in the two regimes, none of the two would be legitimate without it.

Seen from the perspective of legitimate forms of democracy, what is new in qualitization? The new does not so much lie in the metrological and the deliberative forms of qualitization.

Table 6.1 Government and governance

	Government	Governance
Principles of legitimacy	Primary principles: Representation. Parliamentary chain of control. Secondary principle: Deliberation	Deliberation
Modes of regulation	Hard law	Soft law, rules, indicators, standards, dialogue
Regulators	Managers and specialists with a formal mandate	Public and private actors in a variety of roles
Appropriate evaluative approach	Goal-based evaluation	A deliberative process with evolving evaluative criteria

Sources: Own construction inspired by Mörth (2008) and Vedung (1997)

A classical democratic government regime with a clear chain of control often authorizes metrological specialists to solve particular tasks. Legal and political mandates, as well as specific terms of references for specific committees, regulate the space within which metrology can operate. These forms of operation are historically known in the form of statistics, but they continue with a variety of specialized experts in econometrics, psychometrics, and so on. The open debate which complements the official structure of government provides a space in which metrology is subject to scrutiny. The expert may here play a humble role, depending on his/her good argument and the power to convince.

Under a governance regime, deliberation is a key principle rather than a supplement. Experts may be invited to play a consulting role rather than take a starting point in an official, authoritative position. While the tension between knowledge and values, between politics and science, and the role of uncertainty continue to be debatable, these issues are not unknown. There is a literature on issues related to the use of expertise in democracies and the use of scientific knowledge in decision-making (Bauman 1987; Pielke 2007; Prewitt et al. 2012).

In a similar way, a democratic form of government can also allow controlled forms of deliberation. Spaces are carved out within a government structure where experts and others deliberate within boundaries defined by policies, rules, terms of references for committees, and so on. Other examples are scientific councils working for government, advisory boards, or focus groups consisting of citizens, which provide feedback on government policies. Furthermore, deliberations about quality also take place in the arena of an open society and subject government decisions, policies, and evaluation regimes to critical scrutiny. The known weaknesses in deliberative processes (too time-demanding, not action-oriented) are kept under control since deliberation is only a supplement to government.

Deliberations are also already inherent in complex structures of governance. There are debatable issues, such as how to identify the appropriate set of participants in a given deliberative process, how a qualitizing network deliberates about the criteria necessary in its self-evaluation; how deliberative qualitization is distinct from deliberation in general; and how a network concerned with quality engages in deliberation with other networks concerned with other things in society. Still, by definition, there is no fundamental reason why qualitization according to the deliberative model cannot be seen as democratic and normal within democratic regimes, as long as deliberation is not circumvented. Yet, the weaknesses of deliberation are ever-present. It assumes that there is endless time and that action can wait.

But this is precisely where the configurative model of qualitization has a new, powerful, yet problematic potential. A genuine and socio-historically unprecedented problem lies in capacity of the configurative style of qualitization to produce massive constitutive effects, which escape the forms of democratic control known from both government and governance, respectively. The two following sections unfold this argument in further detail in relation to government and governance, respectively.

How Qualitization According to the Configurative Model Challenges Democratic Government

Let us first consider the argument that quality is an important notion in contemporary policymaking and governments sometimes do in fact use qualitization (including qualitization according to the configurative model) as a policy instrument. Examples could be testing in schools or hospital accreditation systems, which both require the smooth operation of complex quality configurations. Politicians do want quality, both implicitly and explicitly. They propose quality reforms and claim that their policies will enhance the quality of schools, hospitals, and other institutions, if not the quality of life.

However, they do so in a discursive mode in which "most political parties can find an element in it that they like and can promote" (Bache and Reardon 2016: 154). The beauty of quality as an element in political rhetoric is that it is always positive. It is even capable of "sucking up" various types of problems (notice how different quality perspectives capture different understandings of underlying problems). All governments commit to quality, and competing political parties all stand for quality; they just want to deliver better quality than the others. Ever-positive quality makes political differences less visible, and qualitization often amounts to depolitization.

Depolitization is sometimes politically convenient. For example, if a minister of education uses an international assessment of school quality to put pressure on schools, the minister can make a powerful political argument without taking responsibility for either the standard-setting (e.g. the quality perspective, the quality inscription), or the implementation of local quality work. It would be naïve to assume that shrewd politicians do not play such games. In our terminology, they would then be (political) agents in a qualitization network that seeks to amplify its constitutive effects. But this is a game they do not fully control. Sometimes international quality comparisons hit a minister of education like a boomerang and endanger his/her political life when he or she is blamed for poor national scores. In other words, politicians may seek benefits from interacting with quality configurations, but they do not totally control the game.

The constitutive effects of qualitization move through time and space in their own complex ways. While the term "unintended effects" is well-known in political and administrative circles, there is often a lack of interest about unintended effects of indicators upon the school system, for example.

The main political interest might lie in demonstrating the power and capacity to set quality control in motion—and less in understanding the practical consequences of these demands (Kauko et al. 2018). The conventional hierarchical structure of governance with a parliamentary chain of control might be unfit to receive and process that kind of complex feedback from the field (Morgan 1986: 36). Most conventional notions of managerialism also assume a form of control that does not resonate well with the complex, dynamic, and non-linear ways in which effects are produced in quality configurations. We cannot assume that managers "manage" constitutive effects of quality configurations. Networks change their form and shape dynamically. Different kinds of actors, including short-term consultants, enter and leave the configurations.

The political capacity to fundamentally reform what is meant by quality in an official government system is limited to taking into account the massive amount of qualitization that takes place in society and taking into account the diverse and complex character of constitutive effects. Direct government control, including responsibility for constitutive effects, is the exception rather than the rule. At the very best, constitutive effects of qualitization are under very limited government control. Even if governments sometimes have a genuine interest in revising policies which demonstrably have dramatic constitutive effects, governments are in a reactive role vis-à-vis quality inscriptions rather than a proactive one.

In some instances, governments do not define quality, and it is unclear who has the authority to do so. When there is a commitment in politics to a particular definition of quality, it is often a form of quality already circulating in large-scale networks and configurations. Many inscriptors of quality are international ones located outside national chains of parliamentary control. Although some are sanctioned by governments, they also have the capacity to operate in a semiautonomous way, such as the OECD which issues reports and recommendations which are not approved by national governments.

Inscriptors reside in "centers of calculation" that are network-based, sometimes totally or partly private, and often international. They are often not subject to government control. Even if governments in OECD countries can be proven to have authorized particular forms of evaluative inquiry into say, the quality of schools, the exact link is not part of any public understanding of transparent government and not under frequent democratic scrutiny. Moreover, OECD statistics are not issued in the name of the governments representing the member states.

The quality inscriptors (e.g. the OECD and credit rating agencies [CRAs] in our examples) are not subject to conventional mechanisms of legal and political accountability. In cases where CRAs are sued, they claim to operate under freedom of expression and bear no legal responsibility. The point is not (only) that quality inscriptors are beyond government control but, furthermore, as a consequence, that the line between politics and qualitizing networks becomes blurred. In sum, a conventional hierarchical steering model of society with government on the top is not consistent with the new realities in which quality configurations operate.

International quality inscriptors establish quality zones which are much larger than government jurisdictions. More often than not, national governments are seen as players in a global competition. This is exemplified by the prominence of global excellence (e.g. research excellence) as a political objective unto itself. Forms of qualitization which homogenize practices within a larger quality zone are often claiming to be unpolitical (Brown 2015: 139). It is merely assumed that everybody within the quality zone has the same goals, such as competitive advantage (Brown 2015: 137). Acceptance of such "common goals" has more or less become a prerequisite for participating in mainstream policymaking (Ozga et al. 2011). In other words, international qualitization defines the parameters for policymaking as much as the other way around.

In Wendy Brown's (2015) more radical interpretation, conventional liberal democracies have transformed themselves into tools for neoliberal agendas. As a consequence, the notion of a liberal democratic policy can no longer be mobilized as a normative bulwark against market logics. An institutional source of democratic inspiration is thereby lost (Brown 2015: 208).

The most radical transformation of the relation between qualitization and democratic government is perhaps found when responsibilization hits governments themselves. They are constituted as quality agents which are held accountable for their own quality work. A striking example is the falling credit ratings of some nations, which led the presidents of otherwise powerful nations (e.g. France) to complain. In a global economy, conventional structures of power and legitimacy are changing. Constitutive effects of qualitization (e.g. the qualitization of government bonds in relation to a market) contribute to this change. In the example from South Africa, notice how Minister of Finance Gordhan had already paid respect to the concerns of CRAs as he prepared the next year's budget. Notice also how a representative from a CRA interfered quite directly in party politics in this country. We see an inverse power distribution between nations and inscriptors compared to what you would expect in a government-based regime. In globalized networks, states are sometimes victims (Ahrne and Brunsson 2008: 82). They are subject to qualitization rather than its master.

In sum, qualitization according to the configurative model extends beyond or even undermines conventional models of democratic government. Definitions of quality are sometimes beyond government control, the authority to define quality is unclear, control is indirect, invisible, or absent, effects of qualitization are complex and not under control, and the fundamental relation between politics and qualitization is sometimes turned around.

Next, let us turn to how qualitization according to the configurative model may or may not fit into the model of democracy denoted by the term governance.

How Qualitization According to the Configurative Model Challenges Democratic Governance

Remember that the primary principle here is not government control but rather the process of deliberation among a plurality of actors involved in governance. There are a number of reasons why the configurative style of qualitization is not regulated by or responsive to deliberation.

First, configurations extend far in time and space. Their totality is often unknown to participants who, as far as they can see, are only connected to the network of actors in a few particular nodes. People who buy bonds may not know who makes the credit ratings and/or how they operate. They may not know the imprint put on these bonds by CRAs. Experts operating in international organizational fields produce organizational recipes but are not accountable for their operational consequences (Strang and Meyer 1994). Parts of the quality configurations that make qualitization possible are therefore often unresponsive to (conventional) democratic accountability or are more or less invisible; they are visible only in other parts of the quality configuration in the form of the traces they leave in quality inscriptions that travel through time and space. Sometimes they make only "half a decision" because they produce a quality inscription but they are not on the scene when it is up to others to do quality work as a consequence (Brunsson 2000).

Teachers who are dissatisfied with Programme for International Students Assessment (PISA) results may not know who produced them, and if yes, how to contact the OECD and file a complaint. Even if national governments stand behind the OECD, OECD publications contain a standard clause describing how OECD statistics are made independently and not in the name of national governments. This gives the OECD a particular "freedom to inscribe," but it also gives the OECD a status in the quality configuration that is unconventional compared to conventional structures of political accountability. The invited educational experts who helped infuse the notion of evaluation culture into the school system in Denmark were only in the country for a few days. Their effects lasted for years. The OECD is not subject to an adequate deliberative process. Assume that teachers who wish to complain about the consequences of PISA decide to write a letter to the editor of their favorite newspaper. It would appear in a national language, and the OECD personnel are unlikely to read it. There is no common language in the large international quality zone demarcated by PISA, and no common critical public. In addition, the relevant OECD specialists have probably moved on to other tasks.

The configurative style of qualitization circumvents democratic deliberation because the constitutive effects it produces move too swiftly through time and space. Messages about quality reach quality agents much faster through the processes, networks, and connections associated with the constitutive effects of qualitization than they would if they were all subject to democratic deliberation. Deliberation presupposes an identifiable set of participants and a common understanding of binding rules if not a sense of community and shared destiny. A forum for deliberation is also needed. The requirements of deliberation are demanding in terms of proximity, capacity, attention, and time.

Quality configurations operate without such narrow restrictions and are therefore functionally superior when it comes to swift movement. Although quality inscriptions sometimes require large, complicated machineries (Dahler-Larsen 2012), once the machineries are in place, they produce quality inscriptions and sends them across large spaces rapidly. When they reach quality agents, qualitization is a *fait accompli. Quality agents are interpellated to step up and do quality work according to perspectives and criteria they might not have had a chance to think about or deliberate on.*

The quality inscription is already there. Quality inscriptors often choose quality inscriptions that afford easy codification and quantification. In turn, quality inscriptions that are (apparently) easy to read and understand (e.g. rankings) are favored (Normand 2016: 13). The movement through time and space of quality inscriptions and a quick format of both production and consumption of quality inscriptions are enforcing each other. Similarly, the contemporary spirit of evaluation systems and machineries for the production of quality inscriptions is that they should be continuous in time rather than appearing in discrete moments. Clearly, they gain temporal advantages if they are ever-present (on-line).

Rosa (2003) offers a theory of social acceleration. Acceleration implies changes in the decay rates of experience and a contraction of timespans defined as the present. His theory of acceleration makes sense in relation to quality inscriptions traveling rapidly. Quality inscriptions abbreviate the distance to the future by transforming concrete experience with diverse quality situations into standardized inscriptions and by calling upon quality actors to foreclose initiatives to improve their quality scores, knowing that others are already on the move.

Rosa (2005) explains how timeframes and failing democracy are connected. At a certain point in history, democracy itself set the pace for political change. Now, however, the dynamic forces of society, including globalized networks, functionally circumvent democratic political *self-determination* (Rosa 2005: 450).

Deliberation is simply not fast enough in an accelerated society. The problem is not merely the practical embeddedness in time and space of infrastructures for deliberation (e.g. people actually having to meet) and the fact that the deliberative process itself takes time. The very formation of will also requires time to mature (Rosa 2005). For example, raising children and instilling values in professionals requires years of socialization. In a similar vein, there is an upper limit to how much the democratic reconfiguration of values can be accelerated.

There is an "eigentime" in human beings as political animals, which presumably explains why there is a deeper truth hidden in the critique of many contemporary forms of qualitization in the configurative style:

"But we never had the time to sit down and discuss this!" There was neither invitation, occasion, nor time to deliberate, to reflect. Nor was there sufficient time to consider new values. If values change slowly, constitutive effects upon practices operate more effectively through inscriptions, inspirations, nudging, pressures, and imitation rather than through deliberation. Constitutive effects move faster and find ways to move fluidly through cracks in the social fabric. The Internet plus nudging is more powerful and faster than deliberation plus the change of convictions.

In Rosa's view, the imagination of the new temporal order is itself a strong, normative force. Acceleration is also sometimes a self-fulfilling prophecy. An accelerated society incorporates its own endogenous logics to enhance acceleration. Similar patterns can be found in constitutive effects of qualitization. One of the ways to influence reality is to install new quality inscriptions, which may lead to more ways in which quality can be encoded, more connection points, and more confusion and unclarity, which may in turn enhance the need for new inscriptions that compensate for the weaknesses in earlier models and call for an overall, integrative model of quality. In the meantime, people should reflect and strategize and thus in fact create the kind of future they are warned about.

A questioning of the temporal and acceleratory compulsions governing modern society is called for (Rosa 2005: 455), since they are antithetical to autonomy (Rosa 2005: 456). This kind of questioning is made difficult when qualitization separates human beings into fragmented roles situated in quality configurations. Actors take part in qualitization in the capacity of experts, inscriptors, managers of quality objects, users of quality inscriptions, consumers, and so on. Quality configurations set these character masks up against each other (as e.g. providers and consumers of quality products and services). They do not recognize conventional political and democratic concepts such as "citizens." They render invisible the common destiny of the actors as participants in a deliberative community. Conventional roles such as teacher–student are reconfigured. While qualitization might well sometimes help dismantle conventional authoritarian patterns in such conventional roles, as when the teacher is subject to anonymous student evaluation, the juxtaposition of the teacher against anonymous voices is not conducive to a deliberative process leading to collective responsibility for better education. The configurative style of qualitizing connects actors into a network, but they are already thereby interpellated into specific, fragmented roles. Experts are interpellated as quality specialists who are called in to give specific technical advice, but are not asked to question the formation of quality configurations, their constitutive effects, and social implications. Producers are held accountable for "quality." Students are asked to participate in something similar to "customer satisfaction surveys."

On top of all this, qualitizing a phenomenon means dismantling opposition. The ever-present positive connotations of quality contribute to the rapid, unreflected impact of qualitization. As a speech act, qualitization builds on the assumption that no meaningful opposition can be formed. Qualitization sets a stage upon which only actors cooperating to measure, reflect on, and improve quality can act, because no one can deny the inherent goodness of quality. Qualitization assumes that everyone must be on the side of the good, and it requires all who speak for the good to express themselves through the term quality. Potentially, qualitization thereby reduces the kind of plurality of the common good that might otherwise be explored in democratic deliberation (Normand 2016: 17).

Quality is formed in the networks and associations characteristic of the configurative model. The handling of problematic aspects of qualitization, especially designing measurements and inscriptions, are usually delegated away from the visible political scene. While quantification may connote "objective" and "standardized" measurement—and in that sense "a move toward a more public form of knowledge" (Porter 1994: 389)—the social configuration that would presumably sustain that kind of knowledge production would be one that facilitates public deliberation. This would require time, social arenas, and public access to the same debatable knowledge. The configurative model works through networks that are organized in a different way. They transmit knowledge rapidly; not all of the agents enrolled in the network know all of the other nodes in the network; the measurement arrives as a *fait accompli* rather than an object for discussion. And the constitutive consequences are sometimes incorporated into the very operation of the network. When the need for debate becomes apparent, effects have already been produced.

In conclusion, while metrological and deliberative forms of qualitization have identifiable roles and functions that fit into various democratic regimes, the kind of qualitization that takes place according to the configurative model is in dissonance with democratic legitimacy. Since the early days of evaluation, evaluators have believed that democracy provided the necessary normative foundation for evaluative work. Qualitization has now taken on a socio-historic form where it operates smoothly without being dependent on democracy. This change in imaginary regarding the overarching purposes of evaluative work (now qualitization) is quite parallel to what Wendy Brown describes as abandonment of the project of collective mastery of political existence (Brown 2015: 221).

So even after considering counterarguments, *quality without democracy* is a phenomenon to be concerned about.

Consequences of Quality Without Democracy

The consequences of qualitization are particularly problematic when they escape both deliberation and government control. As described above, qualitization in the configurative style was particularly prone to do so.

Does the choice of model for qualitization have any consequences for choices of quality perspectives? This is a particularly pressing question, as this style of qualitization is particularly capable of operating without the kind of legitimacy bestowed by democracy.

The metrological model presumably has an elective affinity with the goals perspective, the impact perspective, the standards perspective, the excellence perspective (insofar as clear rankings are measurable), and a user perspective (but only insofar as user responses can be quantified; e.g. in user satisfaction questionnaires). The metrological model is less sympathetic to quality perspectives such as those based on expert judgment or practice, since these perspectives are usually difficult to operationalize into quantifiable scores.

Deliberation and curiosity are necessary in order to discover the complexity and multidimensional meanings associated with quality. The deliberative model therefore has a familiar relation to the quality perspectives described as expert judgment and quality as practice. Both see quality as situation-bound and context-specific. Both see quality as inherently linked with attention, care, and interpretation.

In contradistinction, where the configurative style of qualitization reigns, some of the preferred quality perspectives will be quality as standards, quality as excellence (in the form of rankings), and quality as organizational recipe. This is because the codification of these perspectives facilitate the transportation of quality through time and space particularly well (in contradistinction to, say, experts who must be personally available, goals which must be hooked up with political legitimacy, and practice which is particularly situated and context-bound).

Again, these delineations are presumptive and tentative, although they do suggest that if the social preconditions for each of the three styles of qualitization are changing, the likelihood that particular quality perspectives will dominate is also going to change. In a broad, socio-historical light, these forces altogether may help explain why quality as standards, quality as excellence, and quality as organizational management recipes thrive, whereas perspectives dependent on situated, local conciliation and afterthought are pushed to the periphery of society's radar.

This observation is consistent with analyses of the increasing role of transnational regulation and with the view of a world designed in the way that organizations shape social order by means of abstraction. Many actors, situations, and problems are increasingly believed to be essentially the same or to belong to the same category regardless of their local setting (Ahrne and Brunsson 2008: 85; Strang and Meyer 1994). Another way of saying this is that organizational machinery is in place which helps quality inscriptions create ever larger quality zones.

Furthermore, with more and more entities defined as "organizations," the number of followers and the coverage in time and space of qualitization increases (Ahrne and Brunsson 2008: 85). Qualitization as standards, as organizational recipe, and as excellence is particularly compatible with this trend. The latter even by definition suggests that the whole world is one quality zone in which global competition takes place.

These changes are noteworthy because qualitization in the configurative style is particularly problematic in a democratic light. One of the strongest contributions of this style of qualitization might be the transportation of issues of quality from conventional political hierarchies into alternative social forums, such as markets and networks (Normand 2016: 10). These social forums operate faster than political systems (Rosa 2003: 24). The easy transportation and consumption of quality is itself such a structuring force. Part of this structuring force lies in the formation and juxtaposition of roles such as producers, consumers, and inscriptors of quality into a productive quality configuration. It is a way of changing a social order.

What are the further implications of this change? The "content" of qualitization cannot be separated from its social form. The formation of a particular quality configuration is a "societizing" move in itself; paradoxically, however, it does not make society visible. Qualitization separates actors into fragmented roles positioned in a quality configuration. The subsequent tensions and effects are shaped by character masks in a manner similar to what is known from markets (Bowbrick 2014).

Is there a particular set of ideas or an ideology that is promoted as part of quality without democracy? In the following, I will make the case that there is currently a particular affinity between quality and *neoliberalism.*

A determinism between qualitization and a particular ideological formation should not be exaggerated. Quality is a vague, multidimensional concept that has connected itself with different sets of ideas over more than 2000 years, even if there are also interesting continuities under the surface. The semasiological analysis undertaken in this book does not trace one particular ideology, but instead the concept of quality. Quality sometimes finds an ally in numbers. One of the functions of numbers and measurement was formerly to reduce the element of human subjectivity in commerce and science. This is an idea much in alignment with rationalism. More recently, numbers also play an important role in New Public Management (NPM). Now, contemporary and dominant forms of quality have remarkable overlaps with neoliberalism.

However, the main problem with identifying quality (in its present form) with a particular ideological agenda is that it will too often be interpreted as if qualitization then by definition has one particular ideological "outcome" (to which quality agents are merely victims). This reservation resonates with Bevir (2004: 617), who observes that too many contemporary sociological accounts claim an almost occult relationship between an overarching concept or process and its all too well-known consequences. According to Bevir, even poststructuralists claiming to respect contingency and particularity sometimes fall into the trap of analyzing an idea or discourse as if it were a quasi-structure operating as a totalizing concept. Ideological baggage in particular forms of quality documentation should be studied, not merely assumed (Kipnis 2008).

One of the strengths of quality as a concept, proven through history, is its ability to "suck up" a variety of ideas and values. Ideologies permeate notions of quality but do so flexibly, and they involve actors, sometimes with all of their creativity and capacity to react, reflect, and find both loopholes and new solutions (as we know from both ANT and practice studies) (Wallenburg et al. 2016). Various institutions and experts also promote types of quality inscriptions, such as those compatible with, say, quality as utility or quality as impacts as consistent with "what is needed today." They also seek cross-cutting alliances with users or specialists interested in organizational recipes. In these alliances, there can be an ambiguous mix of psychological, economic, and messianic elements, such as those found in discourses on "quality of life." Quality can be used in a critique of capitalism, but capitalism is also very quick to come up with goods, communication, new lifestyles, and organizational reforms offering promising ways into the future that disarm such criticism. Capitalism has displayed a remarkable capacity to digest criticism (Boltanski and Chiapello 2007). Criticism is polyvalent in its consequences.

On this background, it is prudent to keep an eye on the role of ideology, but not to assume a single, unified ideological teleology in all inscriptions of quality. For example, the place of neoliberal ideology in inspection regimes may have been exaggerated (Kipnis 2008). Many types of regimes use inspection as a disciplinary tool.

In the present context, neoliberalism should not be identified with a very narrow school of thought in economic theory nor does an analysis of neoliberalism require assumptions about how a few economists conspired so that their ideas could rule a global political movement (Mirowski 2016: 35). Neoliberalism is itself a polysemic term. It is a "loose and shifting signifier," describing both schemes for valuation and the conduct of conduct in relation to those schemes (Brown 2015: 20). Most of its social manifestations do not explicitly occur under the label neoliberalism.

The term itself has sometimes been abandoned in order to promote the sociopolitical agenda it represents (Mirowski 2016: 41).

Neoliberalism can perhaps be understood as a form of "generalized normativity" (Jensen and Olsen 2016: 18). There is a particular logic in the sociopolitical development of neoliberalism that helps us understand important aspects of quality as it appears today. This relates to the transformation of the res publica.

In principle, the common good is intangible; it is the object of much imagination. The fact that it can be imagined, however, is an important constitutive principle of a democratic society.

An important debate occurred among economists in the 1920s and 1930s. Could the common good be expressed in terms of an economic calculation? The socialist regimes were criticized for being irrational since they believed in economic planning to accomplish this goal. Economists with (neo)-liberal inclinations had to devise counterarguments. One of these counterarguments relates to the lack of commensurability between the preferences of different individuals. There is a lack of an algorithm in planning that can boil down subjective preferences into one collectively binding social choice. As an alternative, of course, the market can do so through demand, supply, prices, free commerce, and so forth if only consumer sovereignty reigns.

Another problem relates to the epistemic limitations of centralized planning. There is not enough calculative power to gather all of the necessary information (Jensen 2016: 77) and, furthermore, in a complex and dynamic society, fluctuations cannot be represented quickly enough in any central center of calculation. The market, however, is constantly processing the necessary information in terms of supply, demand, and prices. Competition, the dissemination of information, and making sense of it all are integrated into the neoliberal vision of the market (Jensen 2016: 81). Neoliberal thinking thus made a lasting contribution by (1) de-mystifying the notion of the common good and (2) replacing it as far as possible by a vision of a market with a multitude of sovereign consumers.

Breaking up quality objects into quantifiable parts and dimensions and making them comparable and interchangeable is ontologically very much in line with modern instrumental mentality in general (Berger et al. 1973) as well as with the economistic understanding of the common good. *What present forms of qualitization share with the neoliberal agenda in particular is the fragmentation of imaginaries of the common good.* It also shares a mentality that focuses on quantifications: more, faster, better, higher.

In lieu of the common good, neoliberalism redefines res publica in terms of inscriptions, rankings, comparisons, and so on. Qualitization is societizing in a particular way, which paradoxically sometimes makes society invisible. As Bauman (2002) reminds us, the term "society" is itself a metaphor for a common destiny among a group of people. Bauman points out that the particular social conditions necessary for fulfilling the promise of autonomy are withering away. Modernity has become fluid (Bauman 2000). Solid institutions are "melting," as is personal character (Sennett 2002). The character masks of the market, including that of the consumer, have become reified and turned into "autotelic" ideologies themselves (e.g. consumerism) (Bauman 1983).

At the same time, society becomes difficult to imagine. With networks and global connectivities, the interfaces between individuals and the social forces shaping their lives become complex. Causal links and their moral implications become difficult to pin down. Pilots do not bomb civilians, they look at a screen. Doctors do not treat patients, they engage in evidence-based practice. Teachers do not teach students, they enhance the quality of schools. Politicians do not suggest a vision for society. They install mechanism for evaluation and quality assurance.

Responsibility, including inter-human responsibility, becomes invisible as the latter is mediated through the interface of bureaucratic schemes, performance measurement systems, communication technologies, and the like (Bauman 2001). Quality configurations have much in common with other forces that render society invisible. Qualitization reconfigures social agents into roles such as "quality inscriptors," "quality agents," "quality objects," and so on. Debates and normative frictions between them are expressed in terms such as "best practices," "unintended effects," "gaming," and "strategic use of indicators," but these debates and the terminologies mobilized in them already presuppose that the social body has been carved up and fragmented into the roles prescribed by qualitization processes.

There are deep links between the formatting of quality configurations and their structuring sociopolitical force. In Zizek's analysis of the Bologna process, for example, he sees the cutting up of educational systems into commensurable pieces defined by their "transfer value" as one big attack on the public use of reason. In order to secure commensuration and transferability, qualitization cuts public matters into small pieces that are compared and assessed, traded and exchanged.

Quality not only promotes a neoliberal agenda; it helps extend it into domains that monetarization has yet to penetrate. Quality can make little, calculable pieces out of almost all aspects of social life and transform them into rankings, comparisons, gradings, evaluations, and choice options. It can do so even without the currency of money that economists love so much because they thought it was the only means to make everything comparable and exchangeable. Comparison of quality objects makes it possible to imagine that one of them can be substituted for another one. When quality objects can be substituted, the social relations between quality agents become structured as if they were market-like relations. Quality accomplishes the same without relying on money as the great equalizer; in its present version, quality enhances neoliberal economistic mentality without using money.

And while the state has no central overview, there is a vast multitude of centers of calculation that helps not citizens but quality agents of many sorts, each in their fragmented role, to form quality configurations in which quality is defined, transported, chosen, bought, and sold.

The concept of quality is marked by depolitizing tendencies. The concept presents itself in an ever-positive light, apparently disarming value controversies. It is impossible to measure all of quality. Davies (2011) shows how authority to know the unknowable is sometimes achieved. Measurements are pragmatically justified; concepts are infused with esthetic enthusiasm and affective knowledge; and dreams of total knowledge are mobilized as if measurement covers everything if we hope it does.

At the same time, quality inscriptions decompose structures of meaningful life into small, measurable components that are "consumed" by fragmented actors and for which fragmented social actors are held accountable. This fragmentation and decomposition of the res publica into bits and pieces that are measured, assessed, compared, or ranked is a general aspect of contemporary qualitization regardless of whether it happens to be associated more with particular sectors, ideologies, or paradigms.

Whereas micro-quality might be captured and summed up into indicators, the sociopolitical remains more than a sum of its parts. Qualitization as we know it makes the "macro-quality" of sociopolitical matters evaporate. There is an underlying link between the epistemic character of quality inscriptions based on commensuration, quantification, comparison, ranking, and exchange value, on the one hand, and the formation of quality objects into measureable components on the other. "Large," "complex," and "messy" problems, such as genuinely sociopolitical ones, have difficulties being described in terms of the quality vocabulary. Consequently, qualitization means an incapacity to capture and deal with unhandy and wicked sociopolitical problems.

Palonen (2007) provides a distinction which allows us to understand the depolitizing effects of qualitization. While depolitization can be active, "a movement towards closing a horizon," it can also be passive, based on "exhaustion or on a diminishing interest in the horizon of politicking." While both of these strategies may be at work in qualitization, the exhaustion mentioned as part of the passive form of depolitization presumably plays a very important role. It is a classical theme among professionals that quality assurance, documentation, inscriptions, and their consequences, constitute important dimensions in the psycho-social work environments in contemporary workplaces. The notion of work becomes reconfigured in the light of qualitization processes, and so does the meaning of work as a personal experience.

Similarly, Davies (2015) shows how "the happiness industry" is based on new alliances between medicine and economics, between technocracy and neoliberalism. In Davies' analysis, the discourse on quality of life is closely linked to what he calls the competitive–depressive society. Parallel to Beck's analysis of "institutionalized individualism," fundamentally sociopolitical tensions manifest themselves as purely individual problems (unemployment, stress, life planning). Davies suggests that these psychologizing trends should be interpreted in a critical political light (Davies 2015: 267).

It is in this broader perspective that quality without democracy becomes unnerving. Democracy loses its grip. It hands res publica over to qualitization that does not acknowledge res publica and which exhaust the interests and the resources to engage with res publica. Qualitization has no grip on the sociopolitical; or perhaps more precisely, redefines it so that it no longer appears sociopolitical.

Qualitizers enjoy relatively privileged positions in organization and management. Massive investments have been made in quality inscriptions and quality documentation. Many nurses, teachers, and others are interested in leaving their practices on the floor and becoming some kind of quality specialist. It is more prestigious and often better paid to qualitize a practice than to be a practitioner. Here, present society makes a remarkable prioritization, which testifies to the current prominence of quality and qualitization. But the kind of qualitization that is prioritized is one that takes place in networks of organizations reporting to organizations; it is not one that positions itself as a question of how a democratic society attends to its own matters. Nor is it one that talks about res publica.

In sum, quality in its present sociopolitical formation runs on parallel tracks with neoliberalism. For this reason, the analysis of how qualitization leads to a fragmentation of res publica resonates with Brown's (2015) analysis of how neoliberalism is "undoing the demos." There are many parallels, for example, regarding the homogenization of social life, the reconfiguration of social institutions serving common purposes, the desacralization of precious values, the loss of democratic control of goal-setting, the elimination of discussion, the abandonment of a notion of common mastery of political existence, and even the withering away of the very capacity to imagine such a common mastery.

However, Brown's analytical entry point is neoliberalism itself, while mine is the concept of quality. Could that lead to other openings, other imaginaries?

* * *

The picture painted above might be too gloomy, and perhaps my socio-historical perspective has become a socio-hysterical one, as sometimes happens with social criticism. Have I possibly criticized a new and emerging social order with the use of old concepts? It should be remembered that even if neoliberalism plays an important role regarding the meaning and use of the term "quality" in our contemporary society, it does not exhaust the term. Quality is older and richer than that. Perhaps quality also has more interesting futures. What if quality were democratized?

Rosanvallon's view of democracy helps put things into perspective. Democracy is a way for society to institute itself, and evidently it does so in different ways over time. There is no universally defined standard for democracy across all times. There is not unlimited time available for perfect deliberation (Palonen 2002).

Instead, a society institutes itself in specific ways in specific epochs, using the terms and concepts and structuring principles and technologies available at any given time. In democracies, the most important concepts are those that are most difficult to define (Rosanvallon 2009: 45). There is no general reason to desire more or less politics, since both have been problematic at various points in history (Rosanvallon 2009: 55). Instead, the democratic problem is one that remains open. Democratic societies are constantly struggling with the "resonance" between earlier experiences and recent expectations. Democracy sets concepts and distinctions in motion with which it institutes itself. Society carves out a conceptual terrain that is the arena where it works upon itself (Rosanvallon 2009: 95). Could that terrain not be extended to include qualitization?

Quality inscriptions in massive amounts across time and space may merely be an unprecedented socio-historical phenomenon with which democratic societies can deal. Democracy's struggle with quality can be viewed as a learning process.

Maybe present institutions do not have as much self-confidence as they appear to have (Boltanski 2011: 276). As shown by pragmatic sociology, the dominant institutions in contemporary society are much in need of a legitimate, moral framework. The often adopt and "endogenize" critique (Boltanski 2011: 204). Evaluation would not have been invented if it was not possible to imagine that institutions would be at least somewhat responsive to critique.

Maybe qualitization is more ambiguous than often assumed. Qualitization implies institutionalized responsibilization of a variety of agents, but qualitization also implies critical standards against which institutions can be judged. For example, although customer satisfaction surveys used in public institutions sometimes are a vehicle for market-like reforms, they are also a form of social critique. Furthermore, there are moments of meta-qualitization (such as evaluations, reviews, audits and/or public debates of forms of qualitization). One example of such meta-qualitization may take place up to a reform of national tests in schools. In such a moment, policies and institutions become subject to assessment along a variety of valuation registers. Maybe on that occasion, for example, it will be possible to articulate critique against the test system if it requires pupils to sacrifice their own well-being in schools. Maybe parents will see this. Maybe they will create alliances with critical teachers. Maybe there will be a very small reform, but maybe it will be for the better.

Can contemporary societies teach themselves to shift from one orientation to another, depending on situation-specific arrangements, and perhaps be more sensitive to multiple orders of worth? (Thévenot 2001: 71; Stark 2009). No form of qualitization should be seen as something totalizing or definite. Qualitization is a socio-historical product, it can change over time.

What can be done?

References

Ahrne, Göran, and Nils Brunsson. 2008. Organizing the World. In *Transnational Governance*, ed. M.-L. Djelic and K. Sahlin-Andersson. Cambridge: Cambridge University Press.

Bache, Ian, and Louise Reardon. 2016. *The Politics and Policy of Wellbeing*. Cheltenham: Edward Elgar.

Bauman, Zygmunt. 1983. Industrialism, Consumerism and Power. *Theory, Culture and Society* 1 (3): 32–43.

———. 1987. *Legislators and Interpreters. On Modernity, Postmodernity and Intellectuals*. Cambridge: Polity Press.

———. 2000. *Liquid Modernity*. Cambridge: Polity Press.
———. 2001. Consuming Life. *Journal of Consumer Culture* 1 (1): 9–29.
———. 2002. *Det Belejrede Samfund* [Society Under Siege]. Copenhagen: Hans Reitzel.
Berger, Peter L., Brigitte Berger, and Hansfried Kellner. 1973. *The Homeless Mind: Modernization and Consciousness*. New York: Vintage Books.
Bevir, Mark. 2004. Governance and Interpretation: What are the Implications of Postfoundationalism? *Public Administration* 82 (3): 605–625.
Boltanski, Luc. 2011. *Pragmatisk Sociologi* [Pragmatic Sociology. A Reader]. Copenhagen: Hans Reitzel.
Boltanski, Luc, and Eve Chiapello. 2007. *The New Spirit of Capitalism*. London: Verso.
Bowbrick, Peter. 2014. *The Economics of Quality, Grades and Brands*. New York: Routledge.
Brown, Wendy. 2015. *Undoing the Demos*. New York: Zone Books.
Brunsson, Nils. 2000. Organizations, Markets and Standardization. In *A World of Standards*, ed. N. Brunsson and B. Jacobsson. Oxford: Oxford University Press.
Dahler-Larsen, Peter. 2006. Evaluation After Disenchantment? Five Issues Shaping the Role of Evaluation in Society. In *Handbook of Evaluation*, ed. I.F. Shaw, J.C. Greene, and M.M. Mark, 123–140. Thousand Oaks: Sage.
———. 2012. *The Evaluation Society*. Stanford: Stanford University Press.
Davies, William. 2011. Knowing the Unknowable: The Epistemological Authority of Innovation Policy Experts. *Social Epistemology* 25 (4): 401–421.
———. 2015. *The Happiness Industry: How the Government and Big Business Sold Us Well-Being*. London: Verso.
Jensen, Jacob. 2016. Almenvellets Affortryllelse – Neoliberale Anfægtelser af det Fælles Bedste [The Disenchantment of the Common Good – Neoliberal Contestations of the Common Good]. *Slagmark* 74 (Fall): 69–85.
Jensen, Jacob, and Niklas Olsen. 2016. Hvad Er Neoliberalisme? Redaktionelt Forord [What Is Neoliberalism? Editorial Foreword]. *Slagmark* 74 (Fall): 9–22.
Julnes, George, ed. 2012. *Promoting Value in the Public Interest: Informing Policies for Judging Value in Evaluation. New Directions for Evaluation, No. 133*. San Francisco: Jossey-Bass.
Kauko, Jaakko, Risto Rinne, and Tuomas Takala. 2018. *Politics of Quality in Education. A Comparative Study of Brazil, China, and Russia*. New York: Routledge.

Kipnis, Andrew B. 2008. Audit Cultures: Neoliberal Governmentality, Socialist Legacy, or Technologies of Governing. *American Ethnologist* 35 (2): 275–289.
Kushner, Saville. 2017. *Evaluative Research Methods: Managing the Complexities of Judgment in the Field*. Charlotte: Information Age Publishing.
Mirowski, Philip. 2016. Den politiske bevægelse, der ikke turde ytre sit eget navn [The Political Movement Which Did Not Dare Speak in Its Own Name]. *Slagmark* 74 (Fall): 33–52.
Morgan, Gareth. 1986. *Images of Organization*. Thousand Oaks: Sage.
Mörth, Ulrika. 2008. Soft Regulation and Global Democracy. In *Transnational Governance*, ed. M.-L. Djelic and K. Sahlin-Andersson. Cambridge: Cambridge University Press.
Normand, Romuald. 2016. *The Changing Epistemic Governance of European Education, the Fabrication of the Homo Academicus Europeanus?* Switzerland: Springer.
Ozga, Jenny, Peter Dahler-Larsen, Christina Segerholm, and Hannu Simola. 2011. *Fabricating Quality in Education: Data and Governance in Europe*. London: Routledge.
Palonen, Kari. 2002. The History of Concepts as a Style of Political Theorizing: Quentin Skinner's and Reinhart Koselleck's Subversion of Normative Political Theory. *European Journal of Political Theory* 1 (1): 91–106.
———. 2007. *Re-thinking Politics: Essays from a Quarter-century*. Finnish Political Science Association. Jyväskylä University Printing House.
Pielke, Roger A. 2007. *The Honest Broker, Making Sense of Science in Policy and Politics*. Cambridge: Cambridge University Press.
Porter, Theodore M. 1994. Making Things Quantitative. *Science in Context* 7 (3): 389–407.
Prewitt, Kenneth, Thomas A. Schwandt, and Miron L. Straf. 2012. *Using Science as Evidence in Public Policy*. Washington, DC: National Academies Press.
Rosa, Hartmut. 2003. Social Acceleration: Ethical and Political Consequences of a Desynchronized High–Speed Society. *Constellations* 10 (1): 3–33.
———. 2005. The Speed of Global Flows and the Pace of Democratic Politics. *New Political Science* 27 (4): 445–459.
Rosanvallon, Pierre. 2009. *Demokratin som Problem* [Democracy as the Problem]. Hägersten: TankeKraft Förlag.
Sennett, Richard. 2002. *The Corrosion of Character: The Personal Consequences of Work in the New Capitalism*. New York: W. W. Norton.
Sørensen, Eva M., and Jacob Torfing. 2009. Making Governance Networks Effective and Democratic through Metagovernance. *Public Administration* 87 (2): 234–258.

Stark, David. 2009. *The Sense of Dissonance, Accounts of Worth in Economic Life*. Princeton: Princeton University Press.

Strang, David, and John W. Meyer. 1994. Institutional Conditions for Diffusion. In *Institutional Environments and Organizations*, ed. W.R. Scott and J.W. Meyer, 100–112. Thousand Oaks: Sage.

Thévenot, Laurent. 2001. Pragmatic Regumes Governing the Engagement with the World. In *The Practice Turn in Contemporary Theory*, ed. T.R. Schatzki, K.D. Knorr-Cetina, and E. von Savigny, 56–73. London: Routledge.

Vedung, Evert. 1997. *Public Policy and Program Evaluation*. New Brunswick: Transaction.

Wallenburg, Iris, Julia Quartz, and Roland Bal. 2016. Making Hospitals Governable: Performativity and Institutional Work in Ranking Practices. *Administration & Society*: 1–27.

7

Epilogue: What to Do

Conclusion

Let us imagine someone wanted a large transformation of society, including a reconfiguration of res publica. Let us say they wanted to cut all kinds of activities and institutions into little pieces and make them all measurable and comparable in large territories in time and space. Let us say they wanted to do that in ways that presented a fait accompli, often circumventing conventional forms of government control and democratic deliberation. Let us say that in order to do that, it would be necessary to involve many social actors in many ways, and it should happen through a form of responsibilization that would be difficult to refuse. Let us say that to do that, opposition should be minimized. Therefore, the tools involved in that process should be both ambiguous and powerful and positively loaded. What vehicle would they call for which could facilitate such ambitious process?

They would call for the concept of quality.

It has been shown in this book that quality is a vague, open, multifaceted, and rich concept. For this reason, quality inscriptions and measurement practices play a decisive role in forming and fixing what quality means in specific situations. When set in motion together with other

P. Dahler-Larsen, *Quality*, https://doi.org/10.1007/978-3-030-10392-7_7

elements in quality configurations, quality inscriptions have a capacity to produce constitutive effects in such a way that conventional forms of democratic control are circumvented. It has not been argued that all contemporary quality inscriptions are bad or have bad consequences. A good/bad distinction is far too simple. It has been argued, however, that quality inscriptions are conducive to shaping services and institutions of common interest in society. They do so when many interacting factors in quality configurations encircle quality agents in such a way that particular forms of quality work become expected, demanded, or made possible. The problem is exacerbated by the ever-present positivity in the term quality, which reduces opposition, obscures what is going on, and makes it difficult to analyze the underlying tensions.

What to Do?

While one cannot proceed slowly enough in scientific thinking, there is no time to lose in practical matters (Mauss in Rosanvallon 2009: 58). People often ask social scientists to make very specific and immediate recommendations. However, social scientists have little faith in their own recommendations, when they realize that it is not known what would happen if people follow them. Recommendations in relation to quality are difficult to make. The opaqueness and positivity of the concept make misunderstandings likely.

According to our theory, however, qualitization is an active speech act, and it should be possible to consider (1) the pros and cons of qualitization, (2) the pros and cons of any qualitization in a given situation, including its constitutive effects, and (3) the appropriateness of actively contributing to multiplying the effects of qualitization.

Social scientists often try to "be a lot smarter" than the actors they study, a risk that Latour (2003) warns against. I have injected a bit of skeptical afterthought here and there in the following strategies, which intervene at both micro-political and macro-political levels (Bruno et al. 2014: 203). Nevertheless, I might fall into Latour's trap.

Acknowledge Your Part in the Production of Constitutive Effects and Act Accordingly

This strategy includes recommendations such as:

- *Acknowledge that every form of participation in a quality configuration can be productive in one way or another.* If it is true that quality inscriptors and centers of calculation only have consequences because quality inscriptions are circulated in quality configurations, then every little micro-political step in everyday life circumvented by a quality configuration is conducive to the production of constitutive effects. To claim that a quality inscription is produced far away may be true enough, but to deny any responsibility for the production of its local consequences may be a myth which in fact helps promote some constitutive effects rather than others. Pay attention to your own participation and to the micro-politics of qualitization.
- *Do not unknowingly amplify constitutive effects.* Constitutive effects are produced through the active involvement of quality agents. A responsible engagement with qualitization is one that does not inadvertently exaggerate its constitutive effects through managerial recipes or collegial procedures and norms.
- *Do not use the term "unintended effects" as an excuse.* If you are a quality inscriptor or otherwise involved in the production of quality inscriptions, acknowledge that you are involved in complex interaction which has consequences. The term "unintended" promotes the assumption that if you have pure intentions, actual consequences are less morally relevant or less important. It allows a simple, Manichean moral view to distract attention from the complications of real life. Do not assume that other participants in a qualitization configuration are willing to keep their eyes shut in face of these complications so that they can imagine your "original intentions." To act responsibly is to pay attention to the ongoing systemic effects of your own actions.
- *Engage in your work.* There is an ad which says that "When you are driving your car, drive." The recommendation is intended to be funny,

but the problem it addresses is serious enough. Drivers surf the Internet, read and write text messages, and do all kinds of other stuff without being aware how dangerous their lack of attention to traffic is. In a similar vein, a recommendation is "When you are working, work!" Good schools are sometimes good not because of extensive evaluation efforts, but because good teachers do good work there. Schools can honor their traditions. The French teachers speak French. The music teachers play and sing. Teachers have their personal styles and are not burdened by piles of paperwork. There is a sense of being a special school. Overt and covert social selection mechanisms may contribute to that identity, but there is also a sense of responsibility connected to specialness being nurtured on a daily basis and not only due to biased social recruitment. If a school has "quality," it is not necessarily because there is ample qualitization and quality-checking machinery. In a similar vein, it was found in a case study that the makers of very good flutes were not able to explain how they produced these fine instruments. An observational study revealed that it might have something to do with their attention to material, the way they observed all aspects of production, and the way they interacted and talked about the production process (Cook and Yanow 1993). There are both sociological and philosophical reasons to pay attention to such engagement. Sennett (2008) talks about the role of craftsmanship where skill is perfected for what appears to be its own sake. Arendt distinguished between labor, work, and action. Labor is what is necessary to survive. Work is (in her terminology) instrumental and purpose-oriented. Action, however, is the kind of engagement in the world where human beings express themselves and reach a kind of existential fulfillment. Using Arendt's terminology, we should not let the forces of qualitization reduce everything we do to ticking boxes, complying with audits and responding to surveys, which would just be labor and work. We should not forget the meaning of human action. No argument is made here that it is easy to find that kind of fulfillment in modern work organizations. It is also not easy to separate the core tasks in work from all the add-ons such as documentation, quality assurance, marketing, promotion, auditing, and so on. In complex organizations, these functions are parts of the job, too. Nevertheless, qualitization should not provide the only interpretive key or the overarching definition of what is important in work. There are particular challenges in the materiality of work, in craftsmanship, in creativity, in professional conduct, and in existential fulfillment through making a contribution to the world, which can also be understood as interpretive *callings*. So, for example, when teaching, it might be better to teach than to focus on the qualitization of teaching.

- *Ignore qualitization efforts now and then.* Sometimes, medical staff do not fill in all necessary documentation of a treatment of a patient, because there is an emergency with the next patient. Sometimes, researchers should simply write what deserves to be written, regardless of bibliometrics. It is fruitful and liberating to publish what should be published, no matter what. Such writing sometimes leads to new ideas; not complying with dominant forms of qualitization is not the same as not acting responsibly. It is also possible to ignore some qualitization efforts with respect to particular purposes of qualitization only. For example, if someone sells a particular inscription as a device for organizational learning, but all it can do is really to enhance a narrow form of accountability, just provide the necessary information and do not try to sustain the illusion that it supports any kind of learning. Just ignore that claim.

Study Qualitization in Practice and Report the Findings

This strategy implies:

- *Consider the operational costs of quality regimes.* Empirically, not enough is known about the operation of the machineries producing quality inscriptions. There is a real economic and political trade-off between resources allocated to services and those allocated to describing these services as quality objects. Admittedly, some quality inscriptions produce an "exchange value" that is at the same time a "use value" (e.g. the quality accreditation of an educational institution). In turn, these two kinds of value are relative to the larger social systems in which they are defined (how necessary is accreditation?). Yet resource questions do not go away. What percentage of the staff at an institution for higher education should be devoted to making quality inscriptions? Many of the costs of quality machineries are concealed, as practitioners are expected to spend work hours to produce documentation that serve as input into evaluation machineries. To determine the number of work hours devoted to quality inscription, it is therefore not sufficient to use the proportions of categories of staff (such as "auditors" or "internal evaluators") as a proxy. The exact costs are difficult to calculate. Quality specialists involve teachers and students in evaluations and other forms of quality inscriptions for quite some time. Nevertheless, a distinction between teaching and the evaluation of teaching continues to make sense. The resources devoted to the latter at the expense of the former come at a price. They also have overflow effects for the attention and meaningfulness allocated to the former. Determining how much more quality specialists should be paid than the professionals whose practices they describe is also a matter of socio-political prioritization.

- *Be curious about constitutive effects*. Vocabulary is important. Constitutive effects should not be swept under the carpet as "unintended effects." The term constitutive effects is admittedly a tentative one, a sensitizing concept that invites further study. A cultivation of this term, theoretically and empirically, will help make various kinds of effects of qualitization more visible and create a space in which they are reflected upon. Collect the evidence. Tell the stories.
- *Experiment with bringing quality agents together and let them hear each other's narratives*. Quality configurations connect quality agents, but with a distance between them in terms of time, space, and roles. Agents who make quality inscriptions are often separated from those whose work is inscribed. So are managers whose organizations are involved in the trading of quality inscriptions. Not only are these quality agents often democratically unaccountable, they keep themselves at a distance from the constitutive effects of the quality inscriptions they produce. Quality configurations are often organized with extensive consumer–producer interface and with inscriptors even further away. Quality inscriptors do not always know what they are

doing, being out of contact with the consequences of their actions (Gjørup and Hjortdal 2007). When I once asked an international constructor of evaluation systems about how teachers in a country would react to the national school performance indicators he was designing, he said that "after all, we are concerning with steering, not with rowing." To expand on that metaphor, if the boat is not moving, there is no steering. It is a problem that managers do not recognize how dependent they are on people whom they are trying to "steer." Conversely, a reflexive strategy would be one that sensitized quality inscribers to the effects of their activities upon others. This observation calls for new experiments with social fora for collective learning about qualitization. Some might engage in deliberation if they are exposed to new and expanded publics (Whatmore 2009) and formats, such as consensus conferences, deliberative evaluation (House and Howe 2000), or responsible innovation (Stilgoe et al. 2013). A main purpose would be to subject quality inscribers more directly to the consequences of their work and the reactions from others, a strategy starkly different from one seeking to establish trustworthiness by allowing the work of quality inscriptors to be approved by other quality inscriptors (Kristoffersen and Lindeberg 2004). The practical intersection and frictions between our otherwise stylized metrological, deliberative, and configurative styles of qualitization could be explored. Evidently, overlaps already exist. Deliberation could build on available statistics. Metrologists could invite others in their deliberations and cultivate their interests in the constitutive effects of their indicators. More could be done to sensitize those who practice the metrological, the deliberative, and the configurative styles of qualitization to each other's work.

- *Create spaces for evaluative inquiry that recognizes the "rough ground" of value tensions in practice* (Schwandt 2003). Such evaluative inquiries should stay closer to epistemic missions, frictions, and resonances of practices (Fochler and de Rijcke 2017). The theoretical and philosophical framework for this kind of evaluative inquiry is already articulated eloquently (e.g. by Schwandt 2002). Weick (1995) describes a corresponding view of sense-making processes in organizations (beyond formalized quality regimes). While the normal reaction in organizations is to push decisions upwards in the organizational hierarchy, especially during a crisis (Weick et al. 2005), important sense-making capacity is hereby lost. Instead of hierarchy, good collective sense-making requires involvement, experimentation, and dialogue. The key notion in the deliberative model is repeated here, albeit in slightly different terms: The problem-oriented interaction of a variety of people with different experiences and perspectives and their active engagement is necessary for sense-making and a richer understanding of problems and potential solutions. Theoretical and empirical studies of how practitioners in various social domains deal with multiple orders of worth are available (Stark 2009). What is most clearly missing in practice is the social space and time available for evaluative inquiry along these lines, especially in situations where the regimes for quality inscription are already in place and seem to constitute a problem in themselves. An inspiration can be found in statactivism (Bruno et al. 2014). One of the strategies of this activist movement is to disclose how quality inscriptions, performance indicators and the like are produced under pedestrian and problematic circumstances in real life. The underlying studies are often carried out in cooperation between researchers and professionals with first-hand experience (such as policemen).

Contribute to Multiple and Alternative Qualitizations

Under this headline, consider the following:

- *Deprive any particular form of qualitization of its monopoly, if it has one.* Teach young members of your profession that no quality inscription captures all of quality. Set an example. Demonstrate in action that multiple criteria deserve attention. More criteria are not inherently better than a few, but a multiplicity of criteria may help enhance deliberation and reflection by showing that multiple views are possible.

- *Develop concepts of quality that more clearly reveals relativity, particularity, and definitions through social use.* It is possible to imagine speech acts and language games that appeal less to any essential aspects of quality and instead lay bare how the meanings of quality are linked to its pragmatic use. What would happen if we conceived of quality as…? This strategy could be followed by a "civilized" engagement with the concept, which is one that recognizes that there is no inner core in quality to which anyone has authoritative access. This idea challenges the "guarantee" that the metrological style finds in the measurement of essential objects. It also challenges both the extraterrestrial rule-setting in the deliberative style as well as the universal wisdom of solutions achieved by deliberation. There is no similar "guarantee" in the configurative style of qualitization. Instead, the question is which kind of justifications would be regarded as fair, legitimate, and proper in quality configurations that do not simply present quality as a fait accompli? An engagement in this question would reflect Vattimo's "weak thinking"; an approach to knowledge claims that lays bare that there is no ultimate, "secure" foundation. There is no inner core in quality, and there is no authority who knows that inner core.
- *Change vocabularies regarding implementation problems into something more creative.* Imperfect measurements, messy derivations of quality inscriptions, the uneven and inconsistent use of quality regimes, and lack of consistency across time and space are too often understood as results of failed implementation problems or faulty management. The underlying assumption is that one day, there will be perfect measurement. This vocabulary could be changed. Inconsistency provides room for maneuvering. Unclarity invites interpretation. Ambiguity is another word for new reality in the making (Best 2008). There is no such thing as total quality (Weick 2000). A lack of perfect quality regimes indicates a plurality of moral and political orders of worth (Normand 2016: 7; Stark 2009).
- *Play with new forms of qualitization.* One way to play with qualitization is to invent new indicators of quality. After some dissatisfaction with a bibliometric system which gave high priority to publications in

English only, I developed a PLOTE index which measures the proportion of impact (in terms of Google Scholar citations) which flow from publications in Languages Other Than English (LOTE). The invention of new indicators is, evidently, highly ambivalent. Does the world really need more indicators? Pros and cons should be considered carefully, including constitutive effects. New indicators may lead to new inscription machineries. Is it worth the effort? And do new indicators in fact confirm an underlying ideology saying that things only count if they are counted? (A dilemma familiar to those who want to expand GDP to include metrics about climate change, or unpaid housework, or human happiness). If carried out as a "weak" epistemic exercise (weak in the spirit of Vattimo's non-authoritarian philosophy), however, and if observations and reflections are made regarding the social life of an indicator and its consequences, such experiments might have merits. Instead of promoting criticism of a particular measurement of quality for not measuring quality correctly (which inherently conforms to the notion that quality is a thing that can be measured correctly), then perhaps it is more productive to suggest new notions of quality, which are constructive and productive in different ways. At least, there will be multiple criteria to draw from.

- *Build quality configurations with more interesting feedback-loops.* If quality configurations became more self-reflexive, perhaps more intelligent and sensitive forms of qualitization would be developed. For example, a national testing system in schools could be improved by incorporating an up-to-date governance structure where teachers and students provided feedback about how tests work in practice.
- *Contribute to meta-qualitization of quality configurations.* Documenting and reporting on findings about qualitization and using them as feedback may be a good first step. Another step may be to use these findings and observations in macro-political initiatives to form and shape quality configurations (public debate, government committees, statactivism, etc.). The totality of a quality configuration is often invisible from any particular point. A better democratic meta-governance of networks may include creating more publicity around their operations; empowering weaker groups in society as members of networks; and taking part in further evaluation of qualitizing networks (Sørensen

and Torfing 2009). It should be remembered, however, that such processes will perhaps be much more openly political than what is suggested by the de-politicized imagery that sometimes imbue qualitization processes. Instead, politics, interests, and brute contradictions which were swept under the carpet then see the light of the day. In a democratic light, however, the politicization of quality may be refreshing.

Consider Alternatives to Qualitization

> The flow into which you have been thrown is not inherently any more of a quality problem than it is a problem of gender, management, or shamans. (Weick 2000)

So finally, and perhaps most radically, think beyond quality.

- *See qualitization as an option*. Qualitization is a particular kind of speech act defining a situation at hand as something that calls for quality, for a quality inscription, and for the involvement of quality actors. First and foremost, it creates a helpful condition for anything else that happens: The impossibility of being against quality. Consider an example. A group of researchers discusses what to require of the candidates applying for a position at their department. Some evidently argue that research achievements are crucial. Others say that the department's need for teachers in particular subdisciplines is also important. In comes a qualitizing statement: "After all, the only thing that should count is quality." The statement tacitly assumes that some have appealed to criteria that are not quality criteria and therefore not part of "the good." Such statements force others either to go against quality or to offer their particular definition of quality. They can buy into the assumption that the only kind of quality that counts is research quality or they can introduce the notion that quality is comprehensive and includes teaching. The one who wins the quality debate has the upper hand in the selection of candidates. Alternative, it might well be possible to talk about what kind of candidate is needed in relation to two problems: The strengthening of research at the department and teaching needs. These problems can be solved without qualitization. When qualitization is seen as an option, its pros and cons can be considered.

- *Consider political alternatives to qualitization I: Dare to talk about problems.* In debates on public and political issues, there are approaches that can serve as functional alternatives to qualitization. The first is specific talk about specific problems. Quality inscriptions build on quality perspectives that make sense in relation to problems. Yet very general quality talk buries problems. Organizations that dare to talk about their problems in a more direct manner might tackle such problems more directly than organizations that need to transform everything into a general quality vocabulary. When students drop out of school, the problem can be conceptualized as a drop-out problem rather than a quality problem. When patients have problems with infected wounds, this particular problem might be better handled as an infection problem than as a quality problem. Sense-making around such problems and their solutions may simply be more concrete, specific, and helpful than abstractions and euphemisms concerning quality (Weick 1995).
- *Consider political alternatives to qualitization II: Recognize value conflicts.* Qualitization is not usually a helpful way of bringing value controversies to the surface. Qualitization presents issues as matters of the good against an opposition that does not exist. At best, a quality discussion can allow choices between different quality perspectives, different quality inscriptions, and so on. Yet it rarely allows a clear confrontation between different value systems to emerge. *Roe v. Wade*, the abolishment of Apartheid, and global warming are not quality issues. Some political interests and values refuse to be flattened and compressed. Qualitization may do exactly that, which is one of the reasons why it should be considered an option, not a mandatory kind of discourse. Qualitization has unrecognized side effects, especially for the losers of political controversies over values; not only have they lost, they are also portrayed as those who were unable to side with the good or failed to understand the issue. *Quality does not recognize the reasonableness of its opposition.* Conversely, a value conflict is a matter of dif-

fering convictions. It is therefore more dignified to lose a battle over values than a battle over quality.

- *Consider political alternatives to qualitization III: Attend to issues of social distribution.* Third and finally, there are issues of social distribution. It is too often assumed that the concept of quality will make solve social distribution issues less pressing. But who gets the jobs in "high quality work environments"? Who gets to live in neighborhoods which facilitate "quality of life"? Is quality involving the local creativity in art schools or is it attracting the international bigshots? The concept of quality is too inclusive and vague to answer specific questions about the social distributions of advantages and disadvantages. It is sometimes believed to be progressive to recognize a multiplicity of dimensions in quality. However, that still leaves questions of prioritization of values and the distribution of goods. Even if, say, broader notions of research quality are recognized, there is a remaining, painful question of who gets funding and who does not. New and "broader" notions of quality receiving recognition create a new distinction between those who receive funding and those who do not, but the distinction still has to be made. It remains a contested socio-political problem. The same is true when students are admitted to a program in a more "inclusive" way. However, it is not logically possible to broaden the set of admission criteria describing the quality of applications without narrowing it in other respects given the same number of seats available. Perhaps qualitization should not be used to obfuscate social distribution issues. So reconsider when it is appropriate and useful to talk about (1) problems, (2) values, and (3) the distribution of goods, perhaps instead of qualitization.
- *Deprive the term quality of a monopoly on goodness.* Practice rhetorical strategies that cast light on many forms of goodness. Instead of packing different forms of goodness into the concept of quality, only to unpack them later, a diversified, nuanced vocabulary could more directly capture variations in goodness that do not hinge on quality. On the Amalfi Coast, an old monastery has been converted to a retreat for poets, scientists, and composers. There is good, simple food; kind, local staff; and a sense of spirituality. It is a wonderful place to be and a great place

to write. It is not necessary to qualitize this place. A time has come where it is more pertinent to protect the rare and the valuable from qualitization than it is to secure the spread of qualitization to all objects and all spheres of life. I mean this less in a spiritual sense than in a sociological sense. The diversity of forms of life may be better protected if not everything is subject to qualitization. Appreciate engagements, efforts, care, beauty, grace, loyalty, locality, creativity, creation, and other gifts of life without assuming that they owe their existence to qualitization.

References

Best, Jacqueline. 2008. Ambiguity, Uncertainty, and Risk: Rethinking Indeterminacy. *International Political Sociology* 2: 355–374.

Bruno, Isabelle, Emmanuel Didier, and Tommaso Vitale. 2014. Statactivism. Forms of Action between Disclosure and Affirmation. *Partecipazione e Conflitto* 7 (2): 198–220.

Cook, S.D. Noam, and Dvora Yanow. 1993. Culture and Organizational Learning. *Journal of Management Inquiry* 2: 373–390.

Fochler, Maximilian, and Sarah de Rijcke. 2017. Implicated in the Indicator Game? An Experimental Debate. *Engaging Science, Technology, and Society* 3: 21–40.

Gjørup, Jes, and Henrik Hjortdal. 2007. Kronik: Tilgiv Os – Vi Vidste Ikke, Hvad Vi Gjorde [Feature: Forgive Us – We Did Not Know What We Were Doing]. *Politiken*, March 29.

House, Ernest R., and Kenneth R. Howe. 2000. Deliberative Democratic Evaluation. *New Directions for Evaluation* 85: 3–12.

Kristoffersen, Dorte, and Tobias Lindeberg. 2004. Creating Quality Assurance and International Transparency for Quality Assurance Agencies: The Case of Mutual Recognition. *Quality in Higher Education* 10 (1): 31–36.

Latour, Bruno. 2003. The Promises of Constructivism. Paper Prepared for a Chapter. In *Chasing Technology: Matrix of Materiality, Indiana Series for the Philosophy of Science*, ed. D. Idhe, 27–46. Bloomington: Indiana University Press.

Normand, Romuald. 2016. *The Changing Epistemic Governance of European Education, the Fabrication of the Homo Academicus Europeanus?* Switzerland: Springer.

Rosanvallon, Pierre. 2009. *Demokratin som Problem* [Democracy as the Problem]. Hägersten: TankeKraft Förlag.

Schwandt, Thomas A. 2002. *Evaluation Practice Reconsidered.* New York: Peter Lang.

———. 2003. 'Back to the Rough Ground!' Beyond Theory to Practice in Evaluation. *Evaluation* 9 (3): 353–364.

Sennett, Richard. 2008. *The Craftsman*. London: Penguin Books.

Sørensen, Eva M., and Jacob Torfing. 2009. Making Governance Networks Effective and Democratic through Metagovernance. *Public Administration* 87 (2): 234–258.

Stark, David. 2009. *The Sense of Dissonance, Accounts of Worth in Economic Life.* Princeton: Princeton University Press.

Stilgoe, Jack, Richard Owen, and Phil Macnaghten. 2013. Developing a Framework for Responsible Innovation. *Research Policy* 42: 1568–1580.

Weick, Karl E. 1995. *Sensemaking in Organizations.* Thousand Oaks: Sage.

———. 2000. Quality Improvement: A Sensemaking Perspective. In *The Quality Movement and Organization Theory*, ed. R.E. Cole and W.R. Scott, 155–172. Thousand Oaks: Sage.

Weick, Karl E., Kathleen M. Sutcliffe, and David Obstfeld. 2005. Organizing and the Process of Sense-making. *Organization Science* 16 (4): 409–421.

Whatmore, Sarah J. 2009. Mapping Knowledge Controversies: Science, Democracy and the Redistribution of Expertise. *Progress in Human Geography* 33 (5): 587–598.

References

Ahrne, Göran, and Nils Brunsson. 2008. Organizing the World. In *Transnational Governance*, ed. M.-L. Djelic and K. Sahlin-Andersson. Cambridge: Cambridge University Press.

Alder, Ken. 2002. *The Measure of All Things: The Seven-Year Odyssey and Hidden Error that Transformed the World.* New York: The Free Press.

Alexander, Neville. 2013. *Thoughts on the New South Africa.* Pretoria: Jacana.

Andresen, Emilie, and Maj Fjordside. 2015. *Uklare Begreber, Store Forventninger og Nye Roller: Et Studie af Hverdagsrehabilitering som et Eksempel på Samskabelse* [Unclear Concepts, Big Expectations and New Roles: A Study of Everyday Rehabilitation as an Example of Cocreation]. Thesis, Department of Political Science, University of Copenhagen.

Antal, Ariane B., Michael Hutter, and David Stark. 2015. *Moments of Valuation: Exploring Sites of Dissonance.* Oxford: Oxford University Press.

Arnaboldi, Michela, and Giovanni Azzone. 2010. Constructing Performance Measurement in the Public Sector. *Critical Perspectives on Accounting* 21 (4): 266–282.

Bache, Ian, and Louise Reardon. 2016. *The Politics and Policy of Wellbeing.* Cheltenham: Edward Elgar.

Baier, Vicki E., James G. March, and Harald Sætren. 1986. Implementation and Ambiguity. *Scandinavian Journal of Management Studies* 2 (3/4): 179–212.

P. Dahler-Larsen, *Quality*, https://doi.org/10.1007/978-3-030-10392-7

Barnhart, Robert K., and Sol Steinmetz. 1988. *The Barnhart Dictionary of Etymology*. New York: H. W. Wilson.

Barry, Andrew. 2012. Political Situations: Knowledge Controversies in Transnational Governance. *Critical Policy Studies* 6 (3): 324–336.

Bateson, Gregory. 1972. *Steps to an Ecology of Mind*. New York: Ballantine Books.

Bauer, Martin W. 2016. A Word From the Parting Editor, 4760 Pages Down the Line. *Public Understanding of Science* 25 (2): 130–134.

Bauman, Zygmunt. 1983. Industrialism, Consumerism and Power. *Theory, Culture and Society* 1 (3): 32–43.

———. 1987. *Legislators and Interpreters. On Modernity, Postmodernity and Intellectuals*. Cambridge: Polity Press.

———. 2000. *Liquid Modernity*. Cambridge: Polity Press.

———. 2001. Consuming Life. *Journal of Consumer Culture* 1 (1): 9–29.

———. 2002. *Det Belejrede Samfund* [Society Under Siege]. Copenhagen: Hans Reitzel.

Beck, Ulrich. 1992. *Risk Society. Towards a New Modernity*. Thousand Oaks: Sage.

———. 2002. *Fagre Nye Arbejdsverden* [Schöne neue Arbeitswelt]. Copenhagen: Hans Reitzel.

Becker, Howard S. 1996. The Epistemology of Qualitative Research. In *Essays on Ethnography and Human Development*, ed. R. Jessor, A. Colby, and R. Schweder. Chicago: University of Chicago Press.

Beer, David. 2016. *Metric Power*. London: Palgrave Macmillan.

Bereiter, Carl. 2002. *Education and Mind in the Knowledge Age*. Mahwah: L. Erlbaum Associates.

Berger, Peter L. 1964. Some General Observations on the Problem of Work. In *The Human Shape of Work: Studies in the Sociology of Occupations*, ed. P.L. Berger. New York: Macmillan.

Berger, Peter L., Brigitte Berger, and Hansfried Kellner. 1973. *The Homeless Mind: Modernization and Consciousness*. New York: Vintage Books.

Bergh, Andreas. 2011. Why Quality in Education – and What Quality? – A Linguistic Analysis of the Concept of Quality in Swedish Government Texts. *Education Inquiry* 2 (4): 709–723.

Best, Jacqueline. 2008. Ambiguity, Uncertainty, and Risk: Rethinking Indeterminacy. *International Political Sociology* 2: 355–374.

Beuscart, Jean-Samuel, and Kevin Mellet. 2013. Competing Quality Conventions in the French Online Display Advertising Market. *Journal of Cultural Economy* 6 (4): 402–418.

Bevir, Mark. 2004. Governance and Interpretation: What are the Implications of Postfoundationalism? *Public Administration* 82 (3): 605–625.

———. 2007. *Encyclopedia of Governance*. Thousand Oaks: Sage.

Biesta, Gert. 2007. Why 'What Works' Won't Work: Evidence-Based Practice and the Democratic Deficit in Educational Research. *Educational Theory* 57 (1): 1–22.

Bijker, Wiebe E., and John Law. 1992. *Shaping Technology/Building Society: Studies in Sociotechnical Change*. Cambridge: The MIT Press.

Blishen, Edward. 1969. *Blond's Encyclopedia of Education*. London: Blond Education.

Boedker, Christina, and Wai Chua. 2013. Accounting as an Affective Technology: A Study of Circulation, Agency and Entrancement. *Accounting, Organizations and Society* 38 (4): 245–267.

Boltanski, Luc. 2011. *Pragmatisk Sociologi* [Pragmatic Sociology. A Reader]. Copenhagen: Hans Reitzel.

Boltanski, Luc, and Eve Chiapello. 2007. *The New Spirit of Capitalism*. London: Verso.

Bostock, David. 1988. *Plato's Thæetetus*. Oxford: Clarendon Press.

Bowbrick, Peter. 2014. *The Economics of Quality, Grades and Brands*. New York: Routledge.

Boyte, Harry. 2011. Constructive Politics as Public Work: Organizing the Literature. *Political Theory* 39 (5): 630–660.

Brown, Wendy. 2015. *Undoing the Demos*. New York: Zone Books.

Bruno, Isabelle, Emmanuel Didier, and Tommaso Vitale. 2014. Statactivism. Forms of Action between Disclosure and Affirmation. *Partecipazione e Conflitto* 7 (2): 198–220.

Brunsson, Nils. 1989. *The Organization of Hypocrisy: Talk, Decisions and Actions in Organizations*. New York: Wiley.

———. 2000. Organizations, Markets and Standardization. In *A World of Standards*, ed. N. Brunsson and B. Jacobsson. Oxford: Oxford University Press.

Brunsson, Nils, and Bengt Jacobsson, eds. 2000. *A World of Standards*. Oxford: Oxford University Press.

Butler, Linda. 2003. Explaining Australia's Increased Share of ISI Publications: The Effects of a Funding Formula Based on Publication Counts. *Research Policy* 34: 565–574.

Butler, Judith. 2010. Performative Agency. *Journal of Cultural Economy* 3 (2): 147–161.

Buzan, Barry, Ole Wæver, and Jaap de Wilde. 1998. *Security: A New Framework for Analysis*. Boulder: Lynne Rienner.

Byrne, David. 2012. How Music Works. *Smithsonian* 43 (6): 24–26, 29.

Callon, Michel. 1998. An Essay on Framing and Overflowing: Economic Externalities Revisited by Sociology. In *The Laws of the Markets*, ed. M. Callon, 244–269. Oxford: Blackwell.

Callon, Michel, Cécile Méadel, and Vololona Rabeharisoa. 2002. The Economy of Qualities. *Economy and Society* 31 (2): 194–217.

Cape Times, Feb 23 2017. Cape Town: Cape Town Independent News & Media PLC.

Cape Times, Feb 24 2017. Cape Town: Cape Town Independent News & Media PLC.

Castoriadis, Cornelius. 1997. *World in Fragments: Writings on Politics, Society, Psychoanalysis, and the Imagination*. Stanford: Stanford University Press.

Chavarro, Diego, Puay Tang, and Ismael Ràfols. 2017. Why Researchers Publish in Non-mainstream Journals: Training, Knowledge Bridging, and Gap Filling. *Research Policy* 46 (9): 1666–1689.

Cheney, George, Jill J. McMillan, and Roy Schwartzman. 1997. Should We Buy the "Student-As-Consumer" Metaphor? *The Montana Professor* 7 (3): 8–11.

Cohen, Bernard I. 2006. *The Triumph of Numbers: How Counting Shaped Modern Life*. New York: W. W. Norton.

Cook, S.D. Noam, and Dvora Yanow. 1993. Culture and Organizational Learning. *Journal of Management Inquiry* 2: 373–390.

Cook, Thomas D., and Donald T. Campbell. 1986. The Causal Assumptions of Quasi-Experimental Practice: The Origins of Quasi-Experimental Practice. *Synthese* 68 (1): 141–180.

Dahlberg, Magnus, and Evert Vedung. 2001. *Demokrati och Brukarutvärdering* [Democracy and User Evaluation]. Lund: Studentlitteratur.

Dahler-Larsen, Peter. 2006. Evaluation After Disenchantment? Five Issues Shaping the Role of Evaluation in Society. In *Handbook of Evaluation*, ed. I.F. Shaw, J.C. Greene, and M.M. Mark, 123–140. Thousand Oaks: Sage.

———. 2008. *Kvalitetens Beskaffenhed* [The Nature of Quality]. Odense: University Press of Southern Denmark.

———. 2012. *The Evaluation Society*. Stanford: Stanford University Press.

———. 2013. Constitutive Effects of Performance Indicators: Getting Beyond Unintended Consequences. *Public Management Review* 16 (7): 969–986.

———. 2014. Global Inscription Devices and the Politics of Education. *Knowledge Cultures* 2 (4): 90–109.

———. 2015. Book Review: Enhancing Evaluation Use: Insights From Internal Evaluation Units. *American Journal of Evaluation* 36 (2): 283–286.

———. 2016. Tæller Vi Det Der Tæller. Målstyring og Standardisering i Arbejdslivet [Do We Count What Counts? Management by Objectives and Standardization in Working Life]. In *Moderne Arbejdsliv*, ed. M.F. Andersen and L. Tanggard, 109–132. Copenhagen: Klim.

Dahler-Larsen, Peter, and Signe Pihl-Thingvad. 2014. *Resultatmålinger og Stress* [Performance Measurement and Stress]. Odense: University Press of Southern Denmark.

Dahler-Larsen, Peter, Tineke A. Abma, Maria Bustelo, Roxana Irimia, Sonja Kosunen, Iryna Kravchuk, Elena Minina, Christina Segerholm, Eneida Shiroma, Nicoletta Stame, and Charlie Kabanga Tshali. 2017. Evaluation, Language, and Untranslatables. *American Journal of Evaluation* 38 (1): 114–125.

Dambrin, Claire, and Keith Robson. 2011. Tracing Performance in the Pharmaceutical Industry: Ambivalence, Opacity and the Performativity of Flawed Measures. *Accounting, Organizations and Society* 36: 428–455.

Davies, William. 2011. Knowing the Unknowable: The Epistemological Authority of Innovation Policy Experts. *Social Epistemology* 25 (4): 401–421.

———. 2015. *The Happiness Industry: How the Government and Big Business Sold Us Well-Being*. London: Verso.

Dean, James W., Jr., and David E. Bowen. 2000. Management Theory and Total Quality. In *The Quality Movement & Organization Theory*, ed. R.E. Cole and W.R. Scott, 3–21. Thousand Oaks: Sage.

Desrosières, Alain. 2002. *The Politics of Large Numbers: A History of Statistical Reasoning*. Cambridge: Harvard University Press.

———. 2007. Surveys Versus Administrative Records: Reflections on the Duality of Statistical Sources. *Courrier des statistiques – English Series* 13: 7–19.

———. 2009. How to Be Real and Conventional: A Discussion of the Quality Criteria of Official Statistics. *Minerva* 47: 307–322.

———. 2014. Statistics and Social Critique. *Partecipazione e conflitto* 7 (2): 348–359.

Dewey, John. 1931. *Philosophy and Civilization*. New York: G. P. Putnam's Sons.

DiMaggio, Paul, and Walter Powell. 1983. The Iron Cage Revisited: Institutional Isomorphism and Collective Rationality in Organizational Fields. *American Sociological Review* 48 (6): 147–160.

Dörner, Dietrich. 1996. *The Logic of Failure: Recognizing and Avoiding Error in Complex Situations*. Cambridge, MA: Perseus Books.

Droitcour, Judith A., and Mary G. Kovar. 2008. Multiple Threats to the Validity of Randomized Studies. In *Fundamental Issues on Evaluation*, ed. N.L. Smith and P.R. Brandon. New York: The Guilford Press.

Duffhues, Piet, and Wim Weterings. 2011. The Quality of Credit Ratings and Liability: The Dutch View. *International Journal of Disclosure and Governance* 8 (4): 1–21.

Eijffinger, Sylvester C.W. 2012. Rating Agencies: Role and Influence of Their Sovereign Credit Risk Assessment in the Eurozone. *Journal of Common Market Studies* 50 (6): 912–921.

Eisner, Elliot W. 1976. Educational Connoisseurship and Criticism: Their Form and Functions in Educational Evaluation. *Journal of Aesthetic Education* 10 (3/4): 135–150.

———. 2003. Educational Connoisseurship and Educational Criticism: An Arts-Based Approach to Educational Evaluation. In *International Handbook of Educational Evaluation*, ed. T. Kellaghan, D.L. Stufflebeam, and L.A. Wingate. Dordrecht: Kluwer Academic Publishers.

Encyclopedia Britannica. 1972. London: Encyclopedia Britannica Inc.

Encyclopedia of Quality of Life and Well-being Research. 2014. Ed. A.C. Michalos. Dordrecht: Springer.

Englund, Hans, and Magnus Frostenson. 2017. Managing Performance Evaluation Uncertainties in Schools: When Teachers Become Struggling Performers. *European Educational Research Journal* (online): 1–22.

Erkkilä, Tero, and Ossi Piironen. 2014. (De)politicizing Good Governance: The World Bank Institute, the OECD and the Politics of Governance Indicators. *Innovation: The European Journal of Social Science Research* 27 (4): 344–360.

Espeland, Wendy N., and Michael Sauder. 2007. Rankings and Reactivity: How Public Measures Recreate Social Worlds. *American Journal of Sociology* 113 (1): 1–40.

Feldman, Martha A., and Wanda Orlikowski. 2011. Theorizing Practice and Practicing Theory. *Organization Science* 22 (5): 1240–1253.

Fischer, Frank. 2003. *Reframing Public Policy: Discursive Politics and Deliberative Practices*. Oxford: Oxford University Press.

Fochler, Maximilian, and Sarah de Rijcke. 2017. Implicated in the Indicator Game? An Experimental Debate. *Engaging Science, Technology, and Society* 3: 21–40.

Foucault, Michel. 1984. Nietzsche, Genealogy, History. In *The Foucault Reader: An Introduction to Foucault's Thought*, ed. P. Rabinow, 76–100. London: Penguin.

Fountain, Jane E. 2001. Paradoxes of Public Sector Customer Service. *Governance* 14 (1): 55–73.

Funnell, Sue C., and Patricia J. Rogers. 2011. *Purposeful Program Theory: Effective Use of Theories of Change and Logic Models*. San Francisco: Jossey-Bass.

Furusten, Staffan. 2000. The Knowledge Base of Standards. In *A World of Standards*, ed. N. Brunsson and B. Jacobsson. Oxford: Oxford University Press.

Furubo, Jan-Eric, Ray C. Rist, and Rolf Sandahl. 2002. *International Atlas of Evaluation*. New Brunswick: Transaction Publishers.

Galbraith, Jay R. 1983. Strategy and Organization Planning. *Human Resource Management* 22 (1–2): 63–77.

Gawande, Atul. 2014. *Being Mortal, Medicine and What Matters in the End*. New York: Metropolitan Books.

Gibbons, Michael, Camille Limoges, Helga Nowotny, Simon Schwartzman, Peter Scott, and Martin Trow. 1994. *The New Production of Knowledge. The Dynamics of Science and Research in Contemporary Societies*. London: Sage.

Gjørup, Jes, and Henrik Hjortdal. 2007. Kronik: Tilgiv Os – Vi Vidste Ikke, Hvad Vi Gjorde [Feature: Forgive Us – We Did Not Know What We Were Doing]. *Politiken*, March 29.

Gläser, Jochen, and Grit Laudel. 2015. A Bibliometric Reconstruction of Research Trails for Qualitative Investigations of Scientific Innovations. *Historical Social Research – Historische Sozialforschung* 40: 299–330.

Gorz, André. 1980. *Ecology as Politics*. Boston: South End Press.

Habermas, Jürgen. 1991. *The Structural Transformation of the Public Sphere: An Inquiry into a Category of Bourgeois Society*. Cambridge, MA: The MIT Press.

Hackett, Edward J., Olga Amsterdamska, Michael Lynch, and Judy Wajcman. 2008. *The Handbook of Science and Technology Studies*. Cambridge, MA: The MIT Press.

Hallström, Kristina T. 2000. Organizing the Process of Standardization. In *A World of Standards*, ed. N. Brunsson and B. Jacobsson. Oxford: Oxford University Press.

Hardt, Michael, and Antonio Negri. 2001. *Empire*. Cambridge, MA: Harvard University Press.

Harmon, Michael M., and Richard T. Mayer. 1986. *Organization Theory for Public Administration*. Glenview: Scott, Foresman and Company.

Harvey, Lee, and Diana Green. 1993. Defining Quality. *Assessment and Evaluation in Higher Education* 18 (1): 9–34.

Harvey, Lee, and Bjørn Stensaker. 2008. Quality Culture: Understandings, Boundaries and Linkages. *European Journal of Education* 43 (4): 427–442.

Hay, Colin. 2012. Interpreting Interpretivism Interpreting Interpretations: The New Hermeneutics of Public Administration. *Public Administration* 89 (1): 167–182.

Hegge, Hjalmar. 1978. *Mennesket og Naturen* [The Human and the Nature]. Oslo: Universitetsforlaget.

Hermann, Stefan. 2007. *Magt og Oplysning. Folkeskolen 1950–2006* [Power and Enlightenment. The Public School 1950–2006]. Copenhagen: Unge Pædagoger.

Hochschild, Arlie. 2004. Gennem Sprækker i Tidsfælden [Through Cracks in the Time Bind]. In *Arbejdssamfundet* [The Labour Society], ed. M. Hviid and J. Tonbo, 109–131. Copenhagen: Hans Reitzels.

House, Ernest R., and Kenneth R. Howe. 2000. Deliberative Democratic Evaluation. *New Directions for Evaluation* 85: 3–12.

Husz, Orsi. 2012. The Morality of Quality: Assimilating Material Mass Culture in Twentieth-Century Sweden. *Journal of Modern European History* 10 (2): 152–181.

International Encyclopedia of Business and Management. 2002. Ed. W. Malcolm. London: Routledge.

Jacob, Steve, Sandra Speer, and Jan-Eric Furubo. 2015. The Institutionalization of Evaluation Matters: Updating the International Atlas of Evaluation 10 Years Later. *Evaluation* 21 (1): 6–31.

Jensen, Casper Bruun. 2011. Making Lists, Enlisting Scientists: The Bibliometric Indicator, Uncertainty and Emergent Agency. *Science Studies* 24 (2): 64–84.

Jensen, Jacob. 2016. Almenvellets Affortryllelse – Neoliberale Anfægtelser af det Fælles Bedste [The Disenchantment of the Common Good – Neoliberal Contestations of the Common Good]. *Slagmark* 74 (Fall): 69–85.

Jensen, Jacob, and Niklas Olsen. 2016. Hvad Er Neoliberalisme? Redaktionelt Forord [What Is Neoliberalism? Editorial Foreword]. *Slagmark* 74 (Fall): 9–22.

Julnes, George, ed. 2012. *Promoting Value in the Public Interest: Informing Policies for Judging Value in Evaluation. New Directions for Evaluation, No. 133*. San Francisco: Jossey-Bass.

Kaltenbrunner, Wolfgang, and Sarah de Ricjke. 2017. Quantifying 'Output' for Evaluation: Administrative Knowledge Politics and Changing Epistemic Cultures in Dutch Law Faculties. *Science and Public Policy* 44 (2): 284–293.

Kauko, Jaakko, Risto Rinne, and Tuomas Takala. 2018. *Politics of Quality in Education. A Comparative Study of Brazil, China, and Russia*. New York: Routledge.

W.K. Kellogg Foundation. 2004. *Logic Model Development Guide*. Battle Creek: W.K. Kellogg Foundation.

Kelman, Steven, and John N. Friedman. 2009. Performance Improvement and Performance Dysfunction: An Empirical Examination of Distortionary Impacts of the Emergency Room Wait-Time Target in the English National Health Service. *Journal of Public Administration Research and Theory* 19 (4): 917–946.

Kipnis, Andrew B. 2008. Audit Cultures: Neoliberal Governmentality, Socialist Legacy, or Technologies of Governing. *American Ethnologist* 35 (2): 275–289.

Klein, Jacob. 1977. *Plato's Trilogy: Theaetetus, the Sophist, and the Statesman*. Chicago: University of Chicago Press.

Koselleck, Reinhart. 2007. *Begreber, Tid og Erfaring. En tekstsamling* [Concepts, Time and Experience: An Anthology]. Copenhagen: Hans Reitzel. Collection of chapters originally published in Koselleck, R. 2000. *Zeitschichten: Studien zur Historik*. Frankfurt am Main: Suhrkamp Verlag.

———. 2011. Introduction and Prefaces to the Geschichtliche Grundbegriffe. *Contributions to the History of Concepts* 6 (1): 1–37.

Kreutzmann, Gladys. 1994. *Börn og Unges Anbringelser uden for Hjemmet* [Children and Young People's Placements Outside the Home]. Nuuk: Direktoratet for Sociale Anliggender og Arbejdsmarked.

Kristoffersen, Dorte, and Tobias Lindeberg. 2004. Creating Quality Assurance and International Transparency for Quality Assurance Agencies: The Case of Mutual Recognition. *Quality in Higher Education* 10 (1): 31–36.

Kula, Witold. 1996. *Measures and Men*. Princeton: Princeton University Press.

Kushner, Saville. 2017. *Evaluative Research Methods: Managing the Complexities of Judgment in the Field*. Charlotte: Information Age Publishing.

Lamont, Michèle. 2009. *How Professors Think: Inside the Curious World of Academic Judgment*. Cambridge, MA: Harvard University Press.

Latour, Bruno. 1987. *Science in Action: How to Follow Scientists and Engineers through Society*. Stony Stratford: Open University Press.

———. 2003. The Promises of Constructivism. Paper Prepared for a Chapter. In *Chasing Technology: Matrix of Materiality, Indiana Series for the Philosophy of Science*, ed. D. Idhe, 27–46. Bloomington: Indiana University Press.

———. 2004. Why Has Critique Run Out of Steam? From Matters of Fact to Matters of Concern. *Critical Inquiry* 30 (2): 225–248.

———. 2005. *Reassembling the Social: An Introduction to Actor–Network-Theory*. New York: Oxford University Press.

Latour, Bruno, and Steve Woolgar. 1986. *Laboratory Life, the Construction of Scientific Facts*. Princeton: Princeton University Press.

Läubli Loud, Marlène, and John Mayne. 2013. *Enhancing Evaluation Use: Insights from Internal Evaluation Units*. Thousand Oaks: Sage.

Levitt, Theodore. 1972. Production-Line Approach to Service. *Harvard Business Review* 50 (5): 20–31.

Lilford, Richard, Mohammad A. Mohammad, David Spiegelhalter, and Richard Thomson. 2004. Use and Misuse of Process and Outcome Data in Managing Performance of Acute Medical Care: Avoiding Institutional Stigma. *The Lancet* 363: 1147–1154.

Lind, Jonas K. 2016. University Autonomy as Sensemaking: From Formal to Enacted Autonomy. *Paper fremlagt ved EGPA 2016 – European Group of Public Administration, Utrecht, Holland, 24/08/2016–26/08/2016.*

Lindeberg, Tobias. 2007. *Evaluative Technologies: Quality and the Multiplicity of Performance*. Copenhagen: Copenhagen Business School.

Luckmann, Thomas. 1978. Philosophy, Social Sciences and Everyday Life. In *Phenomenology and Sociology*, ed. T. Luckmann, 217–253. Harmondsworth: Penguin.

Lyotard, Jean-Francois. 1982. *Viden og det Postmoderne Samfund* [The Postmodern Condition: A Report on Knowledge]. Aarhus: Sjakalen.

Management Leksikon. 2001. Ed. S. Hildebrandt and C. Waldstrøm, vol. 3. Copenhagen: Børsens Forlag.

Mathison, Sandra. 1991. Role Conflicts for Internal Evaluators. *Evaluation and Program Planning* 14 (3): 173–179.

———. 2011. Internal Evaluation, Historically Speaking. *New Directions for Evaluation* 132: 13–23.

Meyer, John W. 2008. Building Education for a World Society. In *Changing Knowledge and Education*, ed. M.A. Pereyra, 31–49. Frankfurt am Main: Peter Lang.

Meyer, John W., and Brian Rowan. 1977. Institutionalized Organizations: Formal Structure as Myth and Ceremony. *American Journal of Sociology* 83: 340–363.

Meyer, John W., John Boli, and George M. Thomas. 1987. Ontology and Rationalization in the Western Cultural Account. In *Institutional Structure: Constituting State, Society, and the Individual*, ed. G.M. Thomas, J.W. Meyer, F.O. Ramirez, and J. Boli, 12–37. Newbury Park: Sage.

———. 1994. Ontology and Rationalization in the Western Cultural Account. In *Institutional Environments and Organizations*, ed. W.R. Scott and J.W. Meyer, 9–27. Thousand Oaks: Sage.

Mirowski, Philip. 2016. Den politiske bevægelse, der ikke turde ytre sit eget navn [The Political Movement Which Did Not Dare Speak in Its Own Name]. *Slagmark* 74 (Fall): 33–52.

Mjøset, Lars. 2009. The Contextualist Approach to Social Science Methodology. In *The SAGE Handbook of Case-Based Methods*, ed. D. Byrne and C.C. Ragin, 39–68. Thousand Oaks: Sage.

Moe, Terry M. 2005. Power and Political Institutions. *Perspectives on Politics* 3 (2): 215–233.

Moed, Henk. 2018. Towards a Multi-Paradigmatic, Value Free Informetrics: A Reply to Paul Wouters' Book Review "The Failure of a Paradigm". *Journal of Informetrics*. https://doi.org/10.1016/j.joi.2018.03.003.

Morgan, Gareth. 1986. *Images of Organization*. Thousand Oaks: Sage.

Mortensen, Nils. 2004. *Det Paradoksale Samfund* [The Paradoxical Society]. Copenhagen: Hans Reitzel.

Mörth, Ulrika. 2008. Soft Regulation and Global Democracy. In *Transnational Governance*, ed. M.-L. Djelic and K. Sahlin-Andersson. Cambridge: Cambridge University Press.

Mouritzen, P.E., Niels Opstrup, and Pernille Bak Pedersen. 2018. En fremmed kommer til byen. Ti år med den bibliometriske forskningsindikator [*A Stranger Comes to Town. Ten Years with the Bibliometric Research Indicator*]. Odense: University of Southern Denmark Press.

Munro, Eileen. 2004. The Impact of Audit on Social Work Practice. *British Journal of Social Work* 34: 1075–1095.

Nisbet, Robert. 1966. *The Sociological Tradition*. London: Heinemann.

Noordegraf, Mirko. 2016. Reconfiguring Professional Work. Changing Forms of Professionalism in Public Services. *Administration and Society* 48 (7): 783–810.

Normand, Romuald. 2016. *The Changing Epistemic Governance of European Education, the Fabrication of the Homo Academicus Europeanus?* Switzerland: Springer.

Nóvoa, Antonio, and Tali Yariv-Mashal. 2003. Comparative Research in Education: A Mode of Governance or a Historical Journey. *Comparative Education* 39 (4): 423–438.

Olsen, Niklas. 2016. Velfærdsstatens krise og neoliberalismens indtog i Danmark i 1970'erne [The Crisis of the Welfare State and the Arrival of Neoliberalism in Denmark in the 1970s]. *Slagmark* 74 (Fall): 119–138.

Ordbog Over Det Danske Sprog [Dictionary of the Danish Language]. 1976. Det Danske Sprog- og Litteraturselskab. Copenhagen: Gyldendal.

Orlikowski, Wanda J., and Susan V. Scott. 2008. Sociomateriality: Challenging the Separation of Technology, Work and Organization. *The Academy of Management Annals* 2 (1): 433–474.

Øvretveit, John. 2005. Public Service Quality Improvement. In *The Oxford Handbook of Public Management*, ed. E. Ferlie, L.E. Lynn Jr., and C. Pollitt. New York: Oxford University Press.

Oxford Advanced Learner's Dictionary. 2000. A.S. Hornby. Oxford: Oxford University Press.

Ozga, Jenny, Peter Dahler-Larsen, Christina Segerholm, and Hannu Simola. 2011. *Fabricating Quality in Education: Data and Governance in Europe*. London: Routledge.

Palonen, Kari. 2002. The History of Concepts as a Style of Political Theorizing: Quentin Skinner's and Reinhart Koselleck's Subversion of Normative Political Theory. *European Journal of Political Theory* 1 (1): 91–106.

———. 2007. *Re-thinking Politics: Essays from a Quarter-century*. Finnish Political Science Association. Jyväskylä University Printing House.

Patton, Michael Q. 2002. *Qualitative Research and Evaluation Methods*. Thousand Oaks: Sage.

Pawson, Ray, and Nick Tilley. 1997. *Realistic Evaluation*. London: Sage.

Peters, Thomas J., and Robert H. Waterman Jr. 1982. *In Search of Excellence: Lessons from America's Best-Run Companies*. New York: Harper and Row.

Pflueger, Dane. 2016. Knowing Patients: The Customer Survey and the Changing Margins of Accounting in Healthcare. *Accounting, Organizations and Society* 53: 17–33.

Pielke, Roger A. 2007. *The Honest Broker, Making Sense of Science in Policy and Politics*. Cambridge: Cambridge University Press.

Pinch, Trevor J., and Wiebe E. Bijker. 1984. The Social Construction of Facts and Artefacts: Or How the Sociology of Science and the Sociology of Technology Might Benefit Each Other. *Social Studies of Science* 14 (3): 399–441.

Pirsig, Robert M. 1974. *Zen and the Art of Motorcycle Maintenance: An Inquiry Into Values*. New York: William Morrow.

Polanyi, Michael. 1966. *The Tacit Dimension*. Chicago: The University of Chicago Press.

Pollock, Neil, Luciana D'Adderio, Robin Williams, and Ludovic Leforestier. 2018. Conforming or Transforming? How Organizations Respond to Multiple Rankings. *Accounting, Organizations and Society* 64: 55–68.

Porter, Theodore M. 1994. Making Things Quantitative. *Science in Context* 7 (3): 389–407.

———. 1995. *Trust in Numbers: The Pursuit of Objectivity in Science and Public Life*. Princeton: Princeton University Press.

Power, Michael. 1996. Making Things Auditable. *Accounting, Organizations and Society* 21 (2/3): 289–315.

———. 1997. *The Audit Society*. Oxford: Oxford University Press.

———. 2016. Postscript. On Riskwork and Auditwork. In *Essays on the Organizational Life of Risk Management*, ed. Michael Power. Oxford: Oxford University Press.

Prewitt, Kenneth, Thomas A. Schwandt, and Miron L. Straf. 2012. *Using Science as Evidence in Public Policy*. Washington, DC: National Academies Press.

Radaelli, Claudio M., and Fabrizio De Francesco. 2007. *Regulatory Quality in Europe: Concepts, Measures and Policy Processes*. Manchester: Manchester University Press.

Rasmussen, Erik. 1981. *Lighedsbegreber* [Equality Concepts]. Copenhagen: Berlingske.

Reeves, Carol A., and David A. Bednar. 1994. Defining Quality: Alternatives and Implications. *Academy of Management Review* 19 (3): 419–445.

Roberts, John. 2018. Managing Only with Transparency: The Strategic Functions of Ignorance. *Critical Perspectives on Accounting* 55: 53–60.

Rom, Mark C. 2009. The Credit Rating Agencies and the Subprime Mess: Greedy, Ignorant, and Stressed? *Public Administration Review*: 640–650.

Rosa, Hartmut. 2003. Social Acceleration: Ethical and Political Consequences of a Desynchronized High–Speed Society. *Constellations* 10 (1): 3–33.

———. 2005. The Speed of Global Flows and the Pace of Democratic Politics. *New Political Science* 27 (4): 445–459.

Rosanvallon, Pierre. 2009. *Demokratin som Problem* [Democracy as the Problem]. Hägersten: TankeKraft Förlag.

Rothstein, Henry, Michael Huber, and George Gaskell. 2006. A Theory of Risk Colonization: The Spiralling Regulatory Logics of Societal and Institutional Risk. *Economy and Society* 35 (1): 91–112.

Røvik, Kjell A. 2005. *Moderne Organisasjoner: Trender i Organisasjonstenkningen ved Tusenårsskiftet* [Modern Organizations: Trends in Organizational Thinking at the Millennium]. Bergen: Fagbokforlaget.

Sahlins, Marshall. 1976. *Culture and Practical Reason*. Chicago: Aldine.

Säljö, Roger. 2002. My Brain's Running Slow Today. *Studies in Philosophy and Education* 21: 389–405.

Sauder, Michael, and Wendy N. Espeland. 2009. The Discipline of Rankings: Tight Coupling and Organizational Change. *American Sociological Review* 74 (1): 63–82.

Scalet, Steven, and Thomas F. Kelly. 2012. The Ethics of Credit Rating Agencies: What Happened and the Way Forward. *J Bus Ethics* 111: 477–490.

Schutz, Alfred. 1975. *Hverdagslivets Sociologi* [The Sociology of Everyday Life]. Copenhagen: Hans Reitzel.

———. 1978. Phenomenology and the Social Sciences. In *Phenomenology and Sociology*, ed. T. Luckmann, 119–141. Harmondsworth: Penguin.

Schwandt, Thomas A. 1994. Constructivist, Interpretivist Approaches to Human Inquiry. In *Handbook of Qualitative Research*, ed. N. Denzin and Y. Lincoln, 118–137. Thousand Oaks: Sage.

———. 2000. Three Epistemological Stances for Qualitative Inquiry: Interpretivism, Hermeuneutics, and Social Constructivism. In *Handbook of Qualitative Methods*, ed. N.K. Denzin and Y.S. Lincoln, 189–210. Thousand Oaks: Sage.

———. 2002. *Evaluation Practice Reconsidered.* New York: Peter Lang.

———. 2003. 'Back to the Rough Ground!' Beyond Theory to Practice in Evaluation. *Evaluation* 9 (3): 353–364.

———. 2015. *Evaluation Foundations Revisited: Cultivating a Life of the Mind for Practice.* Palo Alto: Stanford University Press.

Schwandt, Thomas A., and Holli Burgon. 2006. Evaluation and the Study of Lived Experience. In *The SAGE Handbook of Evaluation*, ed. I.F. Shaw, J.C. Greene, and M.M. Mark, 99–118. London: Sage.

Scott, W. Richard. 1992. *Organizations. Rational, Natural and Open Systems.* Englewood Cliffs: Prentice-Hall.

Sennett, Richard. 2002. *The Corrosion of Character: The Personal Consequences of Work in the New Capitalism.* New York: W. W. Norton.

———. 2008. *The Craftsman.* London: Penguin Books.

Shewhart, Walter A. 1931. *Economic Control of Quality of Manufactured Product.* New York: D. Van Nostrand Company.

Shore, Cris, and Susan Wright. 2015. Governing by Numbers: Audit Culture, Rankings and the New World Order. *Social Anthropology* 23 (1): 22–28.

Simpson, John A., and Edmund S. C. Weiner. 1989. *The Oxford English Dictionary.* New York/Oxford: Clarendon Press/Oxford University Press.

Sismondo, Sergio. 2008. Science and Technology Studies and an Engaged Program. In *The Handbook of Science and Technology Studies*, ed. E.J. Hackett, O. Amsterdamska, M. Lynch, and J. Wajcman, 13–31. Cambridge, MA: The MIT Press.

Smith, Peter. 1995. On the Unintended Consequences of Publishing Performance Data in the Public Sector. *International Journal of Public Administration* 18 (2–3): 277–310.

Sower, Victor E., and Frank K. Fair. 2005. There Is More to Quality than Continuous Improvement: Listening to Plato. *QMJ* 12 (1): 8–20.

Sørensen, Eva M., and Jacob Torfing. 2009. Making Governance Networks Effective and Democratic through Metagovernance. *Public Administration* 87 (2): 234–258.

Sørensen, Eva M., and Søren K. Foged. 2015. Mål- og Resultatstyring i Kommunerne Efter Krisen [Target and Performance Management in the Municipalities After the Crisis]. *Økonomi og Politik* 88 (1): 46–56.

Stake, Robert E. 2004. *Standard-Based and Responsive Evaluation*. Thousand Oaks: Sage.

Stark, David. 2009. *The Sense of Dissonance, Accounts of Worth in Economic Life*. Princeton: Princeton University Press.

Stern, Elliot, Nicoletta Stame, John Mayne, Kim Forss, Rick Davies, and Barbara Befani. 2012. *Broadening the Range of Designs and Methods for Impact Evaluations: Report of a Study Commissioned by the Department for International Development*, DFID Working Paper 38. London: Department for International Development.

Stilgoe, Jack, Richard Owen, and Phil Macnaghten. 2013. Developing a Framework for Responsible Innovation. *Research Policy* 42: 1568–1580.

Stone, Deborah. 2012. *Policy Paradox*. 3rd ed. New York: Norton.

Strang, David, and John W. Meyer. 1994. Institutional Conditions for Diffusion. In *Institutional Environments and Organizations*, ed. W.R. Scott and J.W. Meyer, 100–112. Thousand Oaks: Sage.

Taylor, David, and Susan Balloch. 2005. *The Politics of Evaluation: Participation and Policy Implementation*. Bristol: Policy Press.

The Cambridge Dictionary of Philosophy. 1995. Ed. R. Audi. Cambridge: Cambridge University Press.

Thévenot, Laurent. 2001. Pragmatic Regumes Governing the Engagement with the World. In *The Practice Turn in Contemporary Theory*, ed. T.R. Schatzki, K.D. Knorr-Cetina, and E. von Savigny, 56–73. London: Routledge.

van Thiel, Sandra, and Frans L. Leeuw. 2002. The Performance Paradox in the Public Sector. *Public Performance and Management Review* 25 (3): 267–281.

Vattimo, Gianni. 2005. *Nihilisme og Emancipation. Etik, Politik, Ret* [Nihilsm and Emancipation. Ethics, Politics, and Law]. Aarhus: Aarhus University Press.

Vedung, Evert. 1997. *Public Policy and Program Evaluation*. New Brunswick: Transaction.

Venturini, Tommaso. 2010. Diving in Magma: How to Explore Controversies with Actor–Network Theory. *Public Understanding of Science* 19 (3): 258–273.

Vostal, Filip. 2016. *Accelerating Academia, the Changing Structure of Academic Time*. New York: Palgrave Macmillan.

Wallenburg, Iris, Julia Quartz, and Roland Bal. 2016. Making Hospitals Governable: Performativity and Institutional Work in Ranking Practices. *Administration & Society*: 1–27.

Webster's Dictionary of Word Origins. 1995. Ed. Merriam-Webster. New York: Smithmark.

Webster's Ninth New Collegiate Dictionary. 1990. Springfield: Merriam-Webster.

Weick, Karl E. 1995. *Sensemaking in Organizations*. Thousand Oaks: Sage.

———. 2000. Quality Improvement: A Sensemaking Perspective. In *The Quality Movement and Organization Theory*, ed. R.E. Cole and W.R. Scott, 155–172. Thousand Oaks: Sage.

Weick, Karl E., Kathleen M. Sutcliffe, and David Obstfeld. 2005. Organizing and the Process of Sense-making. *Organization Science* 16 (4): 409–421.

Whatmore, Sarah J. 2009. Mapping Knowledge Controversies: Science, Democracy and the Redistribution of Expertise. *Progress in Human Geography* 33 (5): 587–598.

White, Lawrence J. 2012. Credit Rating Agencies: An Overview. *The Annual Review of Financial Economics* 5: 1–22.

Wiktionary. 2017. Appendix: Glossary for Quality Management. Retrieved online from https://en.wiktionary.org/wiki/Appendix:Glossary_of_quality_management

Wimbush, Erica, Steve Montague, and Tamara Mulherin. 2012. Applications of Contribution Analysis to Outcome Planning and Impact Evaluation. *Evaluation* 18 (3): 310–329.

Wouters, Paul. 2018. Book Review: The Failure of a Paradigm. Henk F. Moed. Applied Evaluative Informetrics. *Journal of Informetrics* 12 (2): 534–540.

Young, Joni J. 2006. Making Up Users. *Accounting, Organizations and Society* 31 (6): 579–600.

Index[1]

[1] Note: Page numbers followed by 'n' refer to notes.

P. Dahler-Larsen, *Quality*, https://doi.org/10.1007/978-3-030-10392-7

P

Q

Kolibri 360 GmbH
Ferdinand-Jühlke-Straße 7
99095 Erfurt, Deutschland
produktsicherheit@kolibri360.de